THE BROKEN VILLAGE

THE BROKEN VILLAGE

*Coffee, Migration, and Globalization
in Honduras*

DANIEL R. REICHMAN

ILR PRESS
AN IMPRINT OF
CORNELL UNIVERSITY PRESS
ITHACA AND LONDON

First published 2011 by Cornell University Press
First printing, Cornell Paperbacks, 2011
Printed in the United States of America

Library of Congress Cataloging-in-Publication Data

Reichman, Daniel R. (Daniel Ross), 1976–
    The broken village : coffee, migration, and globalization in Honduras / Daniel R. Reichman.
        p. cm.
    Includes bibliographical references and index.
    ISBN 978-0-8014-5012-9 (cloth : alk. paper)
    ISBN 978-0-8014-7729-4 (pbk. : alk. paper)
    1. Honduras—Emigration and immigration—Social aspects.
    2. United States—Emigration and immigration—Social aspects.
    3. Coffee industry—Social aspects—Honduras.   4. Honduras—
Rural conditions.   I. Title.
    JV7419.R45 1011
    305.868'7283073—dc23   2011020007

Cornell University Press strives to use environmentally responsible suppliers and materials to the fullest extent possible in the publishing of its books. Such materials include vegetable-based, low-VOC inks and acid-free papers that are recycled, totally chlorine-free, or partly composed of nonwood fibers. For further information, visit our website at www.cornellpress.cornell.edu.

Cloth printing   10 9 8 7 6 5 4 3 2 1

Contents

FIGURES

Acknowledgments

First, I thank the Department of Anthropology at Cornell University, where this project took shape. In particular, Terence Turner, Dominic Boyer, and Jane Fajans provided valuable advice and critical insight, and influenced the ideas in this book, knowingly or not, at every turn. Ted Bestor was an important mentor in the early stages of this research. Doreen Lee, Tyrell Haberkorn, and Marcus Watson were among many supportive friends and intellectual compatriots.

I also thank María Cristina García in the Cornell Departments of History and Latino Studies, and the directors of the Latin American Studies Program for their guidance and support. Phil Arneson, Terry Tucker, and other members of the Cornell International Agriculture Program realized the importance of this research and introduced me to Honduras as part of an interdisciplinary field trip in 2001, which remains one of the most enjoyable intellectual experiences I have ever had. A National Science Foundation Graduate Research Fellowship provided the material support to bring this project to fruition.

I owe a debt of gratitude to Michael Billig and Misty Bastian at Franklin and Marshall College, who got me started in anthropology. Their clear-eyed view of the importance of a liberal education (and steadfast resistance to intellectual fads) has shaped my own perspective on teaching and scholarship. Mario Blaser deserves thanks for introducing a startlingly immature anthropologist to "real" fieldwork in the Paraguayan Chaco in 1996.

At the University of Rochester, I have benefited from the support and encouragement of my colleagues in anthropology: Tony Carter, Ayala Emmett, Robert Foster, Tom Gibson, Eleana Kim, and John Osburg. Ro Ferreri always lent a hand when I needed it most. The Office of the Provost provided funds to assist in the publication of this book. Rachel Odhner served as a careful and thoughtful research assistant, thanks to a grant from the Rochester sustainability research program. Johanna Fischer ably assisted with copy editing.

Frances Benson, my editor at Cornell University Press, read the manuscript with generous enthusiasm and, with help from Katherine Liu, shepherded a novice author through the publication process with aplomb. Steve Striffler, Elizabeth Ferry, and Edward Fischer provided valuable critical insight at various points along the way.

In Honduras, I thank the Instituto Hondureño de Antropología e Historia (IHAH) for providing institutional support and research clearance. I owe special thanks to Teresa Campos de Pastor and her staff at the Museo de Antropología e Historia de San Pedro Sula for their generosity and kindness. In the interest of confidentiality, I sadly must refrain from thanking individuals in La Quebrada, but to my many friends and collaborators there: *Gracias por todo lo que me enseñaron, por su paciencia, y por su capacidad de reconocer lo bueno en cada persona y cada situación.*

Finally, I thank my family. My parents, David and Libby, always encouraged curiosity, an independent spirit, and a determined lack of pretense (key traits for any would-be anthropologist). Ted and Mary were always there to provide the right balance of support and inquisitiveness. Robert B. Neuman and the late Arlene R. Neuman helped to open my eyes to the world around me. Amy, Beatrice, and Leah have made every day a joy.

THE BROKEN VILLAGE

INTRODUCTION

Integration and Disintegration

This book describes how people cope with rapid social change. It tells the story of the small town of La Quebrada, Honduras, which, over a five-year period from 2001–2006, transformed from a relatively isolated community of small-scale coffee farmers into a hotbed of migration from Honduras to the United States and back.[1] During this time, the everyday lives of people in La Quebrada became connected to the global economy in a manner that was far different, and far more intimate, than anything they had experienced in the past. Townspeople did not generally view this transformation as a positive step toward progress or development. They saw migration as a temporary response to economic crisis, even as it became an ever more inescapable part of their livelihood. The chapters that follow trace the effects of migration across various domains of local life— including politics, religion, and family dynamics—describing how individuals in one community adapt to economic change.

This is not a story about an egalitarian little Eden being corrupted by the forces of capitalist modernization. La Quebrada's residents have lived with social inequality, violence, political conflict, and economic instability for generations. As coffee farmers, their fortunes have long been tied to the vicissitudes of global markets. However, the social changes wrought by migration presented qualitatively new challenges, as a functioning local economy became dependent on migrants working in distant places such as Long Island and South Dakota who lived in ways that most people in La Quebrada struggled to comprehend or explain. The new reality of migration created a sense of confusion that was especially strong in the early stages of La Quebrada's migration boom, when communication between villagers and migrants was rare. The decline of coffee markets and the rise of the migration economy happened so quickly and chaotically that people struggled to understand, evaluate, and give meaning to the changes they were experiencing. Therefore, migration was experienced as sociocultural *disintegration* in 2003–2005, when the bulk of the research for this study was conducted.

People sensed that their lives were becoming determined by faraway, disconnected "others" and governed by forces of which they were conscious but did not fully understand. In this sense, the collective processes of sociocultural integration that came to be known as "globalization" in Western academic and popular discourse were experienced but not fully recognized or articulated through a defined cultural or symbolic narrative. La Quebrada's encounter with "the global" created a profound sense of alienation, as people felt they were taking part in a system that they had no way of adequately comprehending, let alone controlling.

The systems of knowledge and belief through which they understood the world were rooted in a way of life that was being transformed by back-and-forth circuits of international migration. People who had been social "nobodies," including petty criminals, manual laborers, and uneducated teenagers, returned from years working in the United States magically transformed into the nouveau riche. At the same time, historically successful coffee-growing families and local political elites floundered in a struggling economy, while a new group of elites—linked to the migration business—rose in power and wealth, if not social status (a key distinction to which I will return in chapter 2). Some individuals who migrated to the United States were able to find work, amass savings, and return to Honduras triumphantly, while many others were deported or struggled to find steady work in the hostile, dangerous, and unfamiliar environments they encountered.

Young Hondurans who returned from the United States talked about jobs that were completely alien to the lifestyles of people in La Quebrada— shoveling snow, washing windows in giant skyscrapers, and preparing salads in exclusive suburban country clubs. Returned migrants built homes that were replicas of houses they had helped to build in the suburbs of Colorado and New Jersey, bringing back with them new material markers of success such as Jacuzzis, backyard swing-sets, and elaborate barbeque grills. These changes occurred in a place marked by widespread poverty, where the vast majority of the population did not have access to electricity, running water, or basic social services and relied on seasonal coffee production to meet their basic economic needs. There seemed to be no ordering logic to this new way of life.

Within this atmosphere of cultural upheaval, people tried to determine the causes and future directions of these changes and debated whether they were positive or negative, morally good or bad for individuals, families, and communities. These cultural debates could be found in private conversations, street-corner banter, religious sermons, political campaigns, and other everyday encounters that are the raw material from which this ethnography is made. This book focuses on the crisis of meaning produced by La Quebrada's rapid and chaotic integration into global sociocultural processes, and the collective and individual strategies that people developed to reassert some measure of control amidst a period of rapid change.

Readers familiar with Spanish will note that the name *La Quebrada* means both "the stream" and "the broken article." I have chosen to give the town this pseudonym for two reasons, one descriptive and the other evocative. The town is located high in the mountains near the source of one of Honduras's major rivers, and it is bisected by several streams that eventually drain into the Caribbean, which lies approximately one hundred miles to the north. Therefore, "the stream" describes a notable geographic feature of the community.

More important, the sense of being broken implied by *La Quebrada* reflects the period of crisis in which the community found itself over the course of this study. The book's title is, of course, the clearest example of this motif. Some readers will assume from the title that I view the changes experienced by people in La Quebrada as negative social pathologies rather than neutral historical changes (or even signs of progress). This would be a far too simplistic conclusion to draw. Any "break" or rupture with the past presents opportunities for reconstruction and renewal. Although the rapid and chaotic nature of La Quebrada's experience with migration often appeared to usher in a period of crisis, this book focuses on three strategies through which people attempted to reconstruct a moral vision for society in the wake of rapid change.

First, the creation of a fair trade/organic coffee cooperative sought to raise farmer incomes and establish principles of fairness and economic justice through transnational consumer activism. Second, two religious congregations promoted campaigns for personal morality that were intended to counter the socially corrosive effects of migration. Third, a strategy for social justice is found in local discourses about migrant "greed" and flawed moral character, which frequently labeled migrants as the *cause* of social crisis, rather than its victims. These settings involve both religious and secular visions of morality, but in all three cases, people articulated visions of collective welfare and social citizenship by emphasizing the power of *individual behavior* as a way to respond to a perceived state of social decline.

The phenomena that I describe all view *the individual* as the source of social decline and the potential source of social redemption, rather than the nation-state, community, or some other collectivity. Around the world, and especially in Latin America, people have developed new political strategies in response to the perceived breakdown of the guiding visions of *modern* political philosophy, the blueprints for utopia that shaped modern ideas of progress or development, be they socialist or democratic. For some, the demise of secular, collective visions of progress, and the rise of free-market fundamentalism marks a decisive "break" with modernity and the transition to a postmodern age (Harvey 1989; Hopenhayn 2001).[2] The ethnographic and historical sections of this book explore the implications of this systematic political transformation in one very small—yet very suggestive—setting.

On a more abstract level, *the broken village* intentionally complicates one of the most common (not to mention utopian) metaphors for contemporary processes of global integration—the "global village." In this metaphor, *the village* symbolizes geographic proximity, social harmony, and participation in a single, integrated society, in which people from disparate places come to know each other's lives and worlds through the benefits of technology that, we are told, "makes the world smaller." Yet this sense of proximity is broken by an equally powerful set of forces that separate people geographically, politically, and socially. Throughout this book, I describe settings in La Quebrada in which life is simultaneously integrated and disintegrated by global processes. In La Quebrada, everyday life is incredibly proximate yet impossibly distant from life in the United States. People are unified by new kinds of social connection, yet remain separated by borders and barriers of all sorts. La Quebrada is indeed a "global village," but it is a village that has been permanently fractured. In this sense, La Quebrada serves as a model for the present historical moment. If the world we inhabit is indeed a "global village," then it is a broken one.

Within the realm of anthropological theory, "the broken village" refers to anthropologists' collective attempt to understand our own place in a rapidly changing world. There is a strong parallel between the crisis of meaning experienced by people in La Quebrada and anthropologists' own intellectual struggles to come to terms with a world transformed by the intense processes of transnational interaction that came to be known as "globalization" in the 1990s. Like people in La Quebrada whose worldviews were being transformed by processes of globalization, anthropologists have had to reorient a way of understanding society that was once based on the study of small-scale "knowable communities" (Holmes and Marcus 2005) but has needed to account for complex and diverse forms of global sociocultural interconnection. As in La Quebrada, the guiding models of social life that shaped anthropologists' understanding of the relationship between culture, economy, and society were broken and reassembled to adapt to a rapidly changing world.

Anthropologists have long sought to understand and explain local processes of socioeconomic change as effects of macro-level forces such as colonialism, modernization, capitalist expansion, and economic development. In the 1990s and 2000s, anthropology was marked by an unusual sense of methodological and theoretical unease about the ability of existing concepts to accurately explain "the system." Theoretical understandings of how local settings interacted with global economic forces no longer seemed capable of capturing the complexities of contemporary life. This led to intense debate within the academic community about how to situate local-level ethnographic study within broader, perhaps global, contexts without devaluing face-to-face participant observation and how—and indeed, *if*—it was possible to understand the global economy as a structured totality.[3] This debate led to important new understandings of how globalization—understood as a political, economic, or cultural system—did or did not differ from previous historical epochs, but it was marked by a widespread sense that a paradigm shift was in order, rather than any clear theoretical consensus about what globalization actually was.

In the words of Douglas Holmes and George Marcus, two provocative participants in these debates, "globalization is less an object for comprehensive theorizing or empirical investigation than the referent or symptom that conditions diversely posed challenges to disciplines, knowledge practices, and forms of expertise" (Holmes and Marcus 2005, 247). For anthropologists and the people with whom we work, globalization produced a sense that our ideological frames (worldviews, philosophies, theories) were incapable of grasping contemporary reality. This book will seize upon the parallels found in the ideological struggles of anthropologists and our interlocutors in order to understand how our respective worldviews, our orienting models of self and society, are being "broken" and reconstructed.

The Ethnographic Setting

I first came to La Quebrada in the summer of 2001. At that time, agricultural specialists at Cornell University, where I was then a graduate student in anthropology, were carrying out an initiative to promote sustainable and ecologically friendly forms of coffee production among Honduran farmers. During summer break, I was invited by one of the project's directors to spend a month in La Quebrada, trying to understand how local social conditions were shaping people's decisions to participate or not participate in the sustainable coffee program. For my own selfish intellectual reasons, I wanted to see the on-the-ground workings of an agricultural development project up close. The coffee project was funded by the U.S. government, designed by first-world experts, and managed by a complex web of bureaucratic agencies, yet it was supposed to be driven by the needs and desires of community members in the name of "participatory development." I wondered whether this project was marked by a contradiction between "top-down" and "bottom-up" definitions of development—the former created in the minds of the project's directors, and the latter by the project's beneficiaries. How participatory could any international development project really be?

At that time, I was reasonably well-prepared to conduct an ethnographic study in Honduras. I was a fluent Spanish speaker who had traveled and lived in various parts of Latin America, including Honduras. I had never been to La Quebrada—indeed, I had never even seen a picture of it—so my imagination was fueled by bits of information that I had been given by members of the coffee project before I left. I knew the town of about 4,500 people was in the middle of a severe economic crisis that had been caused by a recent drop in world coffee prices. I knew the town was relatively remote and far off the beaten track for tourists or the legions of scholars interested in Honduran Maya civilization.[4] I also knew that fewer people were participating in the ecological coffee project than had been expected, and that the town had a reputation for feuding between political factions, which sometimes escalated to violence. Beyond that, I knew little about the place, and—truth be told—I saw this trip as an interesting and potentially fun opportunity to try to figure out an unfamiliar locale. Little did I know that this trip would spawn a project that would occupy the next ten years of my life.

La Quebrada is a rural place that feels remote, but one can get to either of Honduras's major cities—San Pedro Sula and Tegucigalpa—within a full day of travel. Heading south to La Quebrada from the industrial hub of San Pedro Sula, the differences between country and city in Honduras can be jarring. Leaving the city by car or bus, it is impossible to ignore the signs of American dominance that blanket the landscape. The highway is lined with *maquilas,* export processing facilities where thousands of young Honduran workers manufacture apparel for major U.S. brands.[5] Packed into shipping containers and hooked directly onto waiting semi-trucks, the finished garments travel north to the port city of Puerto Cortés, to be loaded onto ships as quickly as possible. American chains such as Wendy's, Subway, Sears, and Ace Hardware populate the sleek new shopping malls, each one ringed by its own expansive, well-lit parking lot. Cast-off yellow school buses from American school districts clog the roads. Discarded plastic wrappers from Doritos and Cheetos line every roadside ditch.

Once one leaves the Pan-American Highway, however, the exhaust fumes from the semi-trucks begin to dissipate from the air, and the malls and fast food chains give way to roadside stands selling fresh fruit, handicrafts, and whole fish strung out to hang in the hot sun. The shanty-towns and new suburban developments that creep up the muddy hillsides around the cities are quickly replaced by placid little hamlets where groups of young people sit and stare blankly at passing cars for entertainment and children trudge along the roadsides, carrying impossibly large bundles of firewood on their backs.

The trip to La Quebrada requires several hours of travel over rough mountain roads, across creeks and rivers, and through banana groves that give way to pine forests and, finally, coffee farms as the elevation rises. Long stretches of the road pass through undeveloped forest. After cresting the sierra and beginning the short descent into La Quebrada, a bustling, disorganized, and surprisingly vibrant little town appears out of nowhere. I recall traveling to La Quebrada with a young man from a Honduran city, who was visiting the town for the first time in 2004. As we bounced around, perched on the rails of a pickup truck on the way to town, he exclaimed, "Qué salvaje!" (How wild!) as we traveled along a forested ridgeline with a stunning twilight view of the mountains. As we finally descended into town, he incredulously declared, "This town is enormous," noting that block after block of squat, adobe and concrete buildings seemed to rise out of nowhere, scattered willy-nilly around disorganized streets that are the antithesis of the ordered grids found in most Latin American towns. I would later learn that the town's disorganized layout and remote location was a product of its origins as a logging camp carved out of virgin forest.[6]

On my first trip to La Quebrada, I was brought by a member of the Cornell coffee project to a large *beneficio* (coffee mill) that was located at the main entrance to the town. I was introduced to Alex and Hernán López, the two directors of a newly formed coffee cooperative that was working with Cornell to enter the organic and fair trade coffee markets. Both men were coated with a foul-smelling concoction of rotting coffee husks and chicken manure—two important ingredients in an organic coffee fertilizer that they were mixing in concrete sinks that were designed to receive sacks of freshly picked coffee for processing in the *beneficio*. Built by the Honduran government's coffee marketing board in the 1980s and funded by international aid money, the coffee mill had been abandoned for several years when I arrived in 2001 (figure 1). Although it was the largest and (potentially) the most productive facility in town, it had fallen into disrepair and no one was certain who owned it or was responsible for its upkeep. The government program that originally created the mill had ceased to exist, and the mill sat idle for several years. When I arrived in La Quebrada, the sustainable coffee cooperative was using the mill, but legal and political wrangling was required to determine to whom, exactly, the mill belonged.

After brief introductions, I was dropped off in the house where I would be living. My mind was already racing, wondering how a valuable and useful coffee mill could have been abandoned after only a short period of successful operation. The abandoned mill's rusting, looming presence at the main entrance into town eventually came to symbolize the town's economic and political decline for me.

My sense of puzzlement only increased after being introduced to Ramón, the man whose family owned the house we were renting. Ramón was about my age, then in his mid-twenties. His family owned a large coffee farm outside of town, and his late father was, for a time, a formidable political leader of the right-wing National Party.[7] I asked Ramón if he was a member of the new coffee cooperative, assuming he would have been since

Figure 1. The abandoned coffee mill (*beneficio*). Daniel Reichman, 2004

he was renting his home to us and had also rented to other members of the project team. He looked at me in disgust. "I don't want anything to do with those people. I don't get along well with those *barbones* [long-beards], and I don't trust them. *Son como izquierdistas* [They are, like, leftists.]"

Alex and Hernán, the two directors of the coffee cooperative (who did, in fact, have beards) had been longtime rivals of Ramón's family. Onetime communists, they had led a campaign to stop the use of chemical fertilizers that leeched into the town's water supply, ultimately filing a lawsuit against Ramón's father, claiming that he had violated several of the country's environmental regulations by using toxic chemicals to fertilize coffee planted in close proximity to the water source. Alex and Hernán's new organic coffee project was perceived by some community members as a continuation of their antipollution campaign, which was symbolically associated with left-wing politics. Incredibly, Ramón's family had decided to rent a house (at an unusually high rate) to people, like me, that were affiliated with their political rivals.

Trying to avoid venturing any further into a touchy discussion of local politics, Ramón and I began to look at a photo album that we found while unpacking. As we leafed through the pictures, Ramón began to tell me about all the relatives he had in the United States—in Colorado, New Jersey, and various parts of Long Island. He was trying to find cultural common ground to help along our awkward conversation, but he also revealed that he was in the process of arranging his own trip to the United States. He was looking to sell some of the coffee land he had inherited from his father, he said, and would use that money to pay a *coyote* (smuggler) to help him cross the border illegally.

That early encounter with Ramón introduced me to themes that ran through the rest of my study of migration in La Quebrada: local party politics, the rise and fall of coffee farming and the fortunes of the people that depended on it, the lure of emigration to the United States, and the new illicit economy that migration had spawned. When I returned to La Quebrada in 2003, Ramón was gone. His mother told me he was in Baltimore, working as a window washer. His house was shuttered and abandoned, and I moved into it alone to begin fieldwork. The coffee cooperative had also collapsed. Because of a severe decline in world coffee prices, the co-op had had to sell its crop for less than the price of production for two consecutive seasons. Several of its members had left for the United States.

I have studied the relationship between coffee and migration in La Quebrada more or less continually for nine years. Village fieldwork in 2001, 2003, 2004, and 2008 has been supplemented with interviews with key informants in several U.S. communities, along with frequent online interaction with people in La Quebrada. Over the years, I have encountered scores of people whose lives were being transformed, for both good and bad, by economic and social change. Some people who had gone to the United States had been economically successful, while the lives of others were destroyed. Some families were deeply grateful for money that was sent home to them by relatives working in the United States; other families resented the absence of their migrant kin, castigating relatives abroad for their perceived selfishness. Some people felt that migration was the only thing keeping La Quebrada afloat, while others saw it as a sign of the community's downfall. The chapters that follow describe the experiences of people living in the midst of a new, disruptive, sometimes confounding, social reality wrought by dependence on migration.

This book begins with the stories of individual migrants, and places their experiences within progressively wider social and historical contexts. Chapter 1 attempts to answer a deceptively simple question: Why do people leave La Quebrada for the United States? Through biographical profiles of individual migrants, I describe the complex sets of factors that lead individuals to leave Honduras. Conventional wisdom states that migrants seek "a better life," by escaping poverty for the economic opportunity that awaits them in the United States. However, migrants from La Quebrada come from all social classes, and many do not leave out of economic desperation. People define *a better life* and *opportunity* in varied ways, making it ludicrous to suggest an *a priori* definition of "a good life" to which all migrants aspire. In this chapter, migrants explain their individual motivations for leaving Honduras for the United States.

These profiles reveal that migrants are always motivated by the possibility of economic gain, but they wrestle with the fact they must leave behind their families and communities in Honduras, often risking their lives in search of a higher wage. Thus, their social responsibilities to family and community become radically disconnected from their economic responsibilities. Migrants and their families negotiate this tension every day in La Quebrada, weighing the personal, social, and psychological costs of migration against the potential for economic advancement. In this sense, migrants experience a basic element of all capitalist economies in extreme form: They must sever economic production (acquiring the material necessities of life) from social reproduction, performing and maintaining defined roles and obligations within a social group, such as a family (Graeber 2006).

Chapter 2 expands on the inherent tension created by the separation of migrants' economic and social responsibilities, describing how people in La Quebrada evaluate migration decisions in moral terms, celebrating or denigrating migrants in different contexts. The community's dependence on U.S. migration has led to economic progress for some, but this progress has been accompanied by social hardship, as families adapt to the absence of an entire generation of productive adults. People judge migrants as altruistic or selfish, dutiful or greedy, depending on their particular family circumstances and their ability to manage the competing economic and social demands of migration. This chapter describes the local ethics of migrant behavior, focusing on the distinction made between ethical "needy" migrants and unethical "greedy" migrants.

Taken together, chapters 1 and 2 introduce the reader to the contemporary realities of life in La Quebrada. Chapter 3 explains how the community got to this point, and connects its story to macro-level changes that occurred throughout modern Latin America. Migration to the United States from La Quebrada did not become a common practice until the late 1990s. Prior to that time, migration to the United States, however temporary, was almost unthinkable as a strategy to deal with economic hardship. For technological, political, and cultural reasons that I address at various points in the book, Honduran emigration boomed in the 2000s, much later than migration from other Central American countries. In this chapter, I argue that the rise of migration from La Quebrada—and Honduras as a whole—must be placed within the context of post–Cold War history. For much of the twentieth century, "development," however that term was defined, was the goal that shaped political and economic aspirations in La Quebrada. After the Cold War ended in the early 1990s, both the theory and practice of international development changed. The state took a narrower role in the promotion of social welfare, and focused its attention on market-friendly neoliberal policies that would improve Honduras's competitive position in the global economy. In this context, the social welfare function of the state narrowed, and nongovernmental organizations

(NGOs) became increasingly responsible for providing social services in rural Honduras.

Profitability, efficiency, and competitiveness often came at the expense of social stability.[8] Poor people were encouraged to relocate to fast-growing urban centers to work in *maquilas,* and social expenditures were reduced to control inflation. Migrant remittances came to be seen as a key resource in rural development, and U.S. migration came to be viewed as a beneficial economic option that helped to bring much-needed cash to impoverished parts of Honduras. Migration became a path to "development," rather than a symptom of its failure.

Through a biography of Hernán López, the leader of the coffee cooperative and one of La Quebrada's most prominent political activists, chapter 3 describes how the failure of "development" in the context of the Cold War, led to the era of migration in La Quebrada. Here, the image of the abandoned coffee mill provides a fitting symbol: A piece of infrastructure funded and built by the government to improve agricultural production was abandoned due to bureaucratic mismanagement. It was finally brought back to life by an organic coffee cooperative that that was supported by a network of international NGOs. This cooperative eventually failed in the midst of an unprecedented boom in migration to the United States. Through the life of a single individual, chapter 3 describes the shift from the state-driven, nationalistic visions of development to local-level, NGO-driven activity, arguing that migration emerged as a "way out" of economic hardship after the failure of political strategies for development.

Chapter 3 connects the earlier chapters' descriptions of life in La Quebrada to broader cultural and political strategies that have emerged in response to social upheaval. As the government's role in the promotion of social welfare narrowed, new forms of politics emerged to articulate collective visions of social justice and political reform. Chapters 4 and 5 demonstrate how the political debates described in chapter 3 have shifted outside of mainstream political institutions, examples of what Aihwa Ong refers to as the "disarticulation and rearticulation of citizenship" (Ong 2006, 17). Chapter 4 focuses on how two different churches used theology to articulate radically different political and moral visions in the context of migration. In La Quebrada, a relatively ascetic Pentecostal church has banned drinking, dancing, and conspicuous consumption as a way to combat social disintegration. At the same time, a rival "libertine" congregation from a fringe Christian sect has embraced personal affect, glitz, wealth, and other values that are associated with U.S.-driven processes of modernity. These religious debates are fundamentally political discussions about the meaning and direction of social change and the role of the individual as a citizen. People discuss the political and social implications of migrant dependency within religious congregations.

Chapter 5 returns to the topic of coffee production. The coffee project that originally brought me to La Quebrada was another "way out" of economic crisis for Honduran coffee growers based on secular, ethical principles of "social justice" that were defined by international NGOs. Attempts to establish economic justice through consumer choice, I argue, are the secular analog to the evangelical vision of ethical conduct described in chapter 4. Like the churches described in chapter 4, fair trade is a setting where people articulate collective social principles outside the boundaries of the nation-state. These chapters are united by a common theme—the ways that people and groups develop ethical principles of social responsibility and citizenship in a situation where the nation-state seems incapable or unwilling to address the social consequences of globalization. In these cases, the terrain of politics shifts to nontraditional arenas such as ethical consumerism and religious movements, where people express a sense of alienation toward "the system" by focusing their energies on particular symbols of ethical crisis—"greedy" migrants, sinful behavior of non-Christians, and "unfair" and ecologically harmful coffee beans. In each instance, these enemies come to symbolize a new, alienating encounter with globalization, and people work to express principles of social responsibility in response to a changing world.

The realities of life in a global system are apparent to everyone in La Quebrada, where people can rattle off the names of delis in Long Island where their children work, describing how their son or daughter's big holiday bonus will help them buy fertilizer for their coffee fields; where seven-year-old children talk about *Nueva Jersey* as if it were a hamlet down the road; where a religious congregation huddles around a computer monitor in a dark room to listen to the Internet sermon of a Miami-based apostle; and where people joke about how the *coyote de la gente* (human smuggler) has replaced the *coyote del café* (coffee broker) as the town's richest resident. The existence of these global connections is obvious, but their meaning depends on hotly contested cultural, philosophical, and moral points of view.

I must apologize to readers familiar with Honduras who will no doubt wish for more fine-grained detail about my research site to evaluate my findings. I regret the loss of specificity and historical detail that is an inescapable consequence of the use of pseudonyms. I have invented names to protect the identity of many townspeople who are involved in illegal activities such as human smuggling and undocumented immigration. The only real names included in this work belong to historical figures, scholars, and religious leaders. Some readers may find the names unusual, but they are all names that actually exist in La Quebrada, put into combinations of my own making. I have tried to capture the tone and rhythms of life in La Quebrada without giving too much away. Despite my attempts to preserve anonymity, some Honduran specialists will be able to determine the community in which this study is based. I ask that future commentators respect the standard of privacy to which I strive in this work and refrain from publicly revealing the town's name or identifying the real names of the people described here.

I am certain that the experiences of the people I describe are in some way representative of struggles faced by many people in similar situations all over the world. I chose to write about this little town because its story connects several important threads of life under globalization. I hope that this work clarifies these connections and explains La Quebrada's importance for anthropologists and any other group interested in how globalization is changing cultures around the world. Although certain points of my fieldwork were punctuated by fear, frustration, and confusion, I never doubted that the people of La Quebrada had an important story to tell.

1

American Dream, American Work

Fantasies and Realities of Honduran Migrants

Chris Matthews: When I was in the Peace Corps I calculated it would take
350 years for the country I was serving in to catch up to where we
[Americans] were in GNP in the sixties.

Brent Scowcroft: And that's a horrible thought. That gets to one of the real
problems in the world though, and that is the people where you were serving
didn't know much about the United States. Now they watch television
every night. Even in the boondocks they watch television and they see you
shopping on Fifth Avenue and so on and so forth and they think, "Why am I
not shopping on Fifth Avenue?"

Transcript from MSNBC's *Hardball*, television news program, Dec. 2, 2004

Many people are coming to this country for economic reasons. They're
coming here to work. If you can make fifty cents in the heart of Mexico, for
example, or make five dollars here in America, $5.15, you're going to come
here if you're worth your salt, if you want to put food on the table for your
families. And that's what's happening.

Former President George W. Bush, presidential debate, Oct. 8, 2004

The quotations above contain two common explanations of contemporary migration to the United States, one "cultural" and the other
"economic." Former National Security Advisor Brent Scowcroft gives a
cultural explanation of migration, arguing that increased knowledge of
riches available in the United States, thanks to the global media, has altered
individual and collective worldviews in "boondocks" around the world,
leading to disillusionment and new aspirations shaped by consumerist

desires. According to this form of reasoning, the worldwide spread of the Western media disrupts traditional concepts of status and value, leading to rising expectations for personal advancement, which Scowcroft calls "one of the real problems of the world." Alexis de Tocqueville argued long ago (1856) that rising expectations are effectively the same as declining fortunes: They set the stage for widespread disillusionment and collective action as people's lived realities fail to keep pace with their "expectations of modernity" (Ferguson 1999).[1] I characterize this line of reasoning as a "cultural" explanation because it emphasizes how peoples' decisions are shaped by subjective definitions of value, such as the meaning of "success" and "a good life," that vary across cultures, classes, and generations.

The economic explanation of migration decisions, exemplified by President Bush's comments in a presidential debate, views the decision to migrate as a common-sense response to economic conditions rather than one motivated by fantasies or dreams of upward mobility. Migrants are motivated by relatively high U.S. wage rates and the chance to support their families. (Note that Bush corrected himself to assure audiences that migrants were lured by the exact legal minimum wage of $5.15 per hour.) In this view, migrants weigh the benefits of U.S. wages against other factors and make a decision that "anyone worth their salt" would make. They are not lured by Fifth Avenue finery; they just want to "put food on the table," implying that they send earnings home to support kin. These migrants are realists who are motivated by a conscious evaluation of risk and reward and not the pursuit of a television-fueled "American Dream."

The cultural and economic explanations of migration have strong analogs in the social sciences, where the "culture versus economics" dichotomy provides a useful explanatory device to sort through a vast body of literature. Arjun Appadurai, one of the most influential anthropologists of globalization, has emphasized the importance of culture in shaping transnational migration, arguing that the flow of people and media images around the world has dramatically changed individual and collective subjectivity, allowing people to imagine "possible lives" and new aspirations that were once beyond the reach of their consciousness. Television, film, and the Internet have broadened horizons, changed consumer appetites, and, most important, changed people's concepts of membership in a wider community—that is, their identity—creating a situation whereby "scripts can be formed of imagined lives . . . fantasies that could become the prolegomena for the desire for acquisition and movement" (1996, 36).

In their classic synthesis of late-twentieth-century migration to the United States, Alejandro Portes and Rubén Rumbaut (1996) make a similar point. They challenge the view "of migration as a consequence of foreign destitution and unemployment" (10), arguing that one of the key points of distinction between the "new" immigration of the late twentieth century and the "old" immigration of the late nineteenth century is that "contemporary immigration is a direct consequence of the dominant influence attained by the culture of the advanced West in every corner of the globe" (13). In general, contemporary migrants are not directly recruited to come to America to supply labor for industrial expansion as they were in the past. Instead, contemporary migrants tend to have experienced a gap between subjective expectations for success and lived experiences in their home countries. They seek "a car, a TV set, and domestic appliances of all sorts" (13) and wish to improve their standard of living to fit rising expectations. Therefore, people with some education and income (in the case of urbanites) or assets (in the case of small farmers) are far more likely to migrate than the poorest of the poor, who are not exposed to the lure of popular culture and do not have the economic resources to migrate.[2]

Within scholarship on contemporary Latin American migration to the United States, the distinction between "economic" and "political" migration is made to differentiate migrants who leave a particular country in search of economic opportunity versus those who leave to seek refuge from political persecution and war (García 2006). Economic explanations of migration tend to emphasize how macroeconomic changes produce flows of migrants from one place to another. For example, the demand for cheap agricultural labor in the rural United States, coupled with economic decline in rural Mexico, has produced an unprecedented flow of migrants from rural Mexico to the United States.[3]

Although there is no denying that macroeconomic forces produce migrant flows around the world, "structural" explanations, which emphasize the importance of economic systems over individual choices, can minimize the degree that human volition shapes behavior, viewing people as objects who are "pushed and pulled" (as one common model for explaining migration puts it) by macro-level forces. While I certainly do not wish to discredit structural explanations of migration (and, indeed, I will utilize structural approaches throughout this book), face-to-face ethnography offers a different kind of explanation of migration decisions. In this chapter, I investigate the subjective motivations of migrants in La Quebrada to provide a sense of the human complexity of migration decisions. Through a series of ethnographic profiles, I will present detailed examples of the motivations of a group of male migrants, emphasizing the variation in their life experiences. Even within a single community, there are many types of migrants—some leave in search of the consumerist American Dream (à la Brent Scowcroft), while others want to make a quick buck and return to Honduras (à la George Bush), and others migrate simply because it has become "the thing to do" for young men at a certain point in the life cycle. While virtually all migrants speak of being "forced" to go to the United States by economic pressures, they also recognize that they make a choice that other people in similar situations do not make.

Wilmer Ulloa: A "Needy" Migrant

Near the beginning of my fieldwork, a young man named Wilmer told me that he had something to show me. It was a small paper flyer (figure 2) that someone handed to him as he got off the bus in a nearby town. The flyer was money-green, with words printed over a picture of a bald eagle, hundred dollar bills, and an American flag. The text read, "*Gane como en Estados Unidos*!!" (Earn like in the United States). Someone had handed the flyers to all the passengers on the bus arriving from the countryside. Below the headline it said, "American Company needs people willing to improve their income to $500 to $1,000 a month." The flyer listed a woman's name and telephone number, and the location of a meeting place where interviews would be held. The flyer stated that candidates should be "dynamic," "responsible," and have a "desire to succeed." Wilmer suspected that the flyer was intended to recruit workers for a new *maquila* (sweatshop), but he wasn't sure. He didn't have time to go investigate. His pregnant wife was sick and he was taking her to the hospital at the moment he was handed the flyer.

I asked Wilmer if he believed what the flyer said: Could a company in need of workers pay between $500 and $1,000 a month? "Well," he

GANE COMO EN ESTADOS UNIDOS!!

COMPAÑÍA AMERICANA
Necesita personas dispuestas a mejorar
sus ingresos de $ 500 a 1,000 al mes

Requisitos:
• Dinamico   • Responsable
• Deseo de superación

PRESENTARSE ENTREVISTA
MARTES Y JUEVES 10:00 a.m. Y 2:00 p.m.
Sábado: 9:45 a.m.
Hotel los Andes, Salón la Cumbre

Figure 2. "Earn Like in the United States!!" Flyer. 2003

responded, "I have a cousin that works in a *maquila* making hospital scrubs for an American company. He makes about $500 a month, so it's possible, but it's very hard to get a job there. There's no way they would need to hand out flyers to people like me.[4] This thing can't be true. It's probably a Korean *maquila*. They pay badly and treat people even worse. If it really paid that much, people would be lining up to work there."[5] The flyer appeared to be a scam. Wilmer asked me if I believed the flyer's offer, and I said that it appeared too good to be true. We both concluded that a company that paid such high wages (by Honduran standards) would not need to go hunting for employees at the bus terminal.

Wilmer and his wife had just had their first child, and they wanted to live in a home of their own. As it was, they lived in a tiny, dirt-floored, wattle-and-daub shack with Wilmer's father, younger brother, older sister, and niece.[6] Their home was crowded and had no electricity or running water, not because they were unavailable in the neighborhood, but because the family could not afford these services and did not consider them to be necessities. The family owned about five acres of land (*milpa*) three miles from their home, on which they grew maize, beans, squash, cucumbers, onions, tomatoes, and various herbs. They had a plot of coffee but could not fertilize it, and the plants were old and unproductive. The coffee plot provided a tiny income; as Wilmer said, "Hardly more than the cost of the sacks for the harvest."

Wilmer's only valuable material assets were a mule, a saddle, and a wristwatch that had been sent to him by a cousin who lived in New York City. Wilmer dropped out of school at fifteen, and could not read or write. Even by the standards of La Quebrada, he and his family lived a simple, self-sufficient lifestyle, yet they required cash for medicine, school supplies, shoes, clothes, cooking oil, and other necessities. To earn cash, Wilmer would slaughter hogs owned by others, and would walk around town taking orders for the fresh pork in exchange for a percentage of the sales. He was an exuberant, warm, and funny person—a charming salesman—and I used to enjoy going door to door with him to sell the portions of *pierna* (leg) and *costilla* (ribs). He thought that the presence of an American stranger would make people more willing to buy, and I would make up humorous little jingles or rhymes in Spanish to embarrass myself and make people laugh. He paid me in fresh *chicharrones* (fried pork skin or fried pork belly) to go with him, and I gladly accepted, not only because I liked the *chicharrones* but because this task enabled me to meet many people in town in an informal and light-hearted way. I had heard of many unique strategies that anthropologists used to establish rapport in the field, but door-to-door pork salesman was not on the list.

Wilmer felt that farming his family's plot and working as a butcher-for-hire could not provide enough money for him to establish a home of his own. He had taken on small amounts of debt from kin to pay for his wife's medical care during her pregnancy. In the past, he would have been

able to earn some money by picking coffee during the harvest and by selling his own coffee crop, but due to the coffee crisis (see chapter 2), this type
of work would not provide him with enough cash for basic expenses, let
alone the repayment of debt. In 2002 and 2003, a hundred pounds of coffee
cherries sold for about five dollars, and his plot provided about five hundred pounds. Twenty-five dollars does not last long, so Wilmer and the rest
of the family picked coffee on other people's farms. Coffee pickers were
paid about two dollars per hundred pounds, which worked out to between
four and eight dollars a day for a skilled picker. The harvest lasted only a
few months, though, and not every day had plentiful pickings. The family
earned most of the year's income this way, but it was not nearly enough for
Wilmer to move into his own home with his wife and child.

Wilmer told me that he was considering several options to improve his
situation. The first would be to sell his mule and use the money to move
to the city of San Pedro Sula to seek work in a meat-packing plant or
maquila, using his cousin as a connection. The other option would be to
go to the United States and try to find work there as an undocumented
worker.[7] He had heard that some people had found work in slaughter-
houses or poultry-processing plants (Striffler 2002a) and reasoned that if
he was going to do that sort of work, which he enjoyed, he might as well
do it in the United States where he could get paid far more than he would
in Honduras.

He considered the danger and expense of making the trip to the United
States (about $100 dollars, by his optimistic estimate) and debated whether
he should risk his life and separate from his family to seek work in the
United States. He knew that he could not afford to pay a *coyote* (smuggler), so the chances of successful migration were slim. Most people who
travel with a good coyote arrive in the United States on their first attempt,
but it often takes solo migrants several attempts to cross the border. More
important, his father was getting old and was increasingly unable to perform household chores. Wilmer's teenage brother could pick up some of
the slack if he was gone, but maintaining the *milpa,* which was three miles
out of town, was too hard a task for one person.

He also openly worried that someone would try and seduce his young
wife while he was gone, and he launched into a violent tirade, which was
completely out of character, about what he would do to the man that did

so, telling me how he would return from the States and bash the man's head open with a brick. The mere thought of adultery sent him into a rage, offering a glimpse into some of the deeper fears and drives that influenced his decision.

One evening, Wilmer and I were talking about his plans to migrate. I had just read in the news that a tractor-trailer filled with undocumented migrants from Honduras, El Salvador, and Guatemala had been abandoned in the Texas desert by a human smuggler, part of an operation that was directed by a young Honduran woman named Karla Chavez, who lived in the United States. Nineteen people died of heat or suffocation, including one Honduran. Two children from nearby communities were among the fifty-four people who survived the tragedy.[8] One migrant had made a cell phone call to authorities from inside the trailer, but none of the operators could speak Spanish and the desperate plea for help was ignored. I expected Wilmer to be outraged, but he was blasé:

W: It's sad, but everyone knows it's a risk to go to the U.S. *mojado* [illegally, literally "wet"). They just had a bad *coyota* [female smuggler].

D: Does this make you think twice about migrating? Are you worried?

W: Look. Life here is risky. When bad people get desperate, there is violence here. Do you know how many shootings there were here after Hurricane Mitch? Every night you could hear pa pa pa, coming from the countryside. I've been in machete fights [Shows me a scar on his arm]. Of course it's worth the risk. Is it any more dangerous than staying here?

D: Why don't you look for work in the city?

W: Have you been to Choloma? [Choloma is a rapidly growing northern Honduran city where many migrants from the country go to find work in maquilas; see Pine (2008).] It's filled with gangs. There's a lot of violence . . . delinquency . . . and it's expensive to live there. You have to buy your food and pay someone to wash your clothes. Life is hard there. A lot of bad people and violence. It's hard to make it to the U.S., but at least life there is *tranquilo,* and in a couple of years you can come back here and live well [snapping his wrist for emphasis].

Wilmer weighed the risks of illegal immigration against his prospects in Honduras and decided that it was worth the risk to set out for the

United States. He had modest goals compared with many other potential migrants in La Quebrada. He wasn't looking to buy a car or a mansion; he desired a humble home and a set of pots, pans, and dishes to outfit it. He didn't think that he could achieve this goal by working in Honduras, so he thought about going to the United States for a year or two. This wasn't an easy decision. He would have to leave his family and risk being placed in a Mexican prison or U.S. detention center if he was apprehended en route.

Theoretically, Wilmer could migrate either to the United States or to a Honduran city to achieve his goals. Both options require one to pull up roots and move to a potentially dangerous new environment. Staying within Honduras has the benefit of cultural familiarity and proximity to kin, but with the ever-growing number of Hondurans in the United States, migrants do not feel like they will be totally isolated there. The higher wages in the United States outweigh the advantages of staying in Honduras. The newspaper cartoon reproduced in figure 3 nicely summarizes the rationale of many would-be migrants. Here, a man thinks to himself, "I know that if I migrate to the U.S. illegally there is a good possibility that I will lose my life." Then, he looks at the menacing faces of crime and misery, depicted wearing the shaved hairstyles and undershirts favored by gang members, and the "paquetazo" (a series of consumer tax increases passed in 2003 under the guidance of the International Monetary Fund [IMF], which effectively raised the price of some staple foods), depicted wearing a dark suit and sunglasses, and holding a gun. He wonders what would happen if he stays in Honduras, implying that the risks may be worse than those encountered as an undocumented immigrant.

Wilmer did not see any way to improve his situation without leaving La Quebrada. He thought that organic coffee farming could possibly help, but with coffee prices so low, this was a risky proposition, and it would take several years to yield any benefits, if it did at all. No one in La Quebrada had succeeded with organic production, while the new homes built with migrant wealth were testament to the success of the migrant alternative. In general, he saw no future in coffee farming, given the low prices and the poor condition of his plot.

My conversations with Wilmer continued over several months because I eventually moved across the road from him. As I got to know him further, I realized that a rational consideration of material risk and reward was

Figure 3. "But if I stay . . . ?" Cartoon by Luis Chávez. "Dia a Dia," *Diario El Tiempo,* May 20, 2003. Used with permission of the artist

only a part of his decision-making process. Despite its logic, the thought of leaving Honduras for the United States inspired a sense of guilt that manifested itself in several ways.

One night, while Wilmer was in the middle of his deliberations about migration, he knocked on my door. I was typing notes and drinking whiskey from a plastic cup. Wilmer sheepishly asked me for a drink, and I offered him a small cupful of scotch. "Don't tell my sister or my wife," he said. He and his relatives were devout evangelical Christians, who were vehemently opposed to vices such as tobacco and alcohol. If they found out that he was drinking, they would admonish him, and he would have to publicly ask for forgiveness in church. Wilmer then revealed some personal information that was not prompted by my own questions:

W: Is it true that a lot of Hondurans get addicted to drugs or alcohol in the U.S.?

D: I don't know. What have you heard?

W: The son of Doña Sandra went to jail. He was drunk and stabbed the owner of his apartment in New Jersey. There was a group of guys there from here, and they were all drunk, making lots of noise at night. The landlord came in and told them to stop and Doña Sandra's son stabbed him. . . . I heard that the solitude there and the hard work makes you drink. . . . Plus, you have money in your pocket to buy drinks. Some people can't resist, and they drink away all the money they make. They can't send anything here or bring anything back because of vices.[9]

Wilmer rarely drank because he fought off the urge and could not afford to buy alcohol. His question about alcoholism among migrants was a reflection of his own fears and an acknowledgment of his own weaknesses. He wondered whether he could resist the temptation to drink if he had some money in his pocket and was apart from his family and the church, whose strict regulations and emphasis on guilt kept him in line. He was not an alcoholic, but wondered what might happen if he could afford to drink. How could he resist?

For three days after our conversation, I barely saw Wilmer. He started going to church again and stayed away from my house. I asked his cousin what was going on and found out that Wilmer's sister had suspected that he was drinking at my house. When Wilmer indulged, he became guilt-ridden, and he attended church the next day with the rest of his family. He considered his own weaknesses and how he would react to life, as he imagined it, in the United States, and this fear of social isolation played into his decision-making process. Certainly, he was afraid of the dangers of traveling to the United States illegally, but he was equally worried about what would happen once he arrived. Wilmer saw his family as a source of restraint, support, and order that would not be able to help him in the United States. He would be on his own.

About a week after the drinking discussion, Wilmer told me that he had changed his mind. He decided to look for work in a Honduran city instead of migrating to the United States. He could sell his mule and pawn his watch and use the money to move to San Pedro Sula to look for work in a meat-packing plant. His cousin, who was employed, would help him find work. The money from the sale of his things would pay for travel to the city for him, his wife, and infant daughter, as well as food and rent until they got on their feet. This way, he would not have to risk his life by going to the United States, and with some good fortune he could earn the money he needed. He would try to make due in Honduras before he set out for the United States.

Wilmer's story exemplifies the common interpretation of migration as a product of unmet economic needs. He desires to move into a new residence with his family, but does not have the means to do so because of low prices for agricultural commodities and the lack of competitive employment options in Honduras. He considered the lack of security in dangerous, newly urbanized areas like Choloma and decided that the move from country to city would be difficult, concluding that a move to the United States would be preferable. After a few years of sacrifice, he believed that he could return to La Quebrada and begin a more stable, happy life with his family. His decision was not motivated by the desire for upward mobility that is taken to be part of the "American Dream." He merely wanted to maintain his status position in Honduras and saw migration as a way to make necessary income quickly.

However, Wilmer ultimately chose *not* to migrate to the United States. The specter of "greed" and the feelings of guilt that it inspired lurked behind all his decisions. His association of migration with vice and egoistic action reflect the common belief that migration is a sign of excessive self-interest and ambition (described in detail in chapter 2), something that he tries hard to avoid. His eventual decision not to migrate to the United States was not based on his fear of the journey north, nor was it a purely rational consideration of means and ends. Rather, he was worried about his own self-discipline (or lack thereof) and how he would respond from life away from family and church.

Wilmer's story typifies a familiar immigration narrative that could be found in many times and places—from Europe during the Industrial Revolution to contemporary Latin America—the young, male, rural farmer leaves the country in search of new opportunities in the city, hoping to support his family, yet fearful of how his loved ones will cope in his absence. In La Quebrada, however, Wilmer's story was far from typical. People from relatively wealthy families (i.e., those that had some assets to finance the trip north) were more likely to emigrate than the poorest members of the community. These wealthier migrants tended to be labeled as "ambitious" or "greedy" because their behavior was seen as being motivated by a desire for self-advancement rather than the material "needs" of their families.

Alfredo Flores: A "Greedy" Migrant

Alfredo is the only son in one of the wealthiest families in town. His father is a prominent local politician, owner of a large coffee farm, and the manager of several other local businesses. Alfredo is twenty-five, married with two children, and lives in his father's home with his wife and two children. He can barely read or write, and is known among the townsfolk as the quintessential *haragán* (loafer), a lazy person who feels he is above manual labor. His father—an "up by your bootstraps" individualist who built his fortune on his own—refuses to support Alfredo financially, much to the delight of members of the town's gossip ring, who seem to get inordinate pleasure watching a member of this family fall to Earth.

I recall an occasion when the rotund Alfredo tried to hide from his dad by lying on his back in the bed of a pickup truck so that he would not be seen as we cruised through town on our way to a lazy afternoon of leisure. Alfredo's belly poked up above the rails of the pickup bed, so that the people on the sides of the street pointed and laughed, his big paunch revealing that he was whiling away the day, drinking with friends.

He was a jolly, self-deprecating person, and led an outwardly carefree life in La Quebrada. Nevertheless, he faced the burden of high expectations from his family. He rarely worked and was not skilled enough to take over the family businesses. Going to the United States provided a chance for him to start over and make money quickly. He dreamed of returning home triumphantly, disproving the people in town who thought of him as a humorous, benign, and somewhat tragic figure. He was willing to perform any task available to him in the United States and had many friends there who would help him find work. He thought that he could work there for two or three years and return to La Quebrada as a "success"— with a new home and car for his family.

One evening in June, in the middle of the "dead season" between coffee harvests, I was standing on a street corner with Alfredo and a group of his friends, drinking, and he declared his desire to migrate once again. "Puchale. Me voy pa' los yunai, compa" (Damn man, I'm heading for the States), he said with feigned exasperation, kicking a rock against the concrete wall of the *municipalidad* (town hall). "La situación aqui está tremenda." (The situation is bad here.) "¿Que voy a hacer, acá? ¿Cortar café? Mejor que limpie baños en los Estados." (What am I gonna do here? [Wait several months to] Pick coffee? I'd be better off cleaning bathrooms in the States). Alfredo's friends gave him a hard time about not being able to successfully migrate to the United States, but they all sympathized with him. They all had attempted to emigrate illegally or were considering doing so.

Alfredo had tried to migrate illegally five times without success, twice making it as far as Central Mexico before being apprehended by immigration authorities. A month after making his declaration to me, he embarked on his sixth try after scrounging up the cash to pay a coyote to help him pass through southern Mexico by boat, instead of going by bus or on foot. This required him to borrow substantial amounts of money from friends and to sell off some inherited coffee land to pay for the trip. He had taken on tremendous financial risk this time, in addition to the physical risk that always accompanies the journey from Honduras to the United States. His wife was vehemently opposed to the idea. She felt that Alfredo should remain with the family and be satisfied with his life in La Quebrada. She worried about being alone with the children, wondering what he was up to. She realized that Alfredo was determined to go, saying to me, "At this point, after such a great effort, he is going to leave. He won't listen to anyone."

Alfredo left with a group of about twenty men, traveling with a female smuggler who was known for having a high rate of success. He called home en route, once from Chiapas, and then from Reynosa, on the Texas border, the night before he was to cross to the United States. The next couple of days were tense, as Alfredo's wife waited to hear whether he had crossed successfully. I was sitting in the town's Internet center when Alfredo's wife arrived in tears. She had gotten word from the coyote that Alfredo had indeed crossed the Rio Grande, but had been apprehended by U.S. immigration officers and sent back across the border. He attempted to cross again, but was apprehended and placed in the *corralón*, a migrant detention center near Brownsville, Texas.[10] Using an Internet phone, she tried to call some relatives in Texas for help, and she spoke with the coyote to get an update.

Alfredo had used a false identity the second time he was caught by immigration authorities. He later told me that he claimed to be Mexican so that he would not be deported all the way back to Honduras. He was transferred from the *corralón* to the Rolling Plains Jail and Detention Center near Dallas, a newly constructed facility that received overflow from the border zones.[11] He spent four months in prison, eventually being sent back to Honduras by plane.

He returned to La Quebrada a different person. His time in prison hardened his body and darkened his skin. He tried to sustain the jocular, carefree personality for which he was known, but he did not have the same spirit as before. His friends mocked him about being sexually abused in prison and said that he looked like a *campesino* (peasant farmer) due to his muscles and sun-darkened skin. He never told me the details of his time in prison, and what he did reveal was always tempered with sarcasm and humor. He clearly was distancing himself from the ordeal.

In addition to facing shame, physical hardship, and psychological trauma, he had spent his life savings on an unsuccessful journey. He no longer had hopes to one day make it to the States, and he began to work full-time in a *beneficio* (coffee mill), performing the taxing manual labor that he despised. He was happy to be safely reunited with his family after such a traumatic ordeal, but he had the air of a defeated, broken person. He told me that he would never try to migrate again.

Surprisingly, Alfredo's story was *not* taken as a cautionary tale by would-be migrants. It was perceived as something that would not have happened to a more quick-witted or lucky person. One of Alfredo's best friends, Jorge, was not at all fazed by what had happened. He decided to migrate only a few weeks after learning that Alfredo had been apprehended.

Jorge Orellana: The Itch to Go

Like Wilmer Ulloa, Jorge comes from a landless family. His father is mute, and both his parents sell produce at a roadside stand, which is among the lowest-status jobs in Honduras. He is a twenty-three-year-old high school dropout with great intelligence and creativity, but he suffers from a lack of self-control that frustrated his teachers and eventually led to his departure from school.

I once asked him why he wanted to go to the United States, and he gave me the standard response: He was only earning forty lempira a day (about $2.50) and that just wasn't enough. He heard about the money his cousin Santos had made in Long Island and saw the beautiful new home that Santos had constructed using earnings he sent home to Honduras. He wanted a shot at success, and it didn't matter what type of work he would have to do. I asked him if, hypothetically, he was paid a hundred lempira a day in Honduras, instead of forty. Would he still want to leave? If low income really was the cause, how much income was necessary to suppress the desire to migrate? He said, "A hundred would help, but it won't let you buy a house or a car. I would still try and go."

As it turned out, he was able to prove his hypothesis. I helped him get a steady job in the town's brand-new Internet center that paid about a hundred lempira a day. He seemed happy in his job. Although the days were tedious, it was year-round, full-time employment, almost unheard of in La Quebrada, especially for an undereducated person from an unremarkable family. He got to work in the flashiest, most outwardly modern business in town, and he was earning much more money than he ever had before. However, he had to follow a strict schedule, work late into the night, and obey the rules set by his bosses—demands that challenged his undisciplined and erratic personality.

After only a few months of work at the Internet center, Jorge informed me that he was going to use the money he had saved to go to the United States. I was surprised, because I assumed that his stable employment would keep him from leaving. Defending his decision, he summed up his desire to migrate: "I can't explain it to you. Once the itch to go [to the United States] hits you, there's just no way that you can be happy here." He was defending himself by admitting that he could not explain his desire to leave in rational terms—he just wanted to go.

Jorge is the clearest example of a poor migrant whose decision was influenced by exposure to Western media. Even before he began to work at the Internet center, he was lured by the bright lights of American pop culture, and sitting on the Internet all day made "the itch" even stronger. He knew all the words to rap songs by Eminem. He and I talked about the contestants on the reality TV show "Lucha Para Sobrevivir" (*Survivor*), and he watched action movies on Cinemax nightly on a friend's television. Once he started working at the Internet center, he spent most of the day in online chat rooms with people from all over Latin America. Incredibly, he mastered reading and writing by spending hours in online chat sessions. He developed friendships and inconsequential romances with people from around the world, and pop culture was the common denominator in their initial social interactions. They would talk about music, TV, film, and sports to break the ice, and eventually these topics would give way to more personal ones like family, love, and friendship.

The Internet provided a way for Jorge to live out fantasies of upward mobility (exactly the sort of imagined lifeworlds described by Arjun Appadurai [1996]). The ability to use the Internet made a clear statement about status in rural Honduras (less so in urban areas). First, in order to be online, one must be able to read and write. Second, one must live in a community with electricity. Third, one must have the money and skill to use the Internet. Therefore, the simple act of being online suggests that a person is not an illiterate peasant and has some education and access to resources.[12] This is part of the reason why Internet romances are so popular in rural Honduras—"undesirables" are weeded out by the requirements of the medium of interaction. In a country where about 30 percent of adults in rural communities are nonliterate, and less than 50 percent of rural households have electricity, the ability to access the Internet is a sign of worldliness and refinement.[13] In a limited way (albeit one that was very meaningful to him) Jorge was able to transcend his status position in Honduras by interacting online.

Jorge started an online relationship with a young woman from the small city of El Progreso in the northern part of the country. They chatted for hours each day for about a month. Finally, they decided that they would meet in person on Valentine's Day. Jorge shined his shoes, borrowed a slick suitcase, put on his best clothes, and took the bus to El Progreso to meet his *novia de pantalla* (on-screen girlfriend) and her family. The family met him at the bus-stop, and the girl's sister accompanied them on their date. They saw *The Lord of the Rings: The Fellowship of the Ring* in a movie theater (Jorge's second time ever in a theater) and ate lunch at Pizza Hut. (Her father gave her money for the date.) He spent the evening with her family, and came back to La Quebrada happier than I had ever seen him. He told me he was in love, but it was hard to tell whether he was in love with the woman or the fantasies of Western modernity she helped him live out. All of this became moot about a month later, however, when she broke off the relationship.

Jorge was dejected and decided it was time to try to migrate to the United States once again. He had tried to emigrate a year before, and he knew the risks involved. This time, he viewed migration as a personal challenge. In his previous attempt, he had made it just over the Guatemalan/Mexican border before he was caught in a freight train and deported after spending the night in a Mexican jail. He experienced a violent, frightful trip in the train, during which a group of Salvadoran women were raped in a boxcar nearby. When he was caught by the Mexican police, Jorge claims the officer mockingly told him he was paid three hundred dollars by the U.S. government for every migrant he apprehended. Jorge laughed and told the officer, "You'll be making a lot of money off me then, because I'll be back until I make it." He was deported from Mexico by bus, given an orange and a cup of instant noodles to eat.

Jorge obviously knew the risks that migrants faced. He had stable, relatively lucrative employment in Honduras, but he was a dreamer, and the Internet and television fueled his dreams of modern self-fulfillment. It would be far too simplistic, however, to focus only on the media as the source of his impressions of life in the United States. His relationship with his older cousin Santos, one of La Quebrada's migrant success stories, played an important role as well.

Santos Orellana: The Model of Migrant Success

In 1996, at the age of eighteen, Santos left La Quebrada for the United States. He was from the same socioeconomic position as Jorge, his first cousin, and worked as a *jornalero* (day laborer) before he left. He traveled without a coyote and nearly died of exhaustion in the deserts of northern Mexico while trying to reach the United States. In a conversation with me, he claimed to have survived by drinking urine and stealing food from street vendors. In public, he bragged about the speed and ease with which he reached the States and the fact that, unlike the wealthy, he didn't need a coyote to cross the border.

Through a connection with a relative, Santos quickly found work in a chain of upscale delis in Long Island, starting off making less than three dollars an hour. Six years later, after working seventy hours a week for the same business, he was making almost twelve dollars an hour and had saved enough to construct a small, well-furnished home in La Quebrada. He timed his return so that his new home was ready when he arrived, and he brought with him a gas range, television, stereo system, and barbeque grill. His home seemed to mimic the style of the Long Island suburbs where he had lived. It had a neat yard that abutted the street and a small fence to keep out animals. Unlike the large homes in the style of the Spanish hacienda owned by the coffee elite, his was not surrounded by an imposing gate. When I asked about the absence of a gate, Santos's cousin told me that his house didn't need one because, "[He doesn't] have to worry about being robbed. [He] was once a *jornalero.*"

Santos epitomized the triumphant return that many migrants dream about. Only three months after returning, he married a beautiful nineteen-year-old girl. His wedding was the dramatic climax of his American success story. Almost everyone in town attended the service, whether they were invited or not. Truck after truck arrived at the church, their beds crammed with standing passengers. Townspeople milled about outside and crowded the interior. Gawking teens peered through the church's glassless window to get a glimpse of the service. Santos was dressed in a handsome black tuxedo that he brought back from the United States, and the bride wore a sleek, modern, white gown. At the reception, members of the groom's extended family passed around little cocktail franks on toothpicks. They poured Pepsi from two-liter bottles into plastic cups and distributed them to the guests. Instead of tortillas, they served sliced white bread to accompany carne asada and refried red beans. The couple's first dance was to "The Love Theme from the Karate Kid," a sappy American pop song from the 1980s; not a single song with Spanish lyrics was played.

After the wedding, Santos was accused of being "addicted" to everything American and some felt that his wedding was an over-the-top expression of his new American identity. It was the type of event that a *jornalero* could hardly imagine before the days of U.S. migration, and it was a very public display of Santos's new status as a successful returnee. For the dozens of young men who watched the wedding through the windows of the church, the message was clear: Undocumented migration can help you live your dreams.

On another occasion, I was sitting with Jorge on a spotless white leather sofa in Santos's new home, watching a videotape of the Dominican film *Nueba Yol* (Muñiz 1995), a tragicomedy about life as an undocumented migrant in New York. In one of the film's scenes, Fellito, a smooth-talking Puerto Rican friend of the protagonist, Balbuena, tells him that, "In New York, the dollars fly around the street like lettuce. . . . Arriving in New York is like arriving in heaven." Santos laughed and said, "Así piensa todo el mundo acá" (That's what everyone thinks here). Then, looking at Jorge, who lay prone on the couch watching TV and who was planning to leave for the States within a month, he said, "No es cierto. Allá, la vida es muy dura." (It's not true. Life is very hard there.)

Santos had been discouraging Jorge from migrating for some time. Later, I asked Jorge if he would heed the advice. "Look," he told me, "He [Santos] says it's so hard there, but he has a furnished home, a car, cows [counting off the assets on his fingers]. He has no reason to complain." For Jorge, the economic ends justified the means, no matter what his cousin said.

Two months later, I received an instant message from Jorge, saying that he was stuck in Tapachula, an infamous border town in Chiapas, working for food in the safe-house of a coyote. Mexican migration authorities were patrolling the town looking for migrants, and he needed some money to return to Honduras. He promised me that he would go back to work at the Internet center and admitted that he had made a mistake. He claimed to have contracted dengue fever (a lie) to play on my sympathies. I wired him fifty dollars to use as bus fare to get back to Honduras. He returned to La Quebrada a week later and soon went back to his old job at the Internet center.

The fitting coda to this story is that Santos Orellana, the epitome of the migrant dream, decided to return to Long Island after only six months in La Quebrada. He was bored, running low on money, and not as happy in his dream home as he thought he would be. He paid a coyote to go back to the United States and began working at the deli again. His wife felt scared and lonely in the big new home and moved back in with her mother. The home that Santos had spent six years saving for—the embodiment of his success—was left unoccupied.

These profiles convey a sense of the complex set of factors that affect migrant behavior and the difficulty of making generalizations about migrants' motives, even within one town. It is important to remember that all of these cases are from a remote town, in the midst of economic crisis, in one of the poorest countries in the Western Hemisphere. Economic opportunity is, of course, the single most important factor that attracts migrants to the United States, and the relative poverty of Honduras vis-à-vis the United States lurks in the background of all of these descriptions. However, these profiles show that different people have dramatically different motivations, goals, and aspirations when they decide to migrate. In some cases, men choose to migrate (or not to migrate, in Wilmer's case) for emotional reasons. Religious values and responsibility to family affected Wilmer's decision to stay in Honduras, and he associated migration with guilt and personal indulgence. Cultural ideas of masculine honor and pride played into Wilmer, Alfredo, Jorge, and Santos's decisions. Yes, migrants decide to set out for America in search of economic opportunity, but the decision to pull up roots is always shaped by familial responsibilities, changing cultural definitions of success, honor, and self-realization, which are now deeply intertwined with fantasies of wealth and modern consumerism driven by exposure to the mass media.

The subjects of these profiles are all men, and therefore do not do justice to the migration experiences of women in La Quebrada. As I mentioned earlier, far fewer women than men emigrate, and out of this already small number, only a handful of females (fewer than five) had returned to La Quebrada from the United States in 2003–2004. Female returnees speculated that women chose to remain in the United States because they have greater opportunity for economic independence there, while, for men, the reverse is true. Men endure a period of status decline while living and working in the United States, and they dream of returning to Honduras to enjoy a relatively high-status lifestyle.

Women from La Quebrada often found work in the United States as nannies, babysitters, or housecleaners in suburban locations. As one woman put it, "They are doing many of the same things that they do here. But there [in the U.S.] they can get paid well for it, and they have more freedom, because men act differently there." In the "ideal" division of labor in La Quebrada, men are responsible for providing food, either through subsistence agriculture or wage labor, while women are responsible for managing the household, child care, cooking, and caring for the elderly. In reality, women play a much larger role in income generation than some men are willing to admit. In addition to harvesting coffee, women often work in small general stores (*pulperías*) or informally work as maids, cooks, or clothes-washers. There are a significant number of women that work in urban *maquilas* and come back to La Quebrada on weekends. These relatively mobile women tend to be unmarried. If they do have children, they leave them in the care of their mother (the child's grandmother) while they earn money in the city. I did not know of a single case in La Quebrada where a man assumed child care duties or managed the household, nor do I know of a single coffee farm that is managed by a woman. Although scholars have demonstrated how transnational migration has transformed the gendered division of labor within families (Hirsch 2003), women remain largely responsible for domestic labor in La Quebrada.

An interesting aspect of the relationship between gender and migration is that male migrants often have to perform what is traditionally feminine labor while in the United States. They often work as cooks, dishwashers, or janitors. And when they are at home in the United States, where they typically live with other undocumented immigrants, they are surrounded by men and have to prepare their own meals and wash their own clothes. This may partly account for the somewhat exaggerated performances of masculinity that are common among returned migrants such as Santos. The time spent by male migrants in the United States is marked by a temporary inversion of gender norms that is somewhat humiliating (Boehm 2008). This temporary embarrassment fuels males' desire to return and live the life of a successful, respected señor in La Quebrada (Striffler 2007).

These profiles do not capture the full range of migration stories from La Quebrada, but they demonstrate how these decisions are shaped by a complex interplay of economic need, the drive for social status, individual ambition, and a strong sense of responsibility to kin. One of the central insights of anthropology (often used to distinguish anthropology from economics) is that all economic action is ultimately driven by social and cultural values. While people may strategically try to maximize a certain "good," the definition of *good*—which defines the ends of economic action—are shaped by cultural values. The key question for anthropologists is not how people try to rationally pursue certain ends, but how and why they define those end goals in culturally specific ways.

In the following chapter, I will analyze how the distinction between "need" and "greed" reflects changing systems of value in La Quebrada.

Prior to the rise of the migration economy, ideas of virtue, honor, and success were rooted in the social structure of the coffee economy. Migration
has changed the social topography of the community, leading people to
reevaluate and contest cultural definitions of value and success. As Clifford
Geertz wrote, change should not be viewed as "so much a destruction of
traditional ways of life, as a construction of a new one; the sharp social conflict . . . is not simply indicative of a loss of cultural consensus, but rather is
indicative of a search, not yet entirely successful, for new, more generalized
patterns of belief and value" (1973, 150).

2

THE NEEDY, THE GREEDY, AND THE LAZY

The Moral Universe of Migration

The individual ethnographic profiles in chapter 1 demonstrate that migrants from La Quebrada come from all social classes and migrate for a variety of complex reasons. The men I described *believed* that migration would improve their life situations. However, before they decided to leave, they had to balance the potential benefits of migration with physical risks and the negative consequences of emigration for their families and loved ones. Migrants had to leave their families behind in search of a respectable income, and the tension between economic and social responsibilities produced strong feelings of guilt. Male migrants often faced an intractable dilemma: They couldn't provide economically for their families *without* leaving Honduras, yet by leaving, they would be abandoning their families, crops, churches, and neighborhoods. Economic survival threatened social reproduction.

Among residents of La Quebrada, there is great confusion and ambivalence over whether migration should be seen as a positive or negative change. Everyone recognized that many individuals and families had prospered from migrant earnings and remittances. The fancy new homes, shiny cars, and home appliances were testament enough to the material benefits of migration. But most people agreed that a migrant economy was not a viable substitute for coffee farming or some other local economic system that would generate income without breaking families apart. Migrant wealth, concentrated in new homes or vehicles, may have helped a few local businesses (e.g., home construction, auto repair, and a handful of retail shops), but migrants tended to not invest in productive industries that employed people, so remitted income was kept within a small group. Without a sustainable economic base, the children of migrants would have to migrate to maintain their standard of living, threatening the community's survival as parents separated from their children, elderly parents, and other extended kin. Migration was an understandable way for people to cope with the coffee crisis, and it had been beneficial for a fortunate few, but most believed it was a short-term source of income that threatened the long-term survival of the community.

People expressed their ambivalence about migrant dependency in the idioms they used to describe migrants. Some male migrants were described as "haragán" (lazy person, loafer) or "ambicioso" (greedy, selfish, overly ambitious). People also distinguished between those who migrated out of necessity (*migrantes de necesidad*) and those who migrated out of personal ambition or a desire for self-advancement (*migrantes de ambición*). The specific ways that people distinguished between negatively valued "lazy" and "greedy" migrants and neutral or positively valued "needy" migrants demonstrate how people perceive migration as a conflict between the needs of the individual and the needs of the group. Some migrants are called lazy (*haragán*), failures (*fracasado/a*), or ambitious (*ambicioso/a*) for leaving the village, while others are lauded as dutiful, self-sacrificing *conformistas* (Zilberg and Lungo 1999). The moral distinction between these two categories depends on intimate knowledge of migrants and their families—How much land do they own? Is their house made of cement block or wood? Do they own a truck? How much furniture do they own? Do they drink or smoke? How many children do they have? Is their marriage happy? Do they have debts? To whom? The normative distinction between these two types of migration is based on a social distinction that separates legitimate aspiration from illegitimate ambition.

It would be tempting to view moral condemnations of migrants as indicative of the generalized resentment of economic inequality, which is well-known in the ethnography of rural Latin America (e.g., Foster 1965). However, La Quebrada has never been an especially egalitarian place given that it has depended throughout its history on lumber cutting and coffee farming, two forms of production that rely on exploitative forms of wage-labor and have produced stark class differences. The debate over the morality of migration reflects a more basic fact of life in an economy that depends on international migration. Migrants' social responsibilities become radically disconnected from their economic responsibilities. The tension between responsibility to family and the need for higher wages reveals itself in moralistic debates about migrant "ambition." People criticize migrants whom they perceive to value individual gain over the collective welfare of the family.

Honduran Migration in Regional Context

Before continuing, it is necessary to explain the broad patterns of Honduran emigration to the United States as well as the local history of emigration from La Quebrada. Compared with emigration from other Central American countries, Honduran migration to the United States is a recent phenomenon that has been driven by *economic* rather than *political* factors.[1] Honduras did not directly experience the widespread civil war and peasant displacement in the 1980s that was a major factor in the rise of immigration to the United States from neighboring countries such as El Salvador and Guatemala during that period. As figure 4 illustrates, migration from Honduras did not really begin to take off until the 1990s. The Honduran community in the United States is currently one of the fastest-growing immigrant groups in the country. From the 1990 to the 2000 U.S. Census, the official population of Hondurans in the United States rose from 130,000 to 217,000, an increase of 67 percent. A study by the Pew Hispanic Center (2008) listed the total number of Hondurans in the United States at 608,000, compared with 352,000 Nicaraguans, 986,000 Guatemalans, and 1.5 million Salvadorans, suggesting that the Honduran community in the United States has continued to grow rapidly since 2000.

Figures 4 and 5 illustrate how dramatically Honduran migration differs from that of El Salvador and Guatemala. Rates of "legal" Honduran immigration, demonstrated in figure 4, are far lower than those of neighboring countries, while unauthorized immigration rates (roughly approximated by border apprehension statistics) are far higher. Honduras has a relatively high rate of migrant illegality, as well as a migrant population that surged in the 2000s, whereas rates of undocumented immigration from El Salvador and Guatemala (roughly measured by border apprehensions) peaked in the 1980s and have trended downward since. By 2008, there were more "deportable" Honduran immigrants (an unfortunate term that I use only because it is used in the *Yearbook of Immigration Statistics,* compiled by the U.S. Department of Homeland Security) than there were from either Guatemala or El Salvador.[2]

Honduran immigration to the United States began in the 1950s, during the heyday of the Honduran banana economy (Gonzalez 1988).[3] Many of these early migrants were members of the Garifuna ethnic group who worked on the banana boats or in other parts of the fruit industry and interacted with U.S. citizens through business. This led to the creation of a significant Honduran community in New Orleans, an important banana port. As Nora Hamilton and Norma Chinchilla argue for El Salvador, it is likely that these early migrants were mainly middle-class Hondurans who had attained some professional skills working in U.S.-run industries, including the banana trade (2001, 29; Puerta 2003). These early-stage migrants most likely worked in the domestic-service or industrial sectors, or facilitated the fruit import/export business in the United States.

Until the 1990s, *domestic* migration within Honduras was far more common than migration to the United States. People responded to changes in the Honduran economy by moving from one part of the country to the other, and international migration was relatively unusual. For most of the twentieth century, the Honduran economy was dominated by the production of bananas for export, an industry centered in the northern part of the country, along the Caribbean coast. The banana industry was in a state of prolonged decline from the 1960s, while the Honduran coffee industry rose in importance. The centers of the coffee industry were located in small towns at high altitudes in mountainous regions of the country that had not been well-integrated into the banana economy and thus had poor infrastructure and relatively weak political leadership.[4] The export-oriented

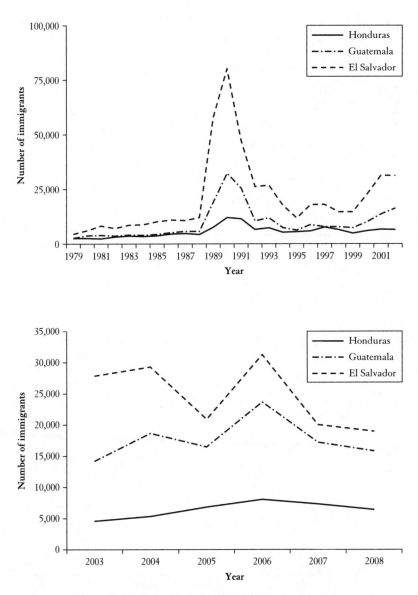

Figure 4. Immigrant admissions to the United States, 1979–2008. *Sources (top):* Statistical Yearbook of the Immigration and Naturalization Service, U.S. Department of Justice; *(bottom):* Yearbook of Immigration Statistics, U.S. Department of Homeland Security, 2003–2009.

Note: The collection of immigration statistics changed slightly after the Department of Homeland Security was established in 2002. These figures cannot be combined into one continuous line chart due to discrepancies in year-to-year data before and after the creation of the DHS.

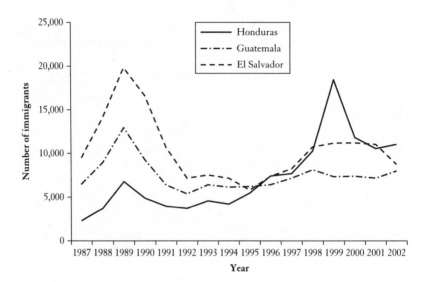

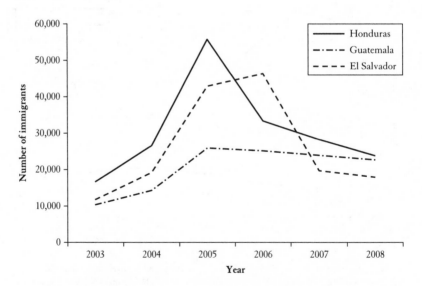

Figure 5. Unauthorized immigration to the United States, 1987–2008. *Sources (top):* Statistical Yearbook of the Immigration and Naturalization Service, U.S. Department of Justice; *(bottom):* Yearbook of Immigration Statistics, U.S. Department of Homeland Security, 2003–2009. See note in figure 4.

cattle and cotton industries also boomed during the 1960s and 1970s, caus-
ing large peasant displacement in the southern part of Honduras as large
tracts of land were converted into cotton farms or cattle ranches (Stonich
1993, 66–68).

Unlike in El Salvador, where this process led the displaced peasantry to
emigrate to Honduras or the United States (Hamilton and Chinchilla 1991;
Mahler 1995), the expansion of large-scale capitalist agriculture mainly led
to internal migration in Honduras. Honduras has relatively low population
density compared to its neighbors, so displaced people were often able to
find new, sparsely populated places to colonize. The social pressures caused
by large-scale export agriculture (especially cotton production) were far
more severe in El Salvador than in Honduras, and many Salvadoran peasants immigrated to the Honduran countryside throughout the 1960s.

In Honduras, industrial development in the northern part of the country (mainly the department of Cortés) attracted rural workers in the 1970s,
and the rapid development of the coffee sector drew migrants from various
parts of the country (Baumeister 1990). Urban industry became increasingly oriented toward the U.S. export market in the 1980s, and growth in
the *maquila* sector attracted migrants to the area around San Pedro Sula,
Honduras' industrial hub.

There was no outright civil war in Honduras in the 1980s, although the
country provided the base of operations for the Contras and other military
forces that were aligned with U.S. interests and supported by millions of
dollars in foreign aid.[5] During this period, Honduras received refugees
from El Salvador, Nicaragua, and, to a lesser extent, Guatemala (most
Guatemalans went north to Mexico). Scholars and policymakers began to
pay attention to Central American migration as a result of the violence of
the 1980s, and as such, there is a substantial amount of material on Salvadoran, Guatemalan, and Nicaraguan migration in which Honduras is
described as a *receiving* country for refugees, rather than a country of ori-
gin for migrants (Enos et al. 1984; Peterson 1986). For all of these reasons,
Honduras did not produce large numbers of immigrants to the United
States until the 1990s.

The relative absence of large numbers of Honduran migrants in the
1980s led to a smaller amount of secondary migration after the passage
of the Immigration Reform and Control Act (IRCA; Pub. L. 99–603,
100 Stat. 3359), a 1986 U.S. law that led to the legalization of three million

immigrants and expanded immigration quotas overall. These changes led to a significant secondary wave of immigration in the early 1990s, as relatives of newly legalized immigrants were able to immigrate under the "family preference" quota system that allocates visas to immediate family members of U.S. citizens. The 1990 Immigration Act (Pub. L. 101–649, 104 Stat. 4978) expanded quotas once again, and Temporary Protected Status was granted to Salvadorans. Taken together, these policies led to increases in Central Americans migration to the United States in the period from 1986 to 1992.

The end of the Cold War in 1989 ushered in a broad neoliberal economic platform in Honduras that prioritized the growth of export-oriented industry, especially garment manufacturing in urban areas, and sought to create a favorable investment climate for foreign capital. This strategy shifted the political focus away from improving social conditions in the countryside and, instead, encouraged rural to urban migration to support urban industrial growth. Migration—whether to urban areas of Honduras or the United States—became an increasingly common path for the struggling rural population.

Economic shocks were coupled with natural disaster. Hurricane Mitch struck in October of 1998, leaving nearly ten thousand Hondurans dead and displacing more than a million people, out of a total population of six million (Ensor 2009). In its aftermath, illegal immigration from Honduras spiked dramatically, with the number of Hondurans apprehended at the southern U.S. border (Entry Without Inspection or EWI) reported by the Immigration and Naturalization Service (INS) rising from 10,600 to 18,800 between fiscal year 1998 and 1999 (see figure 4).[6] Legal immigration remained steady because the number of available visas did not increase. In 1998, Hondurans already in the United States were granted Temporary Protected Status (TPS) that allowed them to remain legally until 2002. TPS was extended in 2001 and again in 2004, allowing Hondurans who arrived before January 1998 to remain in the United States legally until 2006.[7]

Hurricane Mitch damaged lowland areas, especially tobacco and banana crops, far more seriously than it did the coffee-growing regions. Close to 90 percent of the banana crop was affected, leaving 17,000 workers jobless. In the aftermath of the storm, Honduran President Carlos Flores used the fear of migration to plead for U.S. economic aid, "warning that a new wave of migrants will go 'walking, swimming and running up north' unless the United States helps Central America get back on its feet" (Migration News 1998). Migration rates remained high well after Hurricane Mitch. In fact, although EWI apprehensions have fallen from the post-Mitch spike, they rose between 2000 and 2002. A significant characteristic of Honduran emigration to the United States is its extremely high rate of detentions and deportations. As figure 5 demonstrates, far more Hondurans were apprehended and deported at the southern border from 1999 to 2002 than were immigrants from El Salvador and Guatemala. This is especially striking when we consider that legal immigration rates from Honduras are far *lower* than from the other two countries.

La Quebrada: From Coffee Production to Migration

In La Quebrada, migration to and from the United States was virtually unheard of before 1991. For most of its recent history, the town had been a destination for migrants from other parts of Honduras and El Salvador, who moved there to work in the coffee industry or forestry. The Honduran coffee industry experienced rapid growth from the 1960s until the 1980s, and La Quebrada was something of a coffee boomtown during this period (Loker 2004). Most of the current coffee-growers in La Quebrada migrated there from other parts of the region or are the children and grandchildren of these migrants. As in other parts of Honduras, the majority of La Quebrada's coffee is produced by farmers who own less than ten *manzanas* (seventeen acres) of land: 67 percent of coffee producers own less than ten manzanas of land, and 96 percent own less than fifty manzanas (eighty-five acres). In contrast to other parts of Central America, there is no coffee oligarchy in Honduras, and La Quebrada is typical in this regard (Baumeister 1990; Tucker 2008). "Large" coffee farms in La Quebrada would not be "large" by the standards of other coffee-producing countries in Central America.[8]

The coffee sector in Honduras experienced dramatic growth in the 1970s and 1980s, supported by development aid from the U.S. Agency for International Development (USAID). During this period, coffee was regulated by the International Coffee Agreement (ICA), a treaty that established a governing body, the International Coffee Organization (ICO), to control the production and sale of coffee to and from its member countries. With a few exceptions (mostly in the Eastern Bloc and the Middle East) all of the world's countries were members of the ICO. Price control was the major function of the ICO. As Robert Bates (1997, 16) writes:

> By agreement among its members, the ICO constructed an indicator price and used it to set target prices for coffee. In the later years of its existence, the target interval for the indicator price lay between $1.20 and $1.40 a pound. The agency then set quotas for coffee exports so as to force the indicator price into the target range.

The ICA system was a mixed blessing for Honduran coffee farmers. On the one hand, the agreement established a minimum price that provided security from price shocks. On the other hand, the politically driven quota system often gave Honduras an export quota that was far lower than its production capacity, which drove down prices at certain times and led the country to violate the agreement by exporting excess supply (as much as 40% of production) to nonmember countries (Baumeister 1990, 60). Among coffee-growing countries, Honduras was considered one of the "losers" in the ICA system. As a newcomer to the global coffee scene, the country did not have the political clout within the ICO to expand its quota, and the dominant players in the industry—Brazil and Colombia—fought against the influence of the Central American producers (Bates 1997, 174).

The ICA was terminated at the end of June 1989, and, surprisingly, experts predicted that its termination would have a positive impact on the Honduran coffee sector.[9] Although the end of the quota system led to price increases in some years, it led to extreme price volatility that was difficult for small, indebted producers to manage (Goodman 2008, 5). Despite the many flaws in the ICA system, on the whole, it prevented the wild swings in prices that have occurred since its demise. It offered a mechanism to control the cyclical volatility that could lead to social unrest in coffee-growing regions. For small producers who value economic security over the potential for high profits, the ICA system was an important safety net.

The Honduran coffee harvest takes place from November to February; the price paid to Honduran growers in November 1989 was about half of what they had received in January of the previous crop year. The crisis caused by the end of the ICA did not let up until the 1994–1995 crop year, and it was during this crisis period that the first wave of emigration from La Quebrada began. The period from 1991 to 1993 was the genesis of La Quebrada's migration boom, and it was a direct consequence of the ICA's demise. As one farmer told me:

> In 1991, there was a severe drop in the price of coffee [una bajada muy fuerte]. When the price was higher, I took a loan to plant more coffee, but those plants hadn't begun to produce [todavía no daban café] during the price drop . . . God knows if it would have mattered with the price so low. I needed to earn money to pay debts, so I helped my cousin, who was a traveling shoe salesman. We were in Marcala, La Paz [a town near the border with El Salvador with a large regional market]. My cousin knew some Salvadorans, and we became friends. He told me he was going to the States, and had family there to help him . . . you know . . . support him in the trip. I told him about the problems I was having, and he told me I should try to go the States. He ended up helping me in the trip. I ended up with his family in Long Island. We made pizzas in a restaurant owned by some Italians. I stayed for six years. I am a real pizza chef!

This man was the first coffee farmer from La Quebrada to emigrate to the United States. Dozens of his relatives, neighbors, and friends eventually followed his example, building on his social network to migrate to Long Island in the 1990s.

His migration narrative is familiar to anyone who closely follows the coffee trade. In economic terms, coffee has an inelasticity of supply. It takes a long time for producers to respond to signals of a changing market because coffee trees take four years to produce and shocks in the market can be sudden and severe. Many coffee farmers are not aware of changes in the market; nor do they have the resources to respond to changes (Lewin, Giovannucci, and Varangis 2004; Tucker 2008). In the narrative above, the farmer took a loan to increase production during a period of high prices before 1989, but this investment had no hope of generating income for four years. He then was forced to migrate to the United States when he could not pay his debt after the 1989 price collapse.

Emigration to the United States from La Quebrada began during the 1990–1993 crisis. By 1994, there were significant groups of migrants from town living in suburban Long Island and suburban Denver. Coffee prices rose sharply from 1994 to 1998, and this, of course, lessened the appeal of emigration and presented a strong incentive for return migration. As one man who was living in Long Island told me:

> I had people calling me on the phone saying, "You're crazy to be in the States cleaning toilets. I've got millions of lempiras [the Honduran currency] hidden in a *caja de manteca* [box of vegetable shortening] in my bedroom." People thought there was no reason to be in the States when the coffee was so valuable.

The high prices were short lived. Hurricane Mitch hit Honduras in October 1998. Although the coffee crop was not destroyed by the storm, roads were impassable, ports were damaged, and it became almost impossible to market one's crop. Mitch produced a huge flow of migrants to the United States, who helped create a network to assist people from La Quebrada when another historically low period for coffee prices occurred between 2000 and 2004. During this period, hundreds of people emigrated from La Quebrada to the United States, and the possibility of migration began to become a routine strategy for dealing with economic declines. The "first wave" of emigration set the stage for the tremendous upsurge that took place from 1999 to 2004. During this period, migration was transformed from a relatively unusual practice of last resort to a routine part of social life. Coffee farmers now routinely use emigration to manage the cyclical nature of the trade. As the mother of a coffee farmer who emigrated to the United States told me angrily:

> The *coyotes del café* [coffee buyers] used to have the power around here; now it's the *coyotes de la gente* [human smugglers]. People are selling their farms to go the United States!

How does migration fit in with other strategies that farmers use to manage risk in the market? Typically, farmers have capital to invest in production only during periods of high prices. Increased planting leads to expanded production after a four-year period in which the trees mature. The increase in supply consequently depresses prices if demand remains constant, leading to a "crisis" period, in which farmers are forced to cut back due to low prices (Lewin et al. 2004). On a macro level, this cycle eventually resolves itself, but that offers no solace to the farmers who rely on income from the coffee harvest to support their families from year to year.

Farmers respond to cyclical declines in many ways. In La Quebrada, all coffee farmers have a small *milpa* (subsistence plot on which they grow basic grains such as corn and beans), which helps their families survive poor coffee crop years (Tucker 2008). Most have chickens and/or a few pigs. These resources are mere supplements to the coffee farming, which is the primary economic activity. Even during the depths of the 2000–2003 coffee crisis, I did not once come across a farmer who converted a coffee field to *milpa*. Indeed, such a decision would be seen as economic lunacy. Referring to the severity of the coffee crisis, farmers would say sarcastically:

> If this continues, I might have to just turn my *finca* [coffee farm] into *frijol-era* [a bean patch]. What else can we do? Did you hear about so and so who is trying to grow jalapeño chiles for export? That's how bad it has become.

In this quote, we see that conversion of coffee land to a subsistence crop would be an almost unimaginable act of desperation. This farmer even mocks the decision to convert coffee land to another cash crop, jalapeño peppers. If diversification is not a viable option, a more common strategy is to take on more debt. In Honduras, many farmers rely on local money-lenders who charge incredibly high rates of interest (up to five percent *per month*) and then use accumulated debt as leverage to coerce farmers into selling them their entire coffee crop at below-market rates.

Moving to urban areas like Tegucigalpa or San Pedro Sula is another option for indebted farmers. As one man told me:

> When the coffee was really low, I once went to San Pedro Sula and found work as a security guard. My cousin lives there. It is a hard life there . . . very lonely and dangerous for a person from a place like this [the country]. One feels really solitary. The pay for someone like me is very bad. It doesn't add up, so I came back here.

Certainly, rural to urban migration was a common way to deal with agri-cultural downturns before the 1990s, but since that time migration to the United States became—by far—the most common way that farmers in La Quebrada responded to low coffee prices.

The Realities of Migrant Dependency

The new social realities of migrant dependency are visible on the front porch of *Internet Los Catrachos,* a small cinder-block building off the main square that has become the telecommunications hub of this community. The town received electricity only as recently as 2001 and had no telephone service (cellular or landline) until 2008, but it did have two satellite Internet providers, founded in 2003 by two young entrepreneurs, both of whom are returned migrants. These businesses house a handful of computers that use voice over Internet Protocol (VoIP) to make calls to the United States.[10] There, on a dusty corner, sandwiched between the town hall and the dilapidated cathedral, the postmodern division of labor is made manifest in the clientele of the Internet café.[11]

In the morning, men in their teens and twenties begin to stream in, some hopping off the backs of pickups or coffee trucks, others coming by mule or on horseback. Clutching phone numbers scrawled on balled-up scraps of paper, they ask the employee at the Internet café shop to call the U.S. phone number they hold in their hands. Some cannot read the numbers written on the paper, and diffidently hand the paper to the operator with a knowing glance. Others come in bunches, all pooling their money together to call a certain friend or relative in the United States—*pidiendo ayuda*— asking for help in financing their own trip there. Some come from the town, others make the trip from the outlying villages or *caseríos,* tiny rural hamlets that are made up of one or two extended-family households.

Although people come to the Internet café year round, the numbers swell between the months of April and September, when the coffee harvest has ended and there is little available work besides occasional odd jobs that might yield a couple of dollars per day or less. During this time, the desire to migrate intensifies, and crowds gather on the porch, gossiping and weighing their chances at successful migration, partly because there is nothing better to do. Sometimes the young men call a friend's work telephone number in the United States, and they are reprimanded for calling while the person is on the job. Other times, the same phone number appears time and time again, distributed to all the men in a certain *barrio* or village. The calls become so tiresome that the person in the States often changes his number, turns off his phone, or hangs up. The pleas are repetitive: *¿Primo,*

Figure 6. Global Systems, Internet phone calls. Daniel Reichman, 2008

me puede ayudar? [Cousin, can you help me?]; *Aquí la situación es una cosa seria.* [The situation is really serious here.]; *Está tremenda aquí compa.* [It's awful here, compadre.]; *No tengo nada.* [I'm broke.]; *¿Me manda un dinero para irme?* [Can you send me money to go?]

This part of the clientele—the regulars—was a source of comedy for the workers at the Internet café. They memorized the numbers and would try to predict how many times the aspiring migrant would call before giving up. The callers could not—or would not—take a hint, and would sometimes call every day to see if someone could help them. The excuses given by people in the United States were another source of comedy. One of the most common excuses was to say that it was raining or snowing, and there was no work, which created the impression that people did not work in bad weather in the United States. This excuse was based on the fact that many Honduran immigrants worked in house painting, construction, or landscaping. They did not work when the weather was bad, but this excuse was used even by those who did not work outdoors so that they would

Figure 7. Crowds wait to make phone calls on a rainy night. Daniel Reichman, 2004

not have to send money. One day, I checked the U.S. weather report and told the owner, a returned migrant, that it was raining on the East Coast. He said:

> *La gente va a decir que no hay trabajo. Para no enviar. Es lo más seguro.* [People will say that there's no work. So they don't have to send (money). That's for sure.]

Sometimes current events were used as excuses, such as the Iraq War and the East Coast blackout in August 2003. The employees would guess which excuse would be popular on a given day. If people in the United States used the same excuse over and over, rumors would circulate that they were lazy, alcoholic, or spending all of their money on a romantic fling. This is a sign of the intense social pressure put on migrants to produce a surplus to send home as remittances, as described by Sarah Mahler (1995). Any time people called home without being able to send remittances, they were subjected to criticism and gossip.

Not all calls were futile. Migrants who were serious about leaving would already have made a deal with a *coyote* and would call to arrange the logistics of payment and travel. These people had the resources necessary to make long phone calls and pay part of the coyote's fee. Sometimes, returned migrants looking to go back to the States would call their old bosses and inquire about work. It was a surreal experience to see a young Honduran man call a Long Island deli from an Internet phone, nonchalantly ask how business was going, and inquire about whether he could get any shifts next month, but it was a normal part of life in La Quebrada after the arrival of the Internet phone in 2003.

Virtually all migrants from La Quebrada arrive in the United States without visas. Those with some resources hire a coyote for anywhere from $2,000 to $6,000, depending on whether a customer pays in advance or finances the trip with money earned after they arrive in the United States. Groups of friends often set out alone with little more than a few dollars in their pockets, hoping to ride the *trenes de la muerte,* freight trains that travel across Mexico. Members of this group will call relatives asking for fifty dollars, or other small forms of assistance from friends or relatives. The latter group rarely makes it to the United States successfully. Although some have made it, most are apprehended by Mexican police and deported. Some are injured or killed en route. I met two men who had attempted the trip ten times. Certain returnees told me that they could not be happy in Honduras for long. They would build up some capital by working in the States, return to Honduras to live until their money ran out, and then would return to the United States to repeat the process of cyclical migration. As with Santos (described in chapter 1), locals sometimes described cyclical migrants as "addicted" to life in the United States.

By nightfall, the women start to arrive at the Internet café. Most are past their forties and wish to speak with sons and daughters in the States, often to arrange money transfers. A small segment consists of young mothers who bring their children in to speak with their fathers in the States. These people have pre-arranged calling times, and they know their kin's day off, what time they are at work, and when they go to sleep. They request money for diapers, baby formula, fertilizer, visits to the dentist, school supplies, and other mundane necessities. Sometimes the calls are tearful, others have the calculating feel of business transactions. Some people have never spoken over a telephone before. Elderly gentlemen come in, removing their straw hats upon entry. Crowds try to peek through the barred windows to eavesdrop, but they are shooed away. On Sundays, the wait to make a call can be an hour or more, especially after church gets out and entire families have hour-long conversations with loved ones, telling the operator to cut them off at a specific time because they can afford only a certain number of minutes. Migrant families find fellowship in chatting with the dozens of people waiting to call loved ones on Sunday afternoon. Often, a particularly loud talker unknowingly airs her business in front of the waiting crowd. When she leaves, the gossip begins.

Here, a new social order is emerging, in which many of the markers of status that defined life in La Quebrada before the migration boom, such as land ownership, advanced age, and political connections, are being replaced by the valued knowledge of the migrant economy, which is principally held by young returned migrants. The wisdom gained through life experience is now held by young migrants who challenge the social order of the coffee economy. At the same time, new forms of social differentiation emerge within the migrant economy itself. The meaning and value of education, lawful citizenship, and family responsibility have been redefined in the context of the migration phenomenon.

In the past, ownership of coffee land or a store, social connections to politicians, advanced age, and/or a high level of education were signs of high status in La Quebrada. In the past decade, all of these factors have been either devalued or redefined by the decline of coffee and the rise of migration. The declining importance of education is the most surprising. Teachers complain that young people—especially young men—do not see the value of staying in school since they plan on emigrating illegally when they are finished. Education level does not substantially impact one's ability to find work in the States, and college-educated people labor in the same jobs as nonliterate peasants. Three of the town's most accomplished students, all with law degrees from the national university, recently emigrated illegally and live and work in New Jersey alongside uneducated peers with no formal education. One of the town's largest coffee landholders washes dishes in an Atlanta restaurant. Predictably, the study of English has replaced agronomy as the most popular topic of study for the wealthy. There is no English taught in La Quebrada, so many parents, including the town's mayor, send their children to city schools to learn English.

In an economy that depends on wages earned in the United States, the ability to cross the border becomes the most valuable asset one can have. There are several ways to enter the United States, each requiring some combination of money, knowledge, and connections. The simplest way, a legal immigrant visa, is the least common. To my knowledge, no one from La Quebrada obtained an immigrant visa in the past ten years. Obtaining any kind of visa is an option open only to the wealthy, who can demonstrate proof of assets to the U.S. Embassy in order to be granted permission to travel. An embassy interview costs $100 and the would-be traveler must demonstrate significant wealth to convince the embassy that he or she will not overstay a visa. Even if the would-be immigrant can complete the interview process, the chances that he or she will be given a visa through the almost impossibly restrictive U.S. quota system are slim to none.[12] Several coffee growers and their children have obtained tourist visas, which require the same costly interview process, and have overstayed in order to work in the States. A tourist visa is, for all intents and purposes, treated like an immigrant visa by the general public in La Quebrada, and the ability to acquire a tourist visa is a sign of great wealth.

If a person cannot obtain a visa, the next option is to hire a smuggler to help cross the border. This also requires capital, and there are two ways to pay for the trip, which begins in Honduras, crosses into Guatemala, and then crosses into southern Mexico by boat. Once in Mexico, the migrants are smuggled through the country in trailers or buses, staying in designated safe houses along the way. According to a local coyote, the costs change depending on the "going rate" for bribing Mexican immigration officials and the costs of hiring intermediary coyotes at points throughout the trip. The cost of transportation, lodging, and food is insignificant compared to the cost of bribes and fees paid to a network of "subcontractors." And, of course, the coyotes keep some profit for themselves. One way that people pay for the trip is by selling assets such as coffee land, homes, or vehicles. This, however, is an unattractive option in a depressed economy, where people are forced to sell at low rates because they are desperate. I once saw a man, desperate for cash, try to sell fifty acres of coffee land for the equivalent of U.S. $2,000, less than a fifth of its market value. Another option is to use material assets as collateral for the smuggler, and then pay the smuggler in installments with wages earned in the United States.

Either way, traveling with a coyote is an option only for people with some capital or assets. It is not available to the poor, unless they have personal ties to the coyote and he or she trusts them enough to make the trip without putting any money down. This is common for the close kin of people who have previously traveled with the coyote. The relatives are like co-signers in the coyote's loan, and personal ties are necessary to obtain credit with the coyote, as long as the coyote knows that a relative is working in the States and can help make the payments.

The fact that coffee land is now being used as an asset to provide passage to the United States symbolizes the decline of coffee's importance, but also shows how past success is translated into capital in the migrant economy. Land, whether it is used for the production of coffee or to finance passage to the United States, is still used as capital to produce wealth. However, the coffee production employs a network of local people, including harvesters, millers, and merchants, while the use of land as collateral for migrant passage only enriches the coyotes, their lieutenants, and the Mexican and Guatemalan police and border patrol who receive their bribes to facilitate passage. The main coyote in town has not continued to grow coffee on his newly acquired land. He has converted it to pasture for cattle, when possible, and left the rest fallow, waiting for coffee prices to rise. However, the coyote has been so successful in his smuggling operation that he does not plan on investing the time or effort in coffee production.

Coffee and Social Structure

The decline of coffee and the rise of migration have weakened the social bonds that people formed through participation in domestic economic production. It is important to recognize that coffee communities are marked by a volatile economy. Although the price regulations institutionalized by the ICA managed this volatility to a certain degree from 1962 until 1989, there were still continual rises and falls in world coffee prices that affected the fortunes of small farmers.

In his classic studies of San Jose, Puerto Rico, Eric Wolf (1956, 1967) saw coffee communities as being subject to great economic and social volatility, as opposed to the "closed corporate communities" that were well known in Latin American anthropology of that era. Unlike "closed" communities, "open" coffee communities do not have stable patron-client bonds and have relatively weak systems of institutionalized reciprocity. Compared with peasant communities with strong leveling mechanisms and an egalitarian moral economy, coffee communities tend to celebrate the accumulation of wealth as a marker of prestige and honor.[13]

According to Wolf, ascendant growers in Puerto Rico tried to legitimate their position through conspicuous consumption, proving that they had "hit the jackpot" in the coffee casino. In a volatile economic climate with constantly shifting fortunes, public displays of wealth signified who was on top at a given moment. At the same time, the declining classes tried to hold on to lost glory through the same means. Public displays of status translated economic success into social prestige. Wolf called attempts for ascendant elites to prove their new status "redefining behavior," as opposed to the "retaining" behavior of the old elites (Wolf 1967, 519). Wolf saw such behavior as a rational adaptation to the volatile coffee economy. Reinvestment of profits in new homes or vehicles was safer than investing in productive capital since the bottom could fall out of coffee prices at virtually any moment, while fixed assets like cars and homes retained value.[14] Although status plays were driven by particular cultural values, such as ideals of masculinity, Wolf recognized a certain form of economic rationality in the coffee farmers' seemingly irrational form of conspicuous consumption. In this case, "conspicuous consumption" was economically preferable to reinvestment of capital in coffee land. This behavior caused social problems, however. The desire for conspicuous consumption caused ascendant farmers to reduce the amount of wealth they distributed to kin in favor of personal "redefining behaviors"—displays of rising status—and this caused jealousy and envy throughout the community (Wolf 1967, 521).

Given the inherent instability of coffee economies and La Quebrada's history as a community founded by internal migrants who arrived to work in the lumber industry, its social order is highly unstable, even when compared to other coffee communities. Because La Quebrada is a newly formed community, differences in wealth or status do not have deep familial roots. Virtually all the inhabitants of La Quebrada arrived as lumber cutters or coffee entrepreneurs, and this has fostered a strong tradition of socioeconomic mobility.

Prior to the rise of migration and the arrival of returnees, success and high status were associated with a person's ability to hire others to work, rather than work for hire. Those with even a small amount of capital hire *jornaleros* (male day laborers) to perform menial tasks in their *milpas* (maize and bean plots) and *fincas* (coffee farms). Household chores such as washing, cooking, and cleaning are commonly performed by hired women. This status hierarchy is directly tied to the division of labor in the coffee industry, with landowners hiring the landless as day laborers. Although the strong patron-client bonds found in other peasant societies did not exist between particular landowning families and "their" workers, there was a necessary structural relation between landholders and the landless.

Locals see the present as a time of severe crisis and social disintegration precisely because migration has not filled the economic or social void left by coffee's demise. The concepts of status that were formed within the coffee system seem to have no meaning in the migrant economy. Landless people and small farmers relied on wage labor on larger farms to provide the means of subsistence and reproduction. The coffee crisis created a situation where neither landholders nor landless can survive off coffee production, and migration has created an unsustainable economic base that breaks social groups apart, threatens lives, and allows organized crime to thrive.

As Sarah Mahler (1995) and Elana Zilberg and Mario Lungo (1999) noted among Salvadorans, people in La Quebrada tend to explain systemic economic conditions as the results of individual behavior. Accusations of jealousy, envy, greed, and laziness are common idioms that people use to explain the economic crisis in which they find themselves. They blame the crisis on individual character flaws more often than structural forces—such as the decline in coffee prices, restrictive immigration policy, or a corrupt government. These local narratives highlight the failings of individuals as the source of crisis.

The Morality of Migration

The moral criticism of migrants as egotistical, selfish, or greedy parallels the ways that Salvadoran migrants in the United States criticize each other, according to Mahler (1995). She argues that Salvadoran peasants who have migrated to the United States face intense pressure to produce a surplus to send home, which creates an individualistic, dog-eat-dog culture that clashes with the more egalitarian values of prewar Salvadoran rural society. Because the migrants are marginalized from the U.S. mainstream, they exploit one another to extract a surplus. She focuses on the existence of peasant networks of mutual assistance and social reciprocity in rural El Salvador that can no longer be sustained in the United States, where migrants attempt to profit off one another rather than assist each other (216).

This interpretation of migrant competition downplays the social divisions inherent in "open" peasant communities, especially coffee towns. People in La Quebrada indeed exert pressure on migrants to send money home. They depend on migrant earnings. Yet the demands are quite different for different classes of people, and they do not reflect an expectation of generalized reciprocity but rather an expectation that the structure of the coffee-era class hierarchy be maintained.

Need versus Greed.   How do people make moral evaluations of migrant behavior? Two narratives demonstrate how concepts of personal morality are rooted in local class structure, and they shape the social expectations placed on migrants. The first narrative describes certain migrants as "greedy" and "lazy." Although most migrants are incredibly hardworking and make difficult personal sacrifices for their families, they are often accused of laziness and greed by people close to them, even members of their own families. Their behavior is judged according to cultural standards that cannot adequately explain the new economic realities in which the community finds itself.

In interviews and casual conversations, people from all social classes in La Quebrada criticize migrants from landholding families by using the word *ambición*. Locals commonly distinguish between *migrantes de necesidad* and *migrantes de ambición,* which I translate as "migrants of need" and "migrants of greed." *Ambición* is a term of opprobrium, and is thought to be a sin by both the Protestant and Catholic churches in La Quebrada. The Spanish word suggests "greed for power and wealth," as opposed to American English, where it means something more like "earnest desire for success." Although *ambición* can have neutral or positive connotations in Spanish, in this case, *ambición* is the excessive—and socially disruptive—desire for honor or wealth, and is therefore more akin to the English "greed" than it is to "ambition."

The capacity to differentiate between the necessary and the superfluous—that is, to distinguish need from greed—is an example of how moral concepts can serve to legitimate class differences. One class's necessity is another's luxury. All societies draw the line between legitimate desire and greed, and such judgments reflect opinions about socially legitimate action. In English, the word *ambition* is used to describe a positive assessment of individual desire, while *greed* is a negative assessment of the same drive when it crosses the bounds of acceptability. As Pierre Bourdieu (1977, 77–78) argues, the classification of certain forms of desire as virtue and others as vice (such as need vs. greed) is an example of how social hierarchies delimit the conscious possibilities of action for certain groups. He writes:

> [T]he dispositions durably inculcated by objective conditions . . . engender aspirations and practices objectively compatible with those objective requirements, the most improbable practices are excluded . . . which inclines agents to make a virtue of necessity, that is, to refuse what is already refused and love the inevitable. (77)

The French working class has the tendency to "turn necessity into virtue," believing that certain practices—characteristic of the upper classes—are "not for the likes of them" (379–380). Bourdieu sees this as a form of ideological boundary-maintenance. He refers to moral criticisms of "inappropriate" behavior as "calls to [class] order," emphasizing that they legitimate existing class boundaries:

> The calls to order ("Who does she think she is?" "That's not for the likes of us") which reaffirm the principle of conformity—the only explicit norm of popular taste—and aim to encourage the "reasonable" choices that are . . . imposed by the objective conditions also contain a warning against the ambition to distinguish oneself by identifying with other groups, that is, they are a reminder of class solidarity. (1984, 381)

One could easily dispute Bourdieu's assertion that conformity is "*the only* explicit norm of popular taste" (my emphasis), but the key point here is that attempts to transcend the boundaries of class are often considered "unreasonable" or "in bad taste." In La Quebrada, virtually everybody I spoke with claimed that they wished to migrate out of pure necessity, whether it be the need to feed one's family or the need to purchase a new truck or build a new home. However, local gossip suggested that there were certain types of people for whom migration was considered to be a morally acceptable action and others for whom it was not, and that these moral judgments were based on social estimations of "necessity." In this case, the standard of "necessity" approached the minimal limits of human survival. The only migrants who were consistently characterized as "needy" were those who owned no land and faced dire economic circumstances, with insufficient income to house, clothe, or feed their families.

"Migrants of need" are generally the landless poor, while "migrants of greed" own coffee land or some other valued asset. "Migrants of need" make the trip to the United States on their own, while "migrants of greed" pay a *coyote*. The following quote from a landless person, criticizing a coffee farmer for migrating, is representative of the idea that certain migrants are greedy:

> If I had that much money, why would I head out for the States? I could make my life here . . . start a business . . . there's no need to leave your family. People that go with a *coyote* have their things. Why do they go? And those that go with a visa, God forbid.

The idea expressed here is that people who can afford a *coyote* have enough capital to lead a decent life in La Quebrada and therefore do not migrate out of need. The significant point is that those who can afford to pay a *coyote* to smuggle them across the border are considered to be free from "necessity" and act out of greed.

Another major marker of "need" versus "greed" is ownership of a home. Most migrants say they are motivated by a desire to *hacer mi casa* (build my house) and *comprar mi carro* (buy my car) when asked why they want to migrate. Young married men wish to move into their own homes when married, rather than live with parents. I once heard a group of young men making fun of a flashy returned migrant, who owned a new pickup, a shiny revolver, and wore gold medallions but rented—rather than owned—a shabby, pine-board shack. They said, partly in jest, "Is he stupid? It's the *house* first and *then* the car."

This returnee was criticized for spending his money the wrong way. Because the cost of a coyote is enough to construct a modest cinder-block house, those who spend money on coyotes are seen as desiring more than what is socially "necessary" for their class and are accused of "greed."

The term *conformista* (conformist) is sometimes used as a mark of honor, indicating humility and a sense that one is happy with one's position in life. It is the opposite of ambition, and means that one desires only that which is socially appropriate to people of his or her class. Consider the following exchange between me and a landless *jornalero* who was considering illegal immigration:

Q: Would you say that you are migrating out of economic necessity?

A: Look, I'm a conformist. I'm not ambitious. I don't need many things, but right now my work doesn't even provide enough for food. Some people go [to the United States] to get a car or a house. Not me. I'm a real conformist.

This respondent is defending himself against charges of selfishness by saying proudly that he is a conformist, in opposition to an "ambitious" person, who would presumably migrate to gain material wealth while shirking his responsibility to family. He, on the other hand, is truly desperate and is looking for money to provide food for his family. Conforming to social expectations is respected because it displays an acceptance of a given order. This respondent defends himself by saying, in effect, "I know my place. I'm not greedy. I just want to provide for my family."

The social characteristics that distinguish these two categories express a particular concept of virtuous conduct, in which the ceiling of legitimate aspiration parallels the lifestyle of La Quebrada's prosperous coffee growers. Surprisingly, coffee-owning parents often accused their own children of greed because they felt that they sought a lifestyle that was materially "better" than (or at least different from) that of their parents. However, the economic realities of the coffee crisis made it impossible to *maintain* this standard of living, let alone surpass it. Upward mobility in itself was not criticized. Poor migrants were not deemed "too big for their britches" or derided for challenging an existing class order. In fact, returnees who purchased coffee land or opened typical stores were celebrated as success stories. However, migrants who owned land were criticized for desiring more than what been considered "prosperous" by a previous generation. People are defending the *structure* of the coffee society and not the particular people within that structure. Upward mobility itself was celebrated as

long as the definition of "success"—the terms that defined social value—
remained intact.

The Idle Immigrant.   Another common anti-migrant narrative accused
migrants of being lazy or idle. People commonly referred to male em-
igrants as *haragán* (pl. *haraganes*), a Spanish word meaning "idle person," "loafer," or, more specific to this case, "a man who feels he is above
work."[15] The etymology of the word *haragán* is disputed, but it has been
in use in the hispanophone world since at least the eighteenth century,
when it was used in Spain to describe peasant workers who preferred to
relax in the shade, sing, or sleep while the hacienda owner was not present, according to the Real Academia Española's definition from 1758.[16]
Despite being worlds away from imperial Spain both temporally and
geographically, the word's meaning in La Quebrada was quite similar
to the Spanish definition. A *haragán* is a man with a subpar work ethic
who shirks his social responsibility in favor of self-indulgent leisure. Both
in interviews and in neighborly conversation, people would criticize migrants as *haraganes*. This definition surprised me because I tended to
think of undocumented workers in the United States as hardworking
and self-sacrificing people who performed difficult labor to support their
families back home.

That this view that migrants are perceived as lazy was largely uncon-
tested by returned migrants was even more surprising. Returnees seemed
to reinforce, rather than challenge, this misperception. I expected concepts
of wealth and status to change in accordance with the new social realities
of migration, but such concepts die hard, and the presence of returnees had
done little to challenge the idea that migrants were selfish.

Alfredo, profiled in chapter 1, is perhaps the most extreme *haragán* in La
Quebrada, yet he symbolizes the current generation of young males for several reasons. First, the recent crop of migrants inherited coffee land from
their parents and have abandoned it for the United States. Second, their decision is seen as a desire "not to work" because they are not working in coffee
farming. In addition, information about the hardships of life in the United
States is lacking, which allows the paradisiacal impression to survive. Telephone service is new, and impressions of U.S. life are strongly influenced by
U.S. satellite cable television programming, which has been available in La
Quebrada since electricity arrived in 2001. Returned migrants rarely admit

to struggling in the United States. When they do, they are dismissed or ignored (Mahler 1995, 85–86). People believe they are "making excuses" for not having returned with more money or for having sent too little money home while they were away. The successful returnees make those who remain in the United States seem lazy, and people wonder why so-and-so was able to return with money while another person was not.

One would expect the growing number of returnees to challenge such depictions of migrants. There are signs that this may occur in the future, but, on the whole, migrants have done little to challenge these criticisms by presenting their own view of the world. As Mahler (1995) notes, returnees and migrants do not counter the utopian perception of life in the United States held by their countrymen. In many cases, they reaffirm this view, and when they do speak of hardship, people refuse to believe them (1995, 85–88).

Returnees' tendency to maintain the utopian image of the United States creates an unrealistic impression of migrant life. The presence of "successful" migrants makes some families feel that they are receiving too little money from kin in the United States and that perhaps their relatives are wasting money on "vices" in the States. This is especially true among the wives of married men in the States, who resent being left alone and are often suspicious of their husbands. They believe that they should be receiving far more than they actually do, largely because of the myth of easy money in the United States. It is common for people to suspect that migrant relatives are secretly hording some of their income or spending it frivolously, especially on alcohol or extramarital affairs. If the migrants are earning so much in the United States, why are people in La Quebrada not receiving more? The behavior of returnees ends up placing more pressure on migrants by creating unrealistic expectations. This impression is so deeply rooted that people refuse to accept evidence to the contrary, which perpetuates the migratory cycle.

Consider the following joke that I heard dozens of times while in the field:

Did you hear about the guy from La Quebrada who went to the States? Well, on his first day there, a couple of minutes after arriving, he sees a ten-dollar bill on the ground. He's there with a friend who says, "Hey man, are you going to pick that up?" The guy smiles and says, "No, leave it there. I don't feel like working today."

This joke is significant for two reasons. First, it suggests that people do not have to work hard to satisfy their needs in the United States. Money is everywhere. At the same time, the migrants will not work to obtain the money. When I asked a woman in her sixties to explain why the joke was so funny, she replied,

> It's that they [migrants] don't want to work. Not even to get ten dollars. . . . They are some real loafers. [*Es que ellos no quieren trabajar. Ni para sacar diez dólares. . . . Son unos haraganes.*]

This woman's son works as a salad chef in a motel near Mt. Rushmore in South Dakota. Her late-husband was one of La Quebrada's largest land-holders. She called her own son, who sent money home at regular intervals, a *haragán,* largely because her once-prosperous family had fallen on hard times, and she placed the blame on him. The joke seemed to reflect her experience with migrant dependency, and she found it quite funny.

The joke emphasizes the laziness of the migrant pair, as if to say, "Even in a place where there's money everywhere, they still won't even bend to pick it up." Taking the joke into account, it is possible to see why Alfredo is the epitome of the migrant *haragán.* He was given every opportunity to succeed and now must migrate to find work. He is even unsuccessful at migration, having been deported or detained during all of his attempts. The relative ease of Alfredo's upbringing, and his inability to take advantage of it, is analogous to the dollars on the ground that the migrants choose not to pick up. The key is that neither Alfredo nor the other migrants have—in the public's opinion—taken full advantage of what their parents have provided.

Alfredo and his peers are members of the first generation to have been raised entirely in La Quebrada. Their parents were migrants from other parts of Honduras who had some success in coffee growing. Although Alfredo has not been able to migrate successfully, many of his peers, the sons of the coffee elite, have done so. These people face the pressure of rising expectations of success while living in a declining economy. Their parents were able to make a living as coffee farmers after the departure of the lumber industry. However, the coffee crisis has made it almost impossible for young people to achieve the prosperity of their parents, making emigration a popular alternative. The general economic decline that La Quebrada has experienced in the past decade is often blamed on their perceived lack of work ethic. People perceive the economic crisis to be the result of the younger generation's laziness. The *haraganes* bear the responsibility for the hard times in which they live, and are accused not only of abandoning the coffee industry but also of not being able to earn enough in the United States. Whereas Alfredo's parents' generation worked from the bottom up, the current generation is seen as lazy, unwilling to do the work that their parents did to achieve their relatively high status. They bear the responsibility for the general economic decline in La Quebrada, and their decision to migrate is seen as an abandonment of their social obligation. That Alfredo has even failed at migration turns tragedy into farce.

The narrative is an expression of generational decline that places the blame for a structural problem (the coffee crisis) on the shoulders of individual young people. The hard times in La Quebrada are seen as the outcome of decisions made by individual actors, and migration is perceived as an escape from the burden of local expectations and responsibility—a cop-out by the spoiled youth who then waste their opportunity to earn money in the United States. This intergenerational element of remittance economies explains why migrants are so often seen in a negative light, especially when parents depend on their wages for survival.

Migration as Threat to Social Reproduction

One of the most important aspects of an economy based on migration (and especially the dangerous undocumented migration so common in La Quebrada) is that economic production becomes separate from participation in other aspects of social life, especially family life. To earn a decent wage, migrants must separate themselves from the sphere of the household and the day-to-day obligations of kinship. Although transnational communications technologies (phone, e-mail, Internet) allow migrants in the United States to remain connected to social life, these technologies cannot substitute for actual participation in the local community.

In rural Honduras, there is no clear separation between "work" and "home" as there is in most developed capitalist economies. During coffee season, children work alongside their parents and grandparents. Stores are family affairs, located in the front of family homes, with children and elderly people frequently taking part in running the business. Children are constantly being sent to run errands for their parents, bringing workers hot lunches and cold drinks in the fields, picking up supplies at the hardware store, or pitching in to help with the work. Even the owners of large coffee farms and *beneficios* have employed workers come into their homes, where they are paid for a day's work or given a cold drink. "Work" is not conceived as a sphere of life that is separate from the home.

The term *social reproduction* is often associated with the preservation of traditional customs and social practices across generations, as opposed to "transformative conditions and historical questions" (Moore 1986, 329). Social reproduction therefore tends to be associated with static approaches to ethnography that capture the dynamics of a self-perpetuating social system while de-emphasizing processes of conflict and change. However, "social reproduction" does not necessarily need to be set against change. Anthropologists have refined the concept to describe the process through which a social group organizes itself to produce people in accordance with collectively held values (Foster 1995; Fajans 1998; Graeber 2006). The *particular* values through which a society defines itself are always subject to debate and historical change, but collective social processes such as child rearing, socialization/education, marriage, and death are always designed to create certain kinds of individuals in accordance with society's highest values, which tend to be reflected in important life cycle rituals (births, graduations, weddings, funerals).[17]

Most social theory that deals with "production" has tended to sever the production of material goods and the satisfaction of biological needs from the production of *good people*. As David Graeber (2006) writes,

> This approach does, indeed, take it for granted that while any society has to produce food, clothing, shelter and so forth, in most societies the production of such things as houses, manioc, canoes is very much seen as a subordinate moment in larger productive processes aimed at the fashioning of humans. (71)

He continues:

> When value is about the production of people, it is always entirely implicated in processes of transformation: families are created, grow and break apart; people are born, mature, reproduce, grow old and die. They are constantly

being socialized, trained, educated, mentored towards new roles—a process which is not limited to childhood but lasts until death. (75)

It will likely come as no surprise that some migrants from La Quebrada were accused of being "greedy." In anthropological studies of rural Latin America, time-worn concepts such as the "limited-good" (Foster 1965) and other versions of the "moral economy" emphasize group solidarity, generalized reciprocity, and social reproduction over individual initiative. On the surface, the criticism of migrants as "greedy" could appear to be an example of anti-individualist sentiment in rural Latin America. However, this is not the case. In La Quebrada, individual upward mobility is greatly valued, but only up to the point where it becomes "greed." All societies contain normative concepts of right and wrong that limit extreme individualism. Indeed, they could not be considered "societies" if they did not. The difference between these two categories reveals basic principles of individuality and sociality in La Quebrada. The determination of this boundary is not a reflection of a *distinctive* orientation toward a moral economy. These concepts are not timeless ethical principles—they are contested within the political and religious spheres. In La Quebrada, the standards of "need versus greed" are the product of the class structure of the coffee economy, and the rise of a migrant has challenged or transformed these concepts.

Individual ambition is seen as a negative only when it threatens the reproduction of local social structure. La Quebrada is based on a structural relationship between landowners and landless workers; when people who own large amounts of land and a home decide to migrate, their personal ambitions are deemed "greedy" because they are destroying the economic base of the community without developing new alternatives. People value economic upward mobility, as long as individual economic success provides some form of employment for others, maintaining the viability of the local economy.

In this case, the markers of "greed" tend to reflect a pursuit of individual gain at the expense of processes of social reproduction. This does not mean that any ambition beyond the minimal needs of reproduction are seen as antisocial. Migration is seen as negative only when it threatens the community's economic base, which *itself* is based on exploitation and production for profit. Coffee production is seen as far less exploitative and dangerous than the migrant economy because it at least allows families to remain together, with adults caring for children and the elderly. Migrants are greedy because they must leave their families in search of a decent wage, eroding social relationships in search of the economic means of survival. The drive for self-advancement only becomes "greed" when it threatens social reproduction.

This does not explain why the contemporary crisis is so often framed as the product of individual character flaws. I suggest that the local criticism of migrants arises from a profound sense of confusion about how and if La Quebrada can continue to survive as a community if it depends on a remittance economy. Much of the meaning of local gossip lies in the act of telling it. People explain the crisis in whatever terms they have available, and the ability to formulate an explanation of how and why migrants are able to prosper or fail—however humorous, simplistic, or mean-spirited—provides the speaker with a sense of control and comprehension. Gossip, especially critical gossip about migrants' failings, allows people to reassert principles of sociality at a time when the world seems to be turned upside down. Some migrants, like Santos Orellana, leave town with nothing and magically return to live the lifestyle of the coffee elite, while the children of the coffee elite struggle to survive. The journey to the United States is often a magically transformative event that many in La Quebrada—especially the older generation—cannot comprehend. The act of giving one's opinion—no matter what that opinion may be—demonstrates some ability to find meaning in lived reality.

The popular view of migration is necessarily ambivalent, and the negative gossip about migrants always is accompanied by a tacit acknowledgment of their economic importance. Locals know that many families depend on remittances, and that some individuals have achieved economic success. At the same time, they recognize the dramatic negative consequences for the future viability of their community. They tend to express this negative sentiment in incoherent ways, targeting individual migrants, even while knowing that they rely on them economically. They do not know a way out of this cycle.

Until the mid-2000s, the popular ambivalence over migration that I have described here was not reflected in mainstream political or intellectual debates. Migrant remittances now generate more domestic income than any other sector of the Honduran economy, including agriculture and the maquila, so the government views migration as an economic resource.

This is a reasonable position. Places like La Quebrada would be far worse off in the short term *without* migrant remittances than they are with them. Indeed there are many communities in Mexico (Cohen 2004; Striffler 2007) and El Salvador (Pedersen 2003) where long-term processes of back-and-forth migration have allowed remote villages to survive and even prosper. However, as I have suggested here, the unique history of Honduran migration makes it more difficult for individuals, families, and communities to establish long-term social connections with migrants than it has been for migrants from other Latin American countries. In Mexico, for example, there has been a generations-long process of seasonal migration to the United States; many of these Mexican workers obtain seasonal agricultural (H2A) visas, which are extremely difficult for Hondurans to acquire.[18] In 2009, more than 37,000 Mexicans held H2A visas that allowed them to come to the United States as seasonal agricultural workers; only 15 H2A visas were given to Hondurans.

Given that the migration boom from Honduras started in the 1990s, people have not benefited from the family preference quotas for legal immigration that the U.S. government uses to distribute visas. Countries such as Mexico and El Salvador, which had high levels of migration pre-IRCA, benefited from the amnesty program initiated in 1986, which allowed for the legalization of undocumented immigrants who had been in the United States since 1982. Legalization produced a "chaining" effect that generated more migration from those countries (Zolberg 2005, 371–375). Because of the relatively recent genesis of Honduran migration, the proportion of undocumented versus legal Honduran migrants is far higher than that of any other country. The social networks that facilitate migration simply aren't as extensive or strong for Hondurans as they are for Mexicans and Salvadorans.

Migrant remittances play a vital role in the Honduran economy, and a severe decline in remittances would be disastrous in the short term, but this does not mean that a "migration economy"—especially one that depends so heavily on dangerous, illicit forms of migration—can provide an economic system that is sustainable in the long term. In even broader terms, the view of "migration as development" ignores systematic inequalities in favor of short-term revenue generation. In this view, as long as money comes in, the underlying processes through which wealth is produced do not matter. Unfortunately, politicians and intellectuals tend to downplay that communities that depend on migrant remittances face an unsustainable future.

Families are broken apart, and education is devalued. Organized criminal networks led by *coyotes* and drug smugglers attain tremendous social and political clout. Migrants die in the desert. Women disproportionately bear the responsibility for raising children and caring for the aged.

Throughout Latin America, development leaders have argued that migrant money can be put to positive use. The only way to end the need to migrate is to create economic opportunity at home, and they argue that migrant dollars can be used to this end. By embracing migration as "development," governments are trying to be pragmatic and resourceful, but what message are they sending? From the perspective of a would-be migrant, why rely on the largesse of your countrymen in the States when you can join them? Why depend on the "trickle down" from migrant remittances when you can go to the source? Is the government giving up on domestic reform? The desirability of migration demonstrates a lack of domestic economic opportunity and thus the failure of previous development paradigms to create that opportunity. By embracing migration, politicians are looking for a way to end the cycle of migration by creating something at home, but they are tacitly acknowledging migration's effectiveness. The "big questions" of global inequality have faded to the background in favor of a resigned acceptance of migration as a fact of life in a globalized world (Gledhill 1998; Binford 2003; Pedersen 2004). It seems fruitless to ask why these countries must depend on remittances in the first place or to investigate the structural factors that make the worst job in the United States better than the best job in the Honduran countryside. In this political climate, the migrant development platform takes the resigned position that countries like Honduras must "make do with what they have," viewing migrant remittances as an economic resource.

In chapter 3, I trace the history of Honduran social policy to understand how it has arrived at this point. Under a neoliberal economic model that prioritized absolute economic growth over social stability, the basic issues of social equity that guided development policy since the 1950s have been replaced by a narrow focus on short-term income generation and growth, with scant attention paid to the distribution of resources or the long-term social costs of economic activity. As I will argue in chapter 3, the contemporary view of migrant remittances as "development" is the end result of a long and painful process of depoliticization.

3

THE ASHES OF PROGRESS

A Biography after Modernization

Hernán López was the first person that I met in La Quebrada. He was active in all manners of community politics and one of the leaders of a participatory rural development project that was being carried out by U.S. Department of Agriculture (USDA) and Cornell University in 2000 and 2001. He owned about fifty acres of coffee land and was helping to establish an organic coffee cooperative that was preparing for its first harvest when I arrived in La Quebrada in 2001 for exploratory research. Because I was introduced as a Cornell student by a member of the project, Hernán was outwardly cooperative and kind from our first meeting, showing me around the co-op and patiently answering my questions. Our initial relationship was relatively formal, but when I returned to La Quebrada for an extended stay after the initial research, I spoke with Hernán several times a week, picked coffee on his farm, helped him weigh coffee and bring it to the *beneficio,* and frequently turned to him with questions about local politics and history.

Hernán lives in a large, nondescript, concrete home on the top of a hill a few miles from town. He also owns an adjacent *pulpería* (general store), which turns his home into a neighborhood community center, where passersby sit on outdoor benches to wait out rainstorms, buy cold drinks and household staples, or just sit and chat. He has a lush garden where he experiments with different crops and organic techniques. In addition to staple crops like corn, beans, and squash, I noticed a patch of raspberry bushes, a plant I had never before seen in Honduras and have not seen since, as well as carrots, radishes, and other vegetables that are uncommon in the area and demonstrate his curiosity and desire for innovation.

Inside Hernán's home, one immediately notices a bookshelf in the center of the living room, which stands out against the drab cinder-block walls and bare concrete floor. The bookshelf contains titles on indigenous peoples, psychology, the history of philosophy, Marxism (Lenin's *What Is to Be Done?*), pedagogy, and organic farming techniques. The walls of the home are bare. Religious icons, family photographs, and framed school diplomas—common in even the most sparse Honduran homes—are notably absent. Besides the bookshelf, the living room contains a floral print living room set and not much more, except for a shelf that holds bottles of natural medicines purchased from a vendor in the city. An open kitchen, with a typical wood-burning stove and a new (atypical) electric refrigerator, abuts the living room. A hired cook offers visitors a glass of fresh tamarind juice, a homemade pastry, or perhaps a cup of coffee.

A self-described "activista, revolucionario, y cafetalero" (activist, revolutionary, and coffee farmer), Hernán is a socially minded, highly educated farmer, who is as comfortable discussing Marx's critique of the Hegelian dialectic (*My friend, you don't understand the negation of the negation!*) as he is coffee varietals. He is an idealistic, sometimes intimidating man, whose tendency to turn any conversation into a political debate has earned him a reputation for demagoguery and political grandstanding. Trained as a teacher, he is wont to spontaneously lecture on political theory—especially Marx—and his outspoken atheism has made him a polarizing figure in this deeply religious community.

Though small in stature, he exudes toughness, always seeming ready to burst from his own skin in argument. His eyes focus intensely, and his veins bulge from his forearms, which ripple with muscle from years of work on his coffee farm. He sports a pointy Leninesque beard that gives his face a diabolical cast. There are no casual conversations with him. Everything is an intellectual battle, and he seems to get great pleasure from putting his opponents off-guard with bluntness or hyperbole intended to shock (e.g., referring to prominent Honduran politicians as "corrupt, Mafioso, assassin, son-of-a-bitch criminals"; referring to anthropologists as *antropáfagos* (man-eaters); or arguing to me, with an impish grin, that President Bush intentionally destroyed the World Trade Center on September 11, 2001, while brandishing a dusty, battered, floppy disk that, he claimed, provided incontrovertible evidence on the matter, if only the files would open). Once accustomed to his style of argument, one realizes that such pronouncements are made in the spirit of intellectual combativeness rather than reasoned belief. Hernán's rhetorical style is designed to provoke, and he eventually moderates his views after much debate. What he lacks in nuance, he makes up for with passion.

One day, I asked Hernán what his dream for La Quebrada's future would be. He answered with uncustomary restraint and seriousness, showing none of his typical bombast:

> I would like to create a center for sustainable living . . . a community-owned building with land and fields to produce all types of food . . . tilapia ponds, organic orchards, all types of fruits and vegetables, and of course organic coffee for export. We could even have a small hotel for tourists. We would have a recreation center where the youth could play sports, a soccer field, table tennis. I would like to have acupuncture, herbal medicines, and other types of alternative health programs.

Hernán envisions a sustainable land of plenty that is self-sufficient, equitable, environmentally friendly, healthy, and fun. His vision closely parallels the model of eco-development that has become popular throughout Central America in the last two decades, as the "green" politics of sustainability and participatory development became touchstones of social reform (cf. Babb 2004). Eco-tourism, nontraditional export agriculture, and community development are all combined in Hernán's vision.

The story of how Hernán—a self-described radical—came to embrace this relatively moderate political agenda speaks to the general intellectual history of Central America since the Cold War. His youthful belief in large-scale sociopolitical theories of progress—first social democracy, then Marxism—transformed into a belief in participatory local democracy and eco-projects like orchards and tilapia ponds, supported by international organizations. This transformation did not happen overnight. In fact, it was a painful and frustrating process that ended in Hernán's disgusted resignation from politics in 2004.

Honduras after Modernization

The 1980s are often called Latin America's "lost decade," due to the violence, economic upheaval, and political oppression that marked those years. They were especially painful in Honduras, which became the "main girder in the bridge" (LaFeber 1983) for a U.S. foreign policy obsessed with stopping the spread of the Soviet sphere of influence in the Western Hemisphere. Surrounded by countries mired in brutal civil wars, Honduras became the base of operations for many important parts of the Cold War hemispheric struggle, most famously, the training of the Nicaraguan Contras (Grandin 2007).

By decade's end, the Cold War was waning, and new forms of politics had emerged, not only in Honduras but throughout Central America. As democracy was restored in the region, "new" social movements (Laclau and Mouffe 1985; Escobar and Alvarez 1992) rose from the ashes of defeated guerilla armies, and Central American social reformers set their political sights on the cultural rights of particular ethnic groups and environmental preservation rather than on the more systemic issues of economic inequality or dependency that informed politics in previous decades.

After the return to democracy in Honduras in 1990, nongovernmental organizations (NGOs) took on important roles as protectors of social welfare, while national agrarian boards, peasant organizations, and labor unions lost political clout. The political system became decentralized, and individual municipalities were given greater legal autonomy than they had in the past. As the immediate horror of the violence subsided, social reformers turned to more pragmatic forms of politics that yielded many important benefits. However, new social movements pushed basic questions of social equality to the background, as the demands for equal rights and legal representation eclipsed the demands for class equality that shaped the socialist agenda (Laclau and Mouffe 1985). This shift away from a class-based political agenda occurred at a time in history when the gap between the world's rich and poor increased at historically unprecedented rates.[1] These movements shifted the grounds of social policy away from state-level institutions and turned international NGOs into the most visible promoters of social welfare in Honduras.[2]

As NGOs became increasingly important politically, the Honduran economy became more and more dependent on migrant remittances. Between 1990 and 2005, migrant remittances went from an insignificant part of the Honduran economy to the single biggest source of foreign exchange. The rise of migration to the United States in the past two decades serves as a clear symbol of the inability of Cold War development policies to bring about meaningful hemispheric reform and regional economic stability. After decades of agrarian reform, state-led development programs, and billions of dollars of foreign aid spent on international development schemes, remitted wages from people working in the United States have become the most important source of income for many rural communities, including La Quebrada.

Remittances have diffused some of the political economic tensions that were left unresolved after the "lost decade." Without migrant dollars, there would likely be greater competition for low-paying jobs, increased rural to urban migration, and general economic unrest. Because the short-term economic benefits of migration—such as increased incomes and stimulated domestic consumption—have diffused domestic political conflict, migration is often described as a political "escape valve" by Central American intellectuals. Some politicians, notably Mexico's President Vicente Fox, have publicly celebrated migrants as "heroes."

The purpose of this chapter is to explain how historical events have shaped political culture in contemporary Honduras, and to illustrate the relationship between the rise of migration and the transformation of rural politics. The belief that migration is a solution to rural problems—held not only by migrants but also by politicians and intellectuals—is one consequence of the depoliticized climate that arose since the 1980s, when the military leadership effectively destroyed both radical and reformist politics in the country, until opposition to the coup d'état of 2009 reenergized political groups that had been largely pushed to the margins. To see undocumented migration as an economic resource is a rather narrow understanding of progress in that it values the inflow of foreign exchange provided by migrants while disregarding the damaging long-term social consequences of migrant dependency.

The contemporary vision of migration as "development" must be placed in historical context. Since the end of World War II, the Honduran government has tried to improve the condition of rural society through various sorts of modernization programs, such as agricultural intensification, expanded public education, public health initiatives, and land reform. That migrant remittances are perceived as an acceptable substitute to social or economic policy measures demonstrates the rejection of modern ideas of progress based on class compromise and redistribution of wealth, and the valorization of any practice that provides income in the short term.

Hernán's story is, in one sense, uniquely Honduran, but it also reflects more systematic trends in the history of Latin American progressive thought. His political life began with an interest in progressive democracy in the 1950s, then turned to radicalism in the 1970s, and eventually came to embrace participatory democracy, "local" empowerment, and sustainable entrepreneurialism by the early 1990s. His life serves as a model of the general ideological trends that Honduran rural activists have followed since the 1950s.

Learning Modernity: From Catholic Priests to the Cuerpo De Paz

Hernán came of age at a pivotal moment in the history of Honduran politics. During the 1940s, 1950s, and 1960s, the Honduran government began to play an important role in the promotion of public welfare in rural areas, and the state became increasingly representative of a national community rather than a small cadre of elites and neocolonial fruit companies. Swept up by the tides of post–World War II modernization, the Honduran government attempted to improve social conditions through public education, public heath, labor policy, and agrarian reform. Taken together, these policies instilled a new *modern* political philosophy that was initially promulgated by elites but became a part of mainstream culture by the 1960s.

This philosophy was premised on a diachronic notion of progress, founded on the *possibility* of a compromise between labor and capital and a close link between state and nation (the government and the *pueblo* [people]). This new conception of the role and responsibility of government led to rising expectations of socioeconomic progress, following the democratic model of capitalist modernization. Unfortunately, the growth of democracy and the first steps toward a class compromise would be stunted by the political realities of the Cold War in the 1960s.

Hernán was born in 1949 in a provincial coffee town about thirty kilometers (18 miles) from La Quebrada. His hometown was a conservative community devoted to coffee production (for landholders) and subsistence agriculture (for smallholders and landless people). At that time, the town was dominated by the Catholic Church, and his mother was, in his words, "a Catholic fanatic" who constantly prayed to the saints and forced him to say the rosary several times daily. He spent a great amount of time with his paternal grandfather, who, in his words, was a *cacique* (chief or political strongman) who owned cattle land outside of town and was a local political leader.[3] He speaks of his grandfather with great nostalgia as a relic of a bygone premodern era when people gained wealth and status by sponsoring rituals and redistributing wealth:

> My grandfather was *todo un señor . . . un hombre de verdad* [A total gentleman, a real man]. He had eighty-five children with ten women. . . . Can you imagine? And here was a man who lived with *honor*. He was rich and he had land, but he never had to worry because people *respected* him. He buried all his money in the ground. He never went to a bank. . . . No one would even think about robbing him. When someone in the family, or maybe a *campesino,* had a wedding, the entire village was invited and everyone could eat the cake . . . which, back then, was really just bread. And he would sponsor Catholic masses in [the closest parish]. . . . Everyone respected this man. He was a man of the people.

At that time (1949–1954), Honduras was led by president Juan Manuel Gálvez, a member of the National Party, which had long been an ally of the Catholic Church. For most of the first half of the twentieth century, the Honduran army brutally repressed labor movements among urban artisans and workers on the banana plantations. This began to change in the late

1940s. In 1949, Gálvez signed an Organization of American States (OAS) charter guaranteeing the rights of labor organizations (Euraque 1996a, 92). "Two years later, the Honduran congress created the Bureau of Labor and Social Welfare to implement reform measures that included shortening the work day, restricting the use of child labor, and creating worker compensation" (Soluri 2005, 171). In 1954, Honduras was shaken by the largest strike in Central American history, when 35,000 banana plantation workers allied with factory workers in what has been called the Honduran "Paris Commune." This strike led to a wave of labor reforms, assisted by the CIA and U.S. labor-relations specialists, and the country's first national elections in several decades in 1957—the first elections in Honduras with universal suffrage. Dr. Ramón Villeda Morales, a progressive Liberal, was elected in 1957 and proceeded to institute a wave of U.S.-backed state reforms, supported by the Alliance for Progress, which "recommended vigorous land-reform, rapid and broad-based industrialization, and expansion of the functions and resources of the state" (LaFeber 1983, 294).

Hernán was directly affected by the election of President Villeda Morales. His early education was in a parochial school; Honduras had no truly national public school system until the 1950s, and it expanded greatly under the modernization programs led by Villeda Morales.[4] Hernán switched to a public school at age eleven. His move to a public school coincided with the questioning of his mother's faith.

> At the age of twelve, I began to doubt the Catholic religion, and I was fighting with my mother. I began to hear about [Fidel] Castro, Che [Guevara], and the Cuban Revolution on the radio broadcasts, and I expressed my support for the revolutionaries. This outraged my mother since she thought I was disavowing the Catholic Church. . . . She kicked me out of the house when I was sixteen.

Hernán took the Christian value of iconoclasm too much to heart for the taste of his mother and his religious teachers. He acknowledges that his political development was closely linked to adolescent rebellion. At that time, progressive politics were absent from the Honduran Catholic Church, which had not yet been reformed by the Second Vatican Council and the rise of liberation theology, which would significantly change the

church in later years (White 1977). The church symbolized a staid tradi-
tionalism for a young idealist like Hernán. He remembers being a favorite
of the local clergy, who recognized his intelligence at a young age. Knowing that he came from a pious family, they tried to steer him toward a religious life with frequent praise and gifts of sports equipment. He rejected
the church, and this led to intense conflict with his mother. To this day, he
associates religion with his mother, bringing her up in almost every conversation on the matter.

Hernán names Jesus Christ as one of his heroes, but he despises the
Catholic Church. Like many secular intellectuals, he understands the story
of Christ as one of courageous iconoclasm in the face of oppression. He is
familiar with Hegelian and Marxist theories of religion and believes that
organized religion perpetuates the status quo through an ideology of obe-
dience that contradicts the fundamentally revolutionary message of Jesus
Christ. He says:

> I saw the Church as teaching people obedience, not liberation. I was a dy-
> namic person, who felt that power needed to be in the hands of the people,
> and not the nuns and priests. Jesus himself rebelled against the power of the
> priests, who were corrupt, and had turned the temple into a marketplace.

He sees Christ as a person who fought against corruption and hypocrisy
in the Church in hopes that it would realign with the spirit of universal be-
nevolence out of which it was ostensibly created. In this regard, his own interpretation echoes Max Weber's theory of charismatic renewal, in which
the routinization of power structures leads to periodic bursts of charismatic
energy and self-critique. Hernán sees Christ as a historical reformer, not a
religious messiah, and he has carried a strong belief in criticizing authority
throughout his life.

Hernán's rejection of Catholicism was linked to a belief in progressive,
secular government, and his mention of the Cuban Revolution, culminat-
ing in Castro's overthrow of U.S.-backed Cuban dictator Fulgencio Batista
in 1959, as a key event in his life is significant. First, it provides an example
of how the arrival of radio in rural areas changed Honduran culture. Beginning in the 1930s, radios spread from the cities outward, and the development of the battery-powered transistor radio in the 1950s enabled people
in rural areas without electricity to hear about national and international

political events as they occurred. Hernán relied on the radio for information, and his rejection of the legitimacy of religious knowledge was partly based on the new information he was receiving over the airways.

The Catholic Church had been the most important social institution in rural Honduras prior to the 1950s, but the arrival of radio, followed by public schooling, signaled an important change not unlike that observed by Geertz (1957) in Indonesia at the same time, as *abstract* ideological or political affiliations replaced local territorial communities and social networks as the primary modes of social integration in rural areas. As Honduras modernized, rural communities that were based on religious institutions and personal relationships became small components of a national political community.

That Hernán's political awareness was so profoundly shaped by his knowledge of the Cuban Revolution resonates with the experience of much of rural Latin America. As the historian Tulio Halperín Donghi notes, "The Cuban Revolution set the tone of Latin American history in the 1960s" (1993, 301), and the aftershocks of Castro's turn to socialism in 1960 had a significant impact on Honduran history. From the 1960s until the early 1990s, U.S. foreign policy focused on preventing another hemispheric neighbor from becoming "the next Cuba." In Honduras, the U.S. State Department was preeminently concerned with nipping communism in the bud through a combination of military training and economic aid (Euraque 1996a, 108–109, 112).

This policy had a direct impact on Hernán's life. Early in John F. Kennedy's administration, he initiated the Alliance for Progress as a combination of developmentalism and counterrevolution. Guided by modernization theorists, the Alliance intended to use a strong state and applied technology to promote economic development, thereby diminishing the threat of social revolution by initiating broad reform.[5] The Alliance for Progress was intended to alleviate the social tensions that may have otherwise led to a socialist revolution, and it also expanded the "great society" philosophy of activist government beyond the borders of the United States.

In Honduras, the Alliance for Progress found an ally in President Villeda Morales, who held the presidency from 1957 to 1963. Villeda Morales expanded universal public education into rural areas, promoted labor rights, and passed a series of sweeping legislation that intended to redistribute vast tracts of unproductive land to peasants. He also cut off diplomatic relations with Cuba and denounced communism to separate his brand of reformism from Castro's (Euraque 1996a, 114). During this period, organizations such as the Peace Corps and the International Rural Development Bank became active in rural Honduras. Labor unions were given large loans by the U.S. International Cooperation Administration to provide improved housing for fruit company workers (Euraque 1996a, 101), and progressive politics were transforming Honduran society in novel and important ways. A local progressive bourgeoisie had developed around the city of San Pedro Sula, and they allied with labor and peasant groups in the Liberal Party.

While a student in the new public school is his hometown, Hernán befriended a member of the first Peace Corps class in Honduras, Gary Fordham (a pseudonym), who came to his village in 1963. At that time, Hernán was constantly fighting with his mother and considered running away from home. Gary became a mentor and role model to him, often buying him books, speaking with him about world events, and providing food and shelter when he ran away from home. He recalls that his early intellectual development was influenced by the heady democratic idealism of the early 1960s, and that his relationship with Fordham gave him a sense of political optimism and a firm belief in people's ability to change society through secular education. He would listen to current events on the radio with Gary, and they discussed national and international politics.

In 1965, after years of fighting and periodic flights from home, his mother expelled sixteen-year-old Hernán from the family home for good. He had finished the mandatory basic education course and planned to search for work in the U.S.-owned banana plantations of the North Coast, an area that he had never visited before but was, according to him, where "all the action in the country was going on, both politically and industrially." Indeed, there could hardly have been a better place for a young worker imbued with Kennedy-era idealism. The North Coast of Honduras had been economically and politically dominated by U.S.-owned fruit companies since the late nineteenth century and had long been a symbol of U.S. economic imperialism in the region for left-wing Latin American intellectuals, who saw Honduras as the paradigmatic "banana republic." Pablo Neruda best expressed this idea in his poem "La United Fruit Co," published in 1950 in *Canto General,* which has taken on almost iconic significance as an expression against North American neocolonialism in Latin America (Neruda 1991, 79):

> When the trumpet blared everything
> on earth was prepared
> and Jehovah distributed the world
> to Coca-Cola Inc., Anaconda
> Ford Motors, and other entities:
> United Fruit Inc.
> reserved for itself the juiciest,
> the central seaboard of my world,
> America's sweet waist.
> It rebaptized its lands
> "The Banana Republics,"

Despite the neocolonialist legacy of the fruit companies, an unprecedented alliance between an urban bourgeoisie and banana workers in the late 1950s led to significant social democratic reforms (Soluri 2005, 173). By the early 1960s, the North Coast was the locus of much of Villeda Morales' reform efforts. It seemed that Honduras was moving toward a labor-capital compromise, with the North Coast leading the way. The North Coast was the most modern and progressive region in the country, and Hernán wanted to be a part of it.

Radicalization

This progress was halted in 1963, when President Villeda Morales was deposed in a military coup and replaced by Army Colonel Oswaldo López Arellano, a leader of the conservative National Party. In 1965, the year that Hernán set out for the North Coast, the new dictator had scheduled an election under pressure from the United States to reestablish democracy. López Arellano was elected through a process that was clearly a sham, and he took power in 1965. According to Darío Euraque, "The 1963 coup had left mainstream liberalism in disarray" (1996a, 123). The coup deeply affected Hernán, and he decided not to continue with his plans to relocate to the North Coast. He was involved in a nascent romance with the woman who would become his wife and ended up moving in with his paternal grandparents, who lived in the country near La Quebrada.

He was happy living with his grandparents and enjoyed the rural lifestyle. In the following years, he traveled around Central America, worked odd jobs, and got married. He also became increasingly active in agrarian politics and saw the damage that export lumber corporations were inflicting on the environment around La Quebrada. In 1970, Hernán decided to become a teacher and enrolled in the national teacher's college in Tegucigalpa. There, he became increasingly attracted to the political left, which had become more radical throughout the 1960s, following the general political currents of the day. The emergence of the López government temporarily thwarted the efforts of Honduran progressives. In the United States, Kennedy's death led the Johnson administration to turn to more hard-line anticommunist politics, and this rightward shift turned many young Honduran leftists against the liberal-democratic version of progress. López Arellano attacked labor leaders as "subversives" throughout the late 1960s and effectively alienated the Honduran left from mainstream liberalism for several years.

Walter LaFeber details the demise of reformist policies following the coup by López, whom he sees as a martinet controlled by a power block of U.S. businessmen, the military, and wealthy landowners: "The post-1963 Alliance assumed a different form in Honduras. Resembling the larger change in Latin American policy when Johnson replaced Kennedy, increased amounts of U.S. private capital appeared in Honduras as the López Arellano regime rolled back the Villeda Morales labor reforms and provided inviting opportunities for foreign investors" (LaFeber 1983, 181). LaFeber focuses on the Honduran military's role in protecting the interests of the U.S. fruit companies and an emerging cotton and cattle oligarchy at the expense of the peasantry.[6] He sees General López Arellano as a representative of the Vietnam-era shift away from liberal reform in Latin America, which would continue through the Nixon years and reemerge under Reagan in the 1980s.

Hernán's early admiration for the United States, formed during his friendship with Fordham and the days of Kennedy and Villeda Morales, turned to hostility as he entered the university. He organized his first political protest in opposition to a plan funded by the International Bank for Reconstruction and Development (IBRD) for U.S. education specialists to develop a curriculum for Honduran schools. The United States' support of the military dictatorship had eroded popular support for the American government throughout the 1960s. Honduran students were well aware of the 1968 student massacres in Mexico City and believed that the CIA was at least partly responsible.[7] Hernán began to read Marx, Lenin, and Mao Tse Tung and was active in left-wing political groups.

Anti-imperialism, and particularly anti-Americanism, has long been a part of the culture of the Latin American left, and Honduras was certainly no exception. But domestic events turned students' critical energy away from the United States in 1969 when the invasion of Honduras by El Salvador unified Honduran society against a foreign enemy, bringing domestic political rivals together for the cause. Student activism was directed at El Salvador rather than the United States, and the new domestic unity led to a compromise between General López Arellano and his former critics. López Arellano began to institute his own social reforms beginning in the 1970s. Honduran rural society had become increasingly impoverished due to the impact of large-scale export production, and Arellano saw the potential for the sort of rural crisis that had befallen El Salvador and precipitated that country's invasion of Honduras. Working with leaders of labor unions and peasant groups, he revived the sweeping agrarian reform that he had denounced years before, and he established ties to the industrial bourgeoisie that had opposed his coup.

Despite his radicalism, Hernán began working for the Instituto Nacional Agrario (INA), the institution responsible for carrying out agrarian reform in the early 1970s. The INA was responsible for redistributing unproductive *latifundios* to landless peasant groups. That a leftist like Hernán could become an employee of the military government speaks to the uniqueness of Honduran military reformism in the 1970s. In 1975, Hernán was involved in Honduras' most famous and ambitious land redistribution project in the Bajo Aguán valley, a fertile region where thousands of hectares of land had been abandoned by the banana companies. With the financial backing of the state, the INA attempted to develop peasant cooperatives for the production of African palm oil (Macías 2001). The cooperatives were organized and managed by government bureaucrats, who were involved in fraud and embezzlement. Hernán was head of the INA workers union and consistently spoke out against the corruption that eventually led to the cooperative's demise.

The internal problems of the INA became moot, however, in late 1975, when a military coup deposed General López Arellano and replaced him with the more conservative Colonel Melgar Castro, who would then be replaced by General Policarpo Paz García. By 1977, the agrarian reform was essentially halted by the newly conservative government, which was allied with the interests of large landholders who had long opposed the reform (Weaver 1990, 69). After the coup, the agrarian reform process relied on land seizures conducted by peasant groups without support from government agencies. Hernán joined the Honduran Communist Party (PCH) and became active in radical peasant organizations, frustrated with the ineffectiveness of the INA.

Activism took its toll. He developed a severe stomach ulcer in 1977, caused, he believes, by stress. A leader of the PCH arranged for him to travel to the Soviet Union (USSR) for medical treatments. He spent almost a year in the USSR and was disillusioned with the bleak totalitarian society that he encountered there. He was warned of the dangers of speaking critically of the Breshnev government and was convinced that Soviet communism was on the decline. He returned to Honduras in 1979.

The events of 1979 were crucial to the history of Central America and set in motion a series of forces that would quash whatever elements of mainstream progressive politics remained in Honduras. The Sandinistas successfully toppled the Somoza regime in Nicaragua, and the left-wing Farabundo Martí National Liberation Front (FLMN) began its civil war in El Salvador. Honduras became the focus of U.S. foreign policy, led by a hard-line anti-communist Army general named Gustavo Álvarez Martínez. The Honduran military was not under civilian control, and they had been trained and equipped by the United States since the 1960s. Under the new government, General Álvarez was unquestionably the country's political strongman. A fanatical anti-communist, he had trained in Argentina and was the first to impose "dirty war" counterinsurgency tactics, such as death squads, kidnappings, and torture, in Honduras (Armony 2008). The Nicaraguan revolutionaries had conducted operations in the Honduran mountains and developed links with nascent Honduran revolutionary groups. People like Hernán, who had been active in peasant movements and left-wing politics, were labeled as "subversives" and faced unprecedented danger.

Returning to the Local

By this time, Hernán was married with three young children, and decades of work as a political activist were wearing him down. The threat posed by the military leadership led Hernán to back off from his public activism. He decided to move to La Quebrada in 1982 and start a coffee farm on land that was owned by his grandparents and in-laws. He became active in local politics, helping to organize a local committee that pressured the national government to grant La Quebrada autonomous status as a municipality. At the time, Honduran coffee was beginning to grow in importance on the world market. Global demand increased for the mild Arabica varieties that Honduras produced, and Hernán's farm had a run of profitable harvests. The community as a whole was growing and prospering. However, Hernán's personal history as an activist and member of the Honduran Communist Party (PCH) put him in danger of accusations of subversive activity by the paranoid *militares*. In 1985, he was roused from his bed and kidnapped by military police while his children watched. He was held for three weeks under suspicion of subversive activity but does not voluntarily speak about the incident. When I asked what happened, he brusquely responded, "Me jodieron," which is best translated as "They fucked with me."

Although he was unwilling to speak in detail about the 1985 kidnapping, he admits that he was fortunate to survive. By that year, General Álvarez had been deposed by General Walter López, and the dirty war tactics persisted in a less brutal and maniacal form. Hernán says that if Álvarez had still been in power, he would have been murdered. Nevertheless, the events of 1985 left his family traumatized, especially his children. Hernán decided to focus on local political concerns, and in 1986, his efforts to win political autonomy for La Quebrada were rewarded when the community became an official municipality. Hernán was named interim town secretary by governmental decree, pending elections the following year.

At first, the community had almost no infrastructure such as public schools, road maintenance, or water. The leadership had to learn how to work within the political system to achieve funding from the national government for municipal projects. Hernán's initial solicitations show a naïve optimism and belief in the state as a care-giving patron. A letter to

President José Simón Azcona, written months after the formation of the municipality, is revealing. It reads:

> Your Excellency Señor President of the Republic of Honduras, Engineer José Simón Azcona:
>
>   Through this letter, we address you with the love that a community bestows upon you, given the meaning that the transcendental task you accomplished by raising us from the category of village to municipality has for us. This gesture will pass into History as a sublime action that provided a community with the object of its struggle; thanks to this just action, you have become the Favorite Son of this beautiful place, who we wish to keep in our bosom, whether as President of our country or as a simple citizen, because the hope that you gave us when you came here during your campaign has materialized, and for that we want to pay you just and deserved public recognition, as a community should pay tribute to a man that deserves the Honors; we hope that you consider our wishes and one of these days surprise us by stopping by this productive little corner. Señor President: Just as a child needs special treatment for its development, so our Municipality hopes that its creator provides special treatment so that it can reach the short-term goals that we have proposed, which, in broad strokes are . . .

Despite the flowery language, the local government's requests were for basic public goods—a road connecting them to a nearby town, funds for urban improvements, connections to the national electrical grid, a cadastral survey, legal designation of boundaries, and assistance in a potable water project in partnership with CARE, a major humanitarian aid organization. In another letter, Hernán requested a diagnostic study of community needs and asked that the Minister of Planning put them in touch with an international NGO that could spearhead the development process. These seemed like reasonable requests, and they occurred as the country was transitioning to democratic rule. However, Hernán was unprepared for the realities of Honduran party politics.

Prior to electoral reforms passed in 1993, split-ticket voting was not possible in Honduras. Voters could vote only for party tickets rather than individual candidates and therefore could not choose the presidential candidate from one party and a mayor from another. The mayor was elected based on the percentage of votes his or her party's presidential candidate received in a given municipality. Mayoral candidates had vote-getting clout in the national elections, so there was a lot of corrupt dealing to get certain candidates to support a certain party (Taylor-Robinson 2006).

The newly formed government in La Quebrada was open to the influence of Honduran party politics, where favor-swapping, patronage, and bribes are common. National politicians forged links with the new town leadership in a power grab, and a political rift quickly developed in the local government between allies of the Liberal and National parties. Hernán, in typical iconoclastic fashion, refused to ally himself with either party and regretted that local politics had quickly deteriorated into partisan sniping. As he puts it, "The local politicians were only concerned with their own interests and had no concern for the needs of the *pueblo.*"

He had become disillusioned with national bureaucracy while working at the INA, and now he saw that local politics were subject to the same patterns of corruption. The National Party, longtime ally of the military government, took control of local politics and Hernán was cut out of the leadership circle. He began to feud with one of the town's largest coffee growers and most powerful Nationalist politicos. In the meantime, the town remained without potable water, roads, or electricity.

The late 1980s and early 1990s brought sweeping changes to Honduras, due in part to Honduras' strategic position in the Cold War power struggle but also to the wave of democratization that spread throughout the world after 1989. In 1990, the peace plan initiated by Costa Rican president Oscar Arias Sánchez led to the establishment of democratic elections in Nicaragua, ending the threat of guerilla warfare in Honduras or the need for large-scale military aid. The demise of Marxist leadership in Nicaragua, coupled with the breakup of the Soviet Union, ended Honduras' position as "main girder in the bridge" of the United States' hemispheric security strategy. The amount of U.S. aid to Honduras declined dramatically, and much of the remaining funds were intended to strengthen local democratic institutions and decentralize politics. Honduras held democratic elections in 1990, electing the Nationalist Rafael Callejas. Corruption and human rights violations could no longer be excused as necessary evils that ensured "stability." Financial transparency and support of the rule of law became important priorities as "efficiency" and "profitability" replaced stability as the guiding principles of national progress.

With the end of the Cold War communist threat came new interest in strong democracy and human rights, as well as economic policies geared toward market liberalization and global competitiveness.[8] The U.S. Agency for International Development (USAID), the World Bank, and other lending agencies began to focus on fiscal discipline as a requirement for development assistance. The International Monetary Fund (IMF) created a fiscal austerity program for Honduras in 1989, and the USAID could withhold funds as punishment for noncompliance. The structural adjustment programs instituted in Honduras followed the neoliberal model that the IMF and World Bank instituted around the world (Noé Pino 1992). As a response to the debt crisis of the 1980s, highly indebted countries like Honduras aimed to cut spending to stabilize national currencies and attract private capital. Honduras wooed light manufacturing companies—mainly garment sweatshops—with tax-free zones and low labor costs. Investment in nontraditional agricultural products such as berries, cucumbers, mangoes, flowers, and broccoli was encouraged by USAID, and shrimp farming for export became one of the country's most profitable industries.

Centralized social programs were expensive and inefficiently run, and, in this new environment, public expenditures needed to be cut significantly for Honduras to maintain its standing with creditors. This new tight-fisted approach did not bode well for rural areas, especially La Quebrada, which had virtually no public services and was desperately in need of state support. Nongovernmental organizations became increasingly important actors in the social services sector, filling the void left by the cessation of military aid.

In 1989, the breakdown of the International Coffee Agreement caused coffee prices to plummet, intensifying the need for assistance in La Quebrada. During this period, Hernán forged alliances with NGOs that would become important throughout the 1990s. In 1989, the national forestry service, the Corporacón Hondureño de Desarollo Forestal (COH-DEFOR), conducted a feasibility study for a municipal water system and determined that pollution from two coffee farms was contaminating the town's water sources. Hernán began a campaign to stop one of the farmers, his main political rival, from polluting the water from his heavily fertilized field. The influence of Hernán's history as an activist was evident in pamphlets posted around town, in which he used language like, "People of La Quebrada, divided we are many but weak; united we are few but strong" and "Until the final victory," but his goals were far from radical. He sought to develop a communitywide committee for the protection of local watersheds. His request was denied by the town's mayor, so he organized public rallies. Nevertheless, a judge ruled in favor of the polluting landowner under questionable circumstances. Despite affidavits from the national environmental ministry supporting Hernán's claim, the judge ruled that the landowner could continue to pollute. Although his campaign ended in disappointment, Hernán forged professional contacts with agronomists funded by USAID, which was working with CARE to improve hillside agricultural practices in Honduras. He saw his new NGO allies as a way out of the frustrating corruption of mainstream politics.

In the early 1990s, Hernán began to organize an association of elected neighborhood representatives. He focused his energies on local democratic participation, organizing La Quebrada's first open town meeting in 1996, with the assistance of three NGOs. He had come full circle in his political opinions. His early belief in strong centralized government and technical assistance had been challenged by his experiences with bureaucratic corruption and state hypocrisy. His new approach saw the town meeting model of "pure democracy" as the foundation of effective popular rule, and he bemoaned the political flaws and inefficiencies of centralization.

In 1998, the catastrophe caused by Hurricane Mitch led to a tremendous infusion of development aid in Honduras. Hernán had been active in promoting strong systems of local governance in La Quebrada, and development agencies were eager to work in places where, ideally, a broad coalition of political factions developed a community's agenda. Therefore, La Quebrada was a natural fit for community-driven development work. In early 1999, Hernán became the local leader of two related development projects funded by USDA and USAID: (1) a community-driven diagnostic study in which elected neighborhood leaders developed a hierarchy of the community's needs (something Hernán had been working toward for a decade) and (2) an organic coffee cooperative and processing facility, of which Hernán was the co-president.

The coffee cooperative was the victim of bad timing. During its first crop year, world coffee prices hit a fifty-year low, and the co-op sold its crop for below the cost of production. It managed to hang on with a few members for another season, but it failed by 2003. Hernán's sons migrated to the United States and were working as house painters in suburban New Jersey. He had retired from local politics in frustration and spent much of the year in Tegucigalpa, returning to La Quebrada for the coffee harvest. One afternoon in 2004, we were speaking about the fortunes of migrants and whether returnees could help the economic prospects of the community. "Look," he told me, "A few people might come back with a truck or a gold chain from work in the States, but they will never create any long-term future for the people here. That is something that can't be done without *politics*. And here, *politics* are not possible unless you are a criminal."

Hernán's life story encapsulates the transition from modernity to postmodernity in Honduras. His political life began as rural Honduras was beginning to develop as a modern nation-state. He feuded with his mother over the relative value of secular education versus religion, and he eventually became a teacher in the public schools, demonstrating his belief in modern, secular concepts of progress. During the early days of the Alliance for Progress, his exposure to the Peace Corps cemented his faith in progressive democracy. He participated in the agrarian reform movement and state-directed development, but was frustrated by the corruption, inefficiency, and hypocrisy he encountered in the bureaucracy. He turned to Soviet communism as a model of progress, but his belief in communism was shattered by his trip to the USSR in the late 1970s. His persecution by the Honduran military government in the 1980s forced him to adopt a more moderate agenda as a matter of survival. He turned to local democracy and environmentalism in the 1980s and forged alliances with NGOs. By the 1990s, he had lost faith in mainstream government and turned to nongovernmental solutions to local problems. By the time I met him in 2001, he had embraced sustainable entrepreneurship—organic coffee production—which was exactly the sort of market-driven social program that the NGOs were promoting at that time. The failure of the coffee project and his sons' migration had left him disillusioned and cynical about Honduran politics.

In present-day La Quebrada, NGOs play a vital role in local politics. One organization, Proyecto Aldea Global (Global Village Project), has become almost a state within a state.[9] The town's mayor appeals to Aldea Global's leadership for funding for social programs, and this organization has even provided basic infrastructure, like roads and water, that the Honduran government has not been able to provide. Aldea Global is nominally a Christian organization, but it does not actively proselytize, and it works in partnership with American Jewish World Service as well as secular charities such as the Kellogg Foundation. As an NGO, Aldea Global lies outside of the formal electoral system. Of course, it must follow the laws of the country, and it has an internal system of accountability, but the project prides itself on its ability to cut through bureaucratic red tape and deliver results without involving the political establishment. The success or failure of its projects does not translate into political power. Although its leaders stress community involvement, transparency, and participatory approaches, Aldea Global is a nondemocratic organization that relies on external funding from private donors or government grants. NGOs like Aldea Global provide important social services that cash-strapped states cannot. However, their newfound power symbolizes the process of depoliticization that has occurred in rural Honduras. Even "the government" seemed to give up on government, viewing NGO activity as a pragmatic way to provide services with limited resources. The state plays a comparatively minor role in rural development, while the political leadership focuses on export growth in urban manufacturing. The contracting of rural social services to NGOs removes the state from accountability and marginalizes rural politics from the mainstream.

The rising power of groups like Aldea Global is a consequence of the transformation of the social bond between Honduran state and nation, especially in the countryside. One of the ironies of the Honduran transition to democracy, post 1989, is the fact that mainstream political institutions have played a decreasing role in local politics, while NGOs, which are outside the boundaries of democratic governance, have risen in power. It is no wonder that people feel marginalized from domestic politics when NGOs like Aldea Global perform even the most basic functions of government, such as road construction, public health, and other forms of municipal infrastructure. Taking Hernán's story into account, we can see how dramatically the role and responsibility of government has changed since the days of the Alliance for Progress. His story fittingly explains the origins of the current depoliticized climate in La Quebrada.

This chapter has used the biography of a single individual to connect the historical experience of La Quebrada to broad sociopolitical trends that impacted Honduras and other parts of Latin America in the twentieth century. In the following chapters, I describe two movements that provide strategies for social improvement and new forms of citizenship that have emerged in the aftermath of this process of depoliticization in Honduras.

As I have argued, the rise of depoliticized social movements is, at one level, a product of Honduras' unique position in the Cold War geopolitical order. However, much recent anthropology has focused on how the systemic economic changes brought by neoliberalism have produced *systemic* cultural changes in how people think about their role as citizens within a defined collectivity. As the global market surpassed the nation-state as the key organizing principle of social life, the ideological relationship between individuals and nation-states also transformed, leading to new strategies for political action, new understandings of citizenship, and new ways of defining "the social."

The demands of global financial markets led to the "dehyphenization of the nation-state" (Gupta 1998; Turner 2002), turning back the progress made by modern states in domesticating capitalism in the interest of "the nation" during the twentieth century. No international legal system performed the regulatory function of the modern state: Companies established offshore affiliates to avoid taxes, relocated to nations like Honduras to avoid labor standards, or hired undocumented migrants to cut costs. At the same time, there was no guiding political project that reconciled the potential benefits of economic integration with the tenets of "modern" social protection developed in the twentieth century.[10] While regulating institutions such as the World Trade Organization (WTO) facilitated the free movement of capital around the globe, there was no political counterweight to institutionalize social or environmental protections at the global level. In this context, the social welfare function of government was left to transnational NGOs—both religious and secular—that promoted human rights, environmental justice, and fair labor standards through "soft power."

The changing orientation of the nation-state has produced new forms of citizenship and political action. On one side are movements that might be called "expansions" of citizenship. Networks of global activists have responded to the diminished power of the nation-state by developing transnational political projects dedicated to economic justice, environmental preservation, and human rights. On the other side are "contractions" of citizenship, movements that assert the rights of particular social groups against an encroaching global, cosmopolitan threat—such as anti-immigrant activism and various forms of cultural, racial, or linguistic nationalism, based on antiliberal principles that Douglas Holmes (2000) calls "integralism." These changes have all stemmed from the neoliberal "flattening" of citizenship (Strathern 1992) under which the demands of global capitalism erode the bonds of social identity that once served as the bedrock of social life. Once the bond between nation and state is broken, new visions of citizenship emerge to mediate between the individual and the global market.

In chapter 4, I describe two religious movements that provide worshipers with philosophies of self-empowerment, and, I argue, fill the gap left by the narrowed scope of secular visions of political reform. Chapter 5 describes the fair trade coffee movement, one of the few popular strategies that have been devised to improve social conditions in La Quebrada and places like it. Fair trade shifts the responsibility for regulation of the coffee market away from states and international organizations, and toward individual consumers. Although both of these movements contain political elements, they are ultimately products of the process of depoliticization described here.

4

The Devil Has Been Destroyed

Mediation and Christian Citizenship

Jesús es más que un templo de lujo con tendencia barroca.
Él sabe que total a la larga esto no es más que roca.
La iglesia se lleva en el alma y en los actos no se te olvide
que Jesús, hermanos míos, es verbo no sustantivo.

Jesus is more than a luxurious Baroque style temple. He knows that in the
end, this is nothing more than rock. You carry the church in your soul and in
your acts. Don't forget, my brothers, that Jesus is a verb and not a noun.

Pop song by Guatemalan singer Ricardo Arjona, "Jesús verbo, no
sustantivo" (Jesus verb, not noun)

Around Christmas time in La Quebrada, I was shocked by the following scene: Outside a small church, decorative colored lights were strung
along a tree to form the number "666," which is usually taken to be a sign
of the Antichrist, "the number of the beast," in the Book of Revelation. At
night, this number flashed in red, on and off, on and off, casting a blinking
glow across the mud puddles that formed on the street. Only a few doors
down, from another church, one could hear the loud, polka-style beat of
Evangelical Christian hymns pulsing late into the night, punctuated by
cries of "Hallelujah" and "Gloria a Diós," that broke up the pastor's seemingly endless fulminations. Small groups of teenagers congregated outside
the church, chatting and casually listening to the service while they aim-
lessly pedaled circles on their bicycles through the semicircle of light that
the church threw across the darkened street.

The illuminated 666 (examples of which can be seen in figures 8 and 9) was meant to taunt—perhaps torture—the evangelicals in the nearby church. It was put up by members of the Centro Educativo Internacional Creciendo en Gracia (Growing in Grace International Ministries; hereafter called CEG), a rapidly growing congregation that believes that Jesus' sacrifice eradicated all sin from the world.[1] CEG members believe they live in a perpetual state of grace and therefore live free from sin. CEG constantly berates evangelicals for living under the oppressive burden of guilt and fear of temptation, a belief that, they believe, is exploited by ministers who use the insidious presence of the devil to scare their congregations into piety. CEG believes that the devil—and, with it, sin—does not exist. They brazenly display signs like *666* to antagonize the evangelicals, an act that only leads the evangelicals to pray harder.

The conflict between CEG and the evangelicals over the existence of sin and the devil is fundamentally about personal morality in the face of rapid social change. The evangelical church emphasizes the individual's ability to reform society through moral behavior, focusing on the denial

Figure 8. Creciendo en Gracia church exterior in La Quebrada. Daniel Reichman, 2008

of practices that are associated with vice, such as drinking alcohol, gambling, dancing, sex, adultery, and lying. CEG takes the opposite approach, embracing virtually every form of "vice" that the evangelicals prohibit— most of which deal with *consumption* of alcohol, pop music, provocative/ flashy clothing, pornographic TV or film, and the Internet. The evangelicals accuse CEG of *libertinaje* (libertinism), while CEG accuses the evangelicals of living in a state of oppressive, rule-bound sobriety. While CEG embraces all forms of affect, glitz, and modern indulgence, the evangelicals see such things as symptoms of moral decay. Both churches have taken on an important role as sources of moral authority, instructing people how to lead a good and just life at a time when the "old" rules no longer seem to apply (Mintz 1974). Migration to the United States and the demise of the coffee economy has opened possibilities for individuals to craft lifestyles that would have been unimaginable a generation ago, but these forces have also created striking new anxieties about gender, class, family, and morality that are often worked out in religious settings. The evangelicals and CEG have taken opposite stances toward

Figure 9. Creciendo en Gracia liquor store. Daniel Reichman, 2008

the social impact of migration, with CEG celebrating the power of individual freedom, and the evangelicals emphasizing the dangers of absolute individualism.

Because of evangelical religion's theological emphasis on individual moral behavior as the source of social change, many scholars have suggested that it has some elective affinity with neoliberal forms of political subjectivity. The explosive growth of evangelical religion since the 1980s is often perceived to be a spiritual consequence of the "erosion of the basis of popular identification with the state" (Turner 2002) and the turn to the more individuated forms of politics described in chapter 3. Hernán's life history documented the transition from progressive, state-centric modernization to depoliticized postmodernity in rural Honduran politics, and this transition has affected contemporary religious thought and practice.

During the 1960s and 1970s, the era marked by the twin goals of agrarian reform and state-centric modernization, Honduran Catholics came to embrace politicized religious movements that synthesized Catholicism with peasant politics. These movements generally followed the two major modernist ideologies of the Cold War: social democracy and Marxism. In the early 1960s, Catholic Social Movements (CSMs) opposed Communism (mainly Castroism) and followed a reformist democratic model, often funded by USAID, assisted by the CIA and other institutional branches of the Alliance for Progress (White 1977, 276). By the late 1960s, segments of these movements began to embrace Marxism and were influenced by the liberation theology developed by Paulo Freire in Brazil. The Marxist CSMs, especially the "Celebration of the Word of God," directed peasant land seizures and encouraged various strategies of opposition to the dominant capitalist classes. They drew philosophical inspiration from dependency theory and other forms of anti-imperialist thought. In contrast, contemporary movements no longer explain the problems faced by rural society as the consequences of *collective* sociopolitical factors, as did both the democratic and Marxist versions of "social Christianity." Instead, the new churches focus almost exclusively on individual morality and various formulations of "personal responsibility." The individual has become the basic unit of social reform, and secular theories of progress have lost ground to a depoliticized emphasis on individual morality.

In his ethnography of a Pentecostal mega-church in Guatemala, Kevin O'Neill (2010, 3) develops the concept of *Christian citizenship,* arguing that "churches provide a morality with which congregants constitute themselves as citizens (and perform their citizenship) through Christian practices, such as prayer, fasting and examinations of conscience." This chapter takes up the idea of Christian citizenship, arguing that the symbolic idioms that different churches employ to explain the power of the individual in society are essentially *political* theories, even though they shift politics outside of the domain of the state and tend to locate individual action as the site of social change.[2] Any concept of citizenship requires an individual's awareness of his or her place within a defined collectivity that grants specific rights and demands certain responsibilities. In La Quebrada, two rival congregations, the evangelicals and CEG, uphold radically different moral visions of the individual in society, which create different understandings of citizenship.

While both congregations claim to *empower individuals,* the meaning of "empowerment" varies greatly.[3] Debates that occur within the religious sphere in La Quebrada have much in common with fundamental theoretical debates about the potential of religion to provide a philosophical framework for effective social reform in the modern world: Does religion provide a form of personal empowerment (whatever that might mean), or does it hide basic truths behind a mystified aura of doctrinal certainty (as suggested by Ricardo Arjona's lyrics above)?[4] At the conclusion of this chapter, the discussion takes a relatively abstract turn to address these questions. Throughout the book, I have argued that new forms of citizenship focus on the power of the individual, but that can mean many different things. In an attempt to examine the potential and the limitations of religious politics as a basis for citizenship outside the nation-state, we need to examine *how* these religions think about power and individual agency.

Religious Diversity in La Quebrada

La Quebrada has a bewildering array of churches. Almost every street has a small concrete or pine-board building marked by a hand-painted sign that serves as the only indication that these spaces are not mere homes or businesses. In some cases, the church occupies the front of a residential home or even a hastily constructed shack (called *campos blancos,* see figure 10) that might one day blossom into a more impressive structure if the optimistic founders are blessed with success. The large Catholic Church located at the town's center—traditionally, the symbolic heart of rural Latin American towns—is decrepit and usually empty. The evangelical churches, on the other hand, pulse with energy, especially at night, when the streets are dark and empty due to the absence of electricity and a townwide 9 PM curfew.

Until the mid-1980s, La Quebrada was almost entirely Catholic. Protestant evangelicals were active in Honduras since the nineteenth century, but their impact was limited. The country had an insignificant (less than 10 percent) Protestant population until the 1980s. Evangelical missionaries were funded and assisted by fanatical anticommunists in the United States (such as Lt. Col. Oliver North) who saw their religious proselytizing as part of the fight against the spread of Marxism, which was embodied in Catholic liberation theology, a part of the Sandinista revolutionary plat-

Figure 10. A *campo blanco,* or newly constructed evangelical church, called Prince of Peace Church. Daniel Reichman, 2008

form in Nicaragua that threatened to spread through Central America (Stoll 1990, 135–179).

In La Quebrada, all of the non-Catholic churches are relatively new. The first Protestant church was formed in the late 1980s, and the others sprouted up in the 1990s. In numerical terms, Catholicism remains the most popular religion, and it is the baseline against which all other sects define themselves. In 2003, the majority of the adult members of the new churches were born into Catholic families, and most discussions of the relative merits of evangelical churches begin with, "I don't believe in Catholicism because . . ." In La Quebrada, one is a Catholic unless they choose otherwise. Therefore, evangelical religions contain an element of voluntarism that is absent from Catholicism (Martin 1990, 31–42), which makes adherents of the new churches more vocal and enthusiastic about their choice of faiths. Catholics tend to be more passive participants, rarely attending church services more than once a week, while the Protestants tend to be loyal attendees and zealous advocates of their faith. This enthusiasm is helpful to the researcher because people are comfortable explaining *why* they believe in a certain religion versus another. Critique and introspection are inherent in proselytizing faiths because people *choose* to believe in them, often breaking with family tradition.

Iglesia Seguidores de Cristo

I was introduced to La Quebrada's evangelical churches through the Ulloa family. Wilmer Ulloa, profiled in chapter 1, was the older brother of Yadira, a devoted and passionate member of the Iglesia Seguidores de Cristo, La Quebrada's largest Pentecostal Church. Yadira was twenty-four years old, unmarried, and cared for her father, five-year-old daughter, and teenage brother. She worked as a maid year-round and picked coffee during the harvest season. Each day, she washed and mended clothes, prepared meals, chopped firewood, and carried water to the family home. She helped her daughter get ready for school, and cared for her two infant nieces as well, who lived in the house temporarily. She worked tirelessly and was known as one of the fastest female coffee harvesters in town, picking as much as seven hundred pounds in a single day.

The church was the main focus of her life. Every morning, other women of the church would stop by to chat about their plans for the evening. They would discuss what they would wear to church, gossip about other people in the congregation, or discuss the amount of tithes collected the previous night. They were active in collecting funds to start "campos blancos" (see figure 10). They sold raffle tickets, donuts (called *donas* in Honduras), and *pastelitos* (pineapple fritters) door to door to help purchase materials for the new churches. Because a strict bureaucracy is absent within the evangelical community, virtually anyone can start a new congregation. Churches are almost constantly fissuring off into splinter congregations, either due to growth, internal disputes, or the ambition of a pastor who seeks to set out on his own and start a new congregation.

The Seguidores de Cristo church is a Pentecostal Baptist congregation. Its founder is said to have received the Holy Spirit in Rio Piedras, Puerto Rico, in the early 1960s, and his speech in tongues is taken as evidence of his access to divinity. Congregants sometimes speak in tongues during the services, and people are water-baptized after they have spoken in tongues.

The church provided Yadira with a source of entertainment. She lived in a home with no electricity, and, in the church, she could spend a few hours each night singing and clapping to festive music with friends. For Yadira, going to church was a fun alternative to sitting at home, working, or chatting by firelight. It gave her an opportunity to dress up in her best clothes and to proudly walk through town as part of a group that *mattered.* As an unmarried single mother who did not finish high school, her social status was relatively low. The church marked her with a social identity, and she took pride in slowly walking to church with friends each evening, stopping by people's homes to chat along the way. She made sure that people saw her as a *hermana* of the church, and she was a vocal and effective proselytizer. On Sunday market-days, she would stand in the middle of the market stalls, singing and praying with friends, hoping to "win" souls.

As David Martin (1990) has argued, part of the appeal of new Pentecostal churches is that they provide a voluntary association where women like Yadira can be active and valued participants. Her participation in fundraising activities gave her experience and responsibility handling money and a chance to be part of a project that had visible effects in the community. Her proselytizing gave her a public persona as well. Through her participation in the church, she became an important part of one of the town's most powerful subgroups. As a low-status, undereducated young women, she would not have this opportunity in any other group in town. The church gave her a feeling of individual power and pride.

The church's inclusiveness is another part of its appeal. Services follow a weekly schedule that gives everyone a chance to lead the service at some point. Mondays are devoted to bible study; Tuesday is the "Culto de Damas," and services are led by women; Wednesday is "Culto de Niños," and children lead various songs and prayers; Thursday is "Culto en el Hogar," where a particular family hosts services in their home; Fridays, the "Culto de Caballeros," are led by adult men; Saturdays (Culto de Jóvenes) are led by teens; and Sundays are "Culto de Todos," where no group is singled out. The church provides a specific time for each social group to be the focus of attention. Age, gender, and class distinctions exist within the church (in fact, women and men must sit on opposite sides of the church), but every social group is given equal standing as long as they adhere to the tenets of the church. There is an informal weekly prayer meeting for the most active members of the church, and participation in this group of "hard-core" adherents is the most noticeable social division within the church. All but two of the fifteen to twenty "hard-core" participants are women. They fast for a day before the prayer meetings, which last for several hours inside a private home.

The church also provides a network of mutual support that is especially important for single mothers and people who depend on remittances from relatives in the United States. Church members take care of each others' children and run errands for friends when they go to the city to collect remittance checks or shop. Membership in the church creates a bond of trust among people who are not related. The church's strict moral code assures people that members are disciplined and trustworthy. It provides an extended family that is especially important for people who are disassociated from normal bonds of kinship and neighborhood, such as recovering alcoholics or thieves.

The church also provides a therapeutic sense of comfort. Before each service begins, congregants place their heads on the pews and kneel on the ground, facing away from the altar. They quietly pray for forgiveness, murmuring words to themselves. The women usually sob quietly as they do this, while the men, who are far outnumbered by the women, rarely cry. Small groups will sometimes form, in which women's heads are only a few inches from each other on the pews. In this case, the other women can hear what those near them are saying. They hear their friends ask forgiveness from God, and the mutual experience of sorrowful prayer creates a strong bond of sympathy between them. This "silent" prayer lasts for about a half hour before the service starts.

All prayers begin with the same call-and-response welcome, in which the prayer leader says, "Diós le bendiga" (God bless you!), and the crowd responds with the same blessing. Then the leader asks, "Quien vive?" (Who lives?), and the group responds, "Diós." Then the leader responds with "Gloria a Diós" (Glory to God). The congregation begins to sing, a drummer and electric guitar player start out playing softly but build to a false climax just before the pastor begins his sermon. Following the sermon, the congregation sings more energetically, singing becomes even more intense, and this is usually the point where people catch the Holy Spirit and shake, sway, or speak uncontrollably. The presence of the Holy Spirit usually spreads quickly: One person shouts, "Hallelujah!" or "Gloria a Diós," then others respond. Then someone begins to sway or shake, and another follows. Only a handful of people go into these trance-states, but it is taken as evidence of the presence of the Holy Spirit and a sign of the efficacy of the prayer. This is the climax of the service, and then it winds down, with the music becoming softer, and the pastor handing out the offering trays to the congregation. The appearance of the Holy Spirit is a cathartic moment for the group. The service literally begins at a low point, with people kneeling on the ground, sobbing. By the end, their arms are raised, they are clapping and shouting, and the riotous tone of the service lifts the spirits of the congregation. The service takes about two and a half hours on a typical night.

By the time the service ends, people are exhilarated and head home to bed along empty streets. They have a de facto exemption from the town's nighttime curfew. Walking home after church one night with Yadira and her family, her mother asked me how I felt. I said that I felt tired. She looked concerned, and said, "You may be tired, but you should feel totally happy and at peace, because you have heard the word of God. You will sleep in peace." Her words reminded me that the church service serves a daily catharsis that alleviates tension and puts celebrants at ease.

The therapeutic efficacy of the church service rests on the congregants' sense of guilt. The tearful prayers for forgiveness that precede the service are motivated by guilt over sinful behavior. Sin, temptation, confession, and forgiveness are the dominant themes of the service. The church has a strict code of conduct, and the failure to abide by this code produces guilt. In addition to the sins derived from the Ten Commandments that are found in all Judeo-Christian religions—greed, fornication, disrespect of elders, vengeful behavior, blasphemy, lying, and violence—Seguidores de Cristo prohibits drinking, wasteful spending, gambling, the wearing of jewelry, makeup, or provocative clothes, and dancing to pop music.

These codes can be carried to extremes. One afternoon, I saw Yadira in tears and asked her what was wrong. Her cousin had sent her a new skirt from New York, and she was planning on wearing it to church. She showed it to some of her friends, and they told her she could not wear it because it was *chinga* (sexually provocative) because its hemline fell above her knee. Yadira was certain that the skirt went below the knee and accused her friends of trying to make her feel guilty because they were jealous of her new clothes. She was ashamed by the accusation of improper dress and angry at her friends for their "witch-hunt" mentality. Fearing being labeled a sinner by the congregation, she sold the skirt to a neighbor who was not a church member. Even though the skirt fell below her knee, Yadira's fear of accusations of sinful behavior convinced her that her eyes deceived her. In this case, the women of the church were using the fear of sin as a way to enforce conformity. Yadira's skirt was sent from the United States, which they saw as the source of the sinful modernity they so feared.

By far, the consumption of alcohol is the practice that generates the most religious debate in La Quebrada. The evangelicals view alcohol as a demonic vice. As Elizabeth Brusco (1995) argued, alcoholism is often seen as a destructive male practice that drains economic resources away from families. In 2000, the local association of evangelical churches banded together to prohibit the sale of alcohol (leading to the closure of dozens of local *cantinas* and pool rooms) and to end the celebration of the annual *feria patronal* (patron saint's feast). They felt that the patron saint's feast was an example of idolatry, and had become an excuse for public drunkenness, wasteful spending, and other sinful behaviors. The consumption of alcohol is, with few exceptions, a masculine practice in La Quebrada, and the evangelical campaign for prohibition was largely led by women and initiated by the town's first female evangelical mayor.

For the evangelicals, migration—and the United States in general—has become symbolically linked with alcoholism and the sins of ambition and fornication. There is a lingering fear that young men in the United States, away from family, church, and community, with dollars to spend, will give in to these temptations. In this context, much of the electronic media that originate from the United States have been associated with temptation. In 2001, just as the boom in migration was beginning, the town received electrical service and cable television, which gave residents access to nonstop sex and violence on screen, as well as near-constant coverage of the immigration issue from U.S. Spanish-language television. Internet service was established in 2003, quickly leading to a boom in online romances, social networking, and pornography. There are frequent rumors that originate from the evangelical churches about demonic messages hidden in American television shows like Winnie the Pooh, in products like Crest toothpaste, or in pop songs with incomprehensible lyrics.

In various branches of the Protestant tradition, writes David Martin, "discipline and sobriety are as vigorously embraced in ordinary life as ecstasy and release are achieved in the sphere of worship" (1990, 203). This emphasis on sobriety in everyday life creates guilt—behind every prohibition lies a secret craving—and this craving provokes feelings of anxiety. Temptations are signs that the devil is infiltrating one's soul, and life is seen as a constant struggle to avoid diabolical temptation. During services, the pastor asks people to publicly confess to sins. Even young children are put on the spot. The pastor will say, "Have you lied to your parents?" sticking a microphone in front of the child, who usually begins to cry. People publicly confess to both sinful acts and sinful thoughts, such as coveting another person's property or wishing them misfortune. These confessions lead to a release of tension that is built up through feelings of guilt.

In this manner, the church experience rests on the continual production and alleviation of guilt. As Sidney Mintz has eloquently stated, "When the attainment of virtue is made possible by the foreswearing of all those things that can be turned against a man to make him feel guilty, the solution to many of life's problems can seem very clear" (1974, 261). Unlike the Catholics, the evangelicals can directly atone for their sins through prayer, and the presence of the Holy Spirit in the services confirms the efficacy of their prayers. By demonstrating their ability to fight temptation, churchgoers experience a sense of power over their lives. The distinction between possession of power and access to power is crucial. For the Pentecostals, the

Holy Spirit is the ultimate source of power, which acts upon individuals and groups that are able to access it through prayer.

Creciendo en Gracia: Religion without Guilt

If the Seguidores de Cristo church created a sense of individual power or mastery through the production and alleviation of guilt, then the Creciendo en Gracia (Growing in Grace) church was its opposite. It was based on the liberation of worshipers from the burdens of guilt. I first learned of the church when I saw a young man wearing a T-shirt that proclaimed, "The devil has been destroyed! We are all blessed!" The shirt was screen-printed with an image of the vanquished devil—a Halloween-style skull, placed inside a red circle bisected diagonally by a red line, as on a "No Smoking" sign. I asked him about the meaning of the shirt. "There is no more devil," he told me. "There is no more sin. *Todos somos bendecidos.*" (We are all blessed.)

The central tenet of the sect was that, according to the Apostle Paul, the death of Christ had freed the world from sin, and believers lived in a permanent state of grace. The teachings of José Luis de Jesús Miranda, a Puerto Rican "doctor" who refers to himself as an apostle and claims to be both Jesus Christ returned and the Antichrist, were the foundations of their beliefs, which derived from the doctrine, "Salvo Siempre Salvo" (Once Saved, Always Saved). This doctrine states that once a person has been saved, he or she is bound for heaven no matter how they behave on Earth. When a person "grows in grace," they need not worry about sin and punishment because the crucifixion eliminated sin from the world.

The biblical evidence for this belief, according to Miranda, is in Hebrews 2:14–15: "Therefore, since the children share in flesh and blood, He Himself likewise also partook of the same, that through death He might render powerless him who had the power of death, that is, the devil, and might free those who through fear of death were subject to slavery all their lives." The opposite of "death" in this passage is eternal life, entry into heaven. Members of this church believe that Jesus' death guaranteed all believers a place in heaven. Variants of this belief are common in Protestantism. The doctrine of "eternal security" was, for example, associated with the Calvinist concept of predestination, whereby a person had no power over entry to heaven or hell through their behavior on Earth. Creciendo en Gracia also believes in predestination, but in a tautological and risk-free version thereof: Membership in the church is itself a sign of grace, and all members of the church, no matter their actions, are destined for heaven. Whereas Calvinists interpreted the doctrine of predestination as a source of salvation anxiety that led them to do good deeds on Earth, the members of this church take predestination as a free pass to heaven.

The local branch of CEG was founded in 1997, only four years after Miranda was supposedly visited by the Angel Gabriel and began his ministry. The founder of the La Quebrada church discovered CEG after seeing a televised sermon and visiting a branch in San Pedro Sula. In La Quebrada, non-members were quite critical about CEG's theological message and the integrity of its leadership. The local nicknames for Creciendo en Gracia (CEG) were "La Iglesia de los Asesinos" (church of the assassins) or "La Iglesia de los bendecidos" (church of the blessed). The latter was a parodic reference to practitioners' custom of referring to each other as "bendecido/a" (blessed) when they greeted each other on the street. The former name (church of the assassins) referred to a more serious and disturbing set of allegations that residents leveled against one of the church's members who belonged to one of La Quebrada's most wealthy and notoriously corrupt families and had a reputation as a menacing thug. According to local rumor, he murdered the previous husband of his wife to move into the man's home, steal his agricultural supply business, and run off with his wife, who was also the beneficiary of the victim's life insurance policy. He was known as a ruthless person who would do anything for money.

Local critics saw the church as a way for the family to justify its unlawful acts; indeed, dozens of its members were part of the extended clan, employees of the family, or people linked to them through other bonds of patronage or debt. Most townspeople viewed the religion as a sham, joking about the *bendecidos* as *asesinos*. As one man said to me, "Isn't it convenient that the worst family here invents a religion with no sin? Now they have nothing to fear when they die. They think they're going to heaven. They can do whatever they want here on Earth without consequences," he continued, pointing downward at hell with a sly wink. I cannot say whether these allegations were true or not, but it was quite apparent that CEG had a controversial reputation in town.

Unlike the Pentecostals, CEG embraces modernity in every way, right down to the $80,000 BMW that Dr. Miranda frequently mentions in his sermons. CEG broadcasts and webcasts from a flashy studio in Miami and mimics the variety-show aesthetic of TV channels like Univision and Telemundo. It encourages dancing and often makes references to current Hollywood films and other pop cultural products in its sermons, which are peppered with English-language terms. CEG allows female followers to dress any way they like, and Miranda surrounds himself with dozens of scantily clad, attractive young women to whom he refers as his goddesses. In CEG, men and women can consume alcohol without guilt. Miranda once gave an entire sermon on how a Guatemalan bar owner gained prosperity by joining CEG, when his bar, Apo's Beer House (the Apostle's Beer House), became the hot-spot for young Guatemalan partiers. In his weekly sermons, Miranda has referred to the tiny church in La Quebrada and has even mentioned the pastor by name, suggesting that their little group is gaining importance in this global, mass-mediated world, which they largely experience through CEG's sermons and cable television.

After the town's ban on alcohol was lifted in the late 2000s, the first liquor store in the town center was started by members of CEG. As seen in figure 9, the exterior of the store is marked with the number 666, and the storefront is emblazoned with the word *APOSMARKJH*, which means "Apostles, Mark of Jesucristo Hombre (JH)," demonstrating allegiance to CEG and belief in Miranda's claim that he is "Jesus Christ, Man." There could be no clearer sign of CEG's conflict with the evangelicals than a liquor store in the town's center painted with name of Jesus Christ and the so-called number of the beast.

Mediation and Power

One common trait of both the Pentecostal Iglesia Seguidores de Cristo and Creciendo en Gracia is that they criticize the alienated representations of power in other religions, seeking to restore the power of individuals to autonomously chart their own course in life. In this context, the word "alienated" means that individual agency is displaced onto some external object or actor that is seen to be the ultimate source of power. The Pentecostals ask why Catholics bestow such power on religious icons and priests, while members of CEG ask how the Pentecostals can preach deliverance from suffering while upholding oppressive rules that produce guilt, attributing great power to the devil, and placing so much power in the hands of pastors, who are able to distinguish vice from virtue. In their own way, both religions are attempting to restore the power to act to individual subjects, criticizing other faiths that alienate or externalize that power by attributing too much power to objects or people that *mediate* between God and Earth.[5]

False Idols

The Pentecostals explicitly challenge the mediation of divine power by defining themselves against Catholics. Roman Catholicism is the Honduran national religion, and the Pentecostals view it as an anachronistic form of idolatry. In interviews, Protestants consistently ridiculed the Catholic faith in icons. Interestingly, not a single informant focused on the Catholic belief in Papal authority, nor did they criticize the consumption of the Eucharist.[6] Virtually everyone mentioned idol worship as Catholicism's greatest flaw.

The strong association of Catholicism with idolatry stems from the centrality of the image of the crucifix to Catholics. More important, it reflects the popularity of statues of the Virgin of Suyapa as an object of devotion for Hondurans. Suyapa, the patron saint of Honduras, is represented in tiny cedar statues, no more than three inches tall, which are found in every Honduran Catholic church, on vehicle dashboards, and in homes and businesses. The cult of Suyapa began in the mid-eighteenth century (a Saturday in February 1747, according to legend) in a poor village outside of Tegucigalpa. Suyapa is said to have miraculously appeared to a peasant, Alejandro Colindres, and his son Jorge when they got lost at night on their way home from work. Suyapa, in the form of a tiny statue that has the power to heal the sick, has been the national symbol of Honduras since the 1920s. The national cathedral is located in the village of Suyapa (on the outskirts of Tegucigalpa), as is a smaller shrine in which the original idol is housed. The fiesta of Nuestra Señora de Suyapa is celebrated each year as a national holiday, and hundreds of thousands of pilgrims visit the site to pray and seek healing. Suyapa is the symbol of Honduran Catholicism, and she is strongly associated with the narrative of the Honduran nation.

The Protestants' criticism of Catholic idolatry is a challenge to the alienation of divine power. As the pastor at the Seguidores de Cristo church put it:

> What does a crucifix or statue mean to God? We do not pray to the image of god. We pray to God in all his glory. As I like to say, you can have a cross on your chest and the devil in your head [una cruz en el pecho y el diablo en el techo].

In contrast, the Protestants emphasize their direct relationship with divinity. The Pentecostal Church does not venerate religious icons or images of any kind. There is no cross image in the church, only a banner that says, "Gloria a Diós." Services are conducted in informal vernacular speech, and the sanctuary itself is nondescript. The pastor dresses neatly but informally, does not own a car, and lives a lifestyle that is similar to that of church members. The only expensive items used in the church are large speakers and musical instruments, which project the content of the service outward to the community and are therefore useful expenditures used to proselytize. All of the church's energies are devoted to speaking, singing, and shouting directly to divinity. No resources are wasted on decoration or the maintenance of a bureaucracy. The pastor is an approachable layperson who does not live extravagantly and travels through town on a bicycle.

This contrasts starkly with the intimidating formality of the Catholic church, in which iconography, formal hierarchy, and even language itself stand between worshipers and divinity. The words of Don Felipe, a peasant farmer in his sixties and member of the Seguidores de Cristo, strikingly demonstrate the difference between the "clear" (unmediated) message of the evangelicals and the message of the Catholics:

> My parents went to [Catholic] church all the time. . . . [M]y mother went several times a week when I was young, and I went too . . . and I didn't understand anything the priest said. It was all in a language called Latin. Daniel, here in Honduras, we, the poor, don't speak Latin. We speak Spanish or Castilian, as some people call it. I would sometimes ask the nuns questions about stories from the Holy Bible, but not the priest. I could look up at pictures or the statues to learn. Now, the word of God is clear. The Holy Bible tells the truth that God passed down to Jesus his son. We don't pray to statues. Listen up [oiga bien]! The word of God is clear for all to hear. Now everything is really clear [clarito].

Although Catholic priests no longer conduct mass in Latin, the local priests are foreigners who speak with accents. They only occasionally come to La Quebrada; mass is normally given by a Guatemalan nun, accompanied by young women who live in a local convent. There are no lay Catholic preachers in La Quebrada. Worshipers must ask forgiveness by confessing to the priest, who only visits from time to time. In contrast, Don Felipe's emphasis on the clarity of the message of Pentecostalism draws attention to its relatively unmediated truth. Whereas Catholicism is formal, intimidating, and external to the local community, Pentecostalism is informal, accessible, and local.

Taken together, the Pentecostal rejection of priestly authority, faith in icons, and linguistic conventions are all challenges to the mediation of power. The Pentecostals emphasize clarity and direct communication with divinity that gives the worshiper direct access to divine power. They can see the results of their faith in the appearance of the Holy Spirit, revealed through speech in tongues and trances. The ultimate source of power is still transcendent, but worshipers can mediate between the transcendent and the mundane without the help of a priest or an icon. Through personal discipline and ecstatic worship, people attain the power to mediate between the sacred and profane worlds.

False Doctrines

Whereas the Pentecostal Church relies on a relatively unmediated relationship of holiness, Creciendo en Gracia relies on posters, recorded music, broadcast sermons, T-shirts, and webcasts to spread its message. In almost every way, Creciendo en Gracia embraces affect, glitz, and indulgence. During services, sultry young singers in provocative costumes sing to the latest hip-hop beats. Worshipers watch recorded music videos and view sermons on the Internet. A modified seal of the President of the United States of America (visible on the left in figure 8) is the congregation's symbol. Note the small *SSS* on the upper right corner of the shield, which stands for "Salvo Siempre Salvo" (Once Saved, Always Saved).

As mentioned above, the church emphasizes its opposition to both Catholic and Pentecostal Baptist concepts of guilt and self-denial, celebrating that women can dress as they wish and wear makeup. Dancing, stylish clothing, makeup, and alcohol are permitted and even celebrated. Some of CEG's promotional materials openly mock women who wear long skirts of the type favored by the Pentecostal Baptists, which CEG refers to as "ropa Cristiana" (Christian clothes). One promotional poster shows a woman clad in *ropa Cristiana* who dreams of wearing pants, short hair, and stylish clothes. In the poster, she is chained to a vicious guard-dog called "commandments," while lit sticks of dynamite called "law" threaten to explode. To her right is a kneeling, pathetic-looking man, chained to the shadowy figures of the clergy, who warn him, "Remember, we forgive, but we never forget," while holding a scythe and an axe.

This poster depicts people imprisoned by religious doctrine, then set free by the more permissive faith provided by CEG. Traditional religion is depicted as oppressive and dangerous. The same poster shows a sandwich formed by "Paul" and "José Luis" as bread, with "Moses" as the meat in the middle. Miranda, the apostle, considers himself to be continuing the work of Paul, freeing the world from the blinding religious law of Moses, replacing the Pentecostal rules with a doctrine of permissive grace.

CEG's message of individual liberation is, in some ways, a message of "unalienated" power. However, CEG's doctrine is rooted in the absolute authority of Miranda. He determines right from wrong, and individual liberation does not include the freedom to question him. Although the effect of his ministry is to give worshipers a sense of agency and free will, in direct opposition to the strict Pentecostals, worshipers follow his every command and utterance.

Miranda carries the message of God. God, through the Angel Gabriel, communicated the gospel to him, and he carries it to the people. A letter posted on the CEG Web site makes this point, contrasting the false doctrines of Pentecostalism with the apostolic message of CEG:

Dear Brothers of CEG:
One of the articles posted on your website got my attention. In the final part, it reads: Dear Brother, the power of the Holy Spirit did not arrive in Pentecost, but rather, God communicates the gospel through our Apostle José Luis de Jesús Miranda and upon hearing it and believing in him, we are stamped with the Holy Spirit. . . . I would like you to explain this segment to me because it really surprised me.

Miranda responded as follows:

> For two thousand years, religion has thought that the Holy Spirit arrived in
> Pentecost, but nevertheless, no one discovered anything there. There were
> some mystical manifestations of trembling and unknown languages, but
> there wasn't any discovery. . . .
>   Nobody in more than twenty centuries has been able to discover these
> truths until the edification of the Apostle José Luis De Jesús Miranda ar-
> rived. Now, through him, the believers are stamped with the Holy Spirit,
> upon hearing the authentic gospel of Christ resuscitated in his words.

As this exchange makes clear, hearing and seeing the apostle speak the
gospel provided a religious experience. The CEG services were not designed to access divine power directly. The apostle received the truth from
the Angel Gabriel, and he spread the word to the congregation. For this
reason, viewing a sermon over the Internet or a satellite feed was just as
effective as participating in a church service. Being a spectator was a religious experience in itself. The poster reproduced in figure 11 illustrates
the apostle's ability to mediate between God and humanity, and the importance of new media technologies to CEG's message. In this image, the
apostle holds out a Bible (presumably interpreting it), speaking into a microphone. Above him, a satellite orbits the Earth, and the words "We are
living in the days of the mediator, Jesus Christ, man" are printed between
outer space and the apostle, just under the satellite.[7] The satellite, which
mediates between Earth and sky, is analogous to the apostle, who mediates
the word of God for humanity. This poster draws attention to—indeed,
celebrates—the highly mediated nature of its religious message, transmit-
ted mainly via satellite feeds and Internet sermons.

Pentecostals are the "target audience" for CEG. Creciendo en Gracia
defines itself in opposition to the Pentecostals, and Miranda himself is a
converted Puerto Rican Pentecostal. Miranda contrasts his own revelation
to that described in the biblical story of Pentecost (Acts 2), in which the
Prophet Joel delivers the message that speech in tongues is a sign of salvation. Miranda says that this story contains "mystical manifestations of
trembling and unknown languages, but there wasn't any discovery." In
contrast, he received a version of the gospel that presents the possibility of
a new life of freedom and "grace" to Pentecostals who, like the figures in
the poster, are imprisoned by strict doctrines.

Figure 11. "We Live in the Days of the Mediator." Poster advertising *Creciendo en Gracia* convention in Honduras (called *Alturas*). Used with permission of a CEG representative

The Pentecostals define themselves against the Catholics and preach the unmediated relationship between people and the Holy Spirit. Creciendo en Gracia defines itself against the Pentecostals, believing that that the rigid codes of conduct force the Pentecostals to live in a state of rule-bound paralysis. The Pentecostals' attribution of power to the devil limits their own autonomy, and CEG offers an alternative that gives individuals control over their lives. In this sense, Pentecostalism is to Catholicism as CEG is to Pentecostalism. Each doctrine places progressively more emphasis on individual liberty and present worshipers with the possibility for a "closer" relationship to the true source of power.

Native Materialism

Why, one might ask, would CEG worshipers need to believe in Miranda at all? Why not dispense with religion altogether and take the doctrine of liberation to its logical conclusion? Why ascribe power to anything beyond the individual? This line of reasoning echoes the most polemical Marxist interpretations of religion that divide the world into "true" material forces and "false" (or, at least, secondary) symbolic representations. Interestingly, a local theater group in La Quebrada produced a short play that parallels this interpretation, criticizing the ideological effects of religious belief and emphasizing a masculine form of materiality.[8] Called "Los Santos Comilónes" (The Gluttonous Saints), the skit, summarized below, demonstrates what I mean by "masculine materiality":

An old woman, dressed in traditional peasant garb, is at work cooking in a rustic *comedor* (diner), its walls lined with religious icons and statues (held by actors). A tall *gringo* (mildly insulting slang for American), sunburned, wearing sandals, shorts, and a tank-top, enters the building. A few seconds later, a flamboyant transvestite enters as well, wearing a bright purple skirt, a long-haired wig, and gaudy makeup. The gringo and the transvestite begin to talk to one another and order their food, making a lot of noise and generally being rude. The old woman smiles and seems happy just to have customers despite their rude behavior. The gringo and the transvestite read a newspaper together as they await their meals. They laugh, and the transvestite flirts with the gringo. The old woman delivers their food, but they continue to be absorbed in the newspaper and their flirting. As they read the newspaper and flirt, the saint statues descend from the walls and eat their meals off their plates. The statues also eat the rest of the food the old woman is preparing in the kitchen. The old woman, the transvestite, and the gringo remain oblivious. The play ends as the woman and the customers react with great surprise and anger that someone has eaten their food. The "gluttonous" saints have returned to the walls, and the audience erupts in laughter.

This skit could be interpreted as a political commentary, but it was not intended as such. Themes of gender and religion are more important. All of the actors in the play were young men, including those who portrayed the transvestite and the old woman. Acting is not considered to be a masculine activity, and some of the actors were accused of being homosexuals. They played the characters in over-the-top comedic styles to distance the behavior of the characters from their own personas. The gringo—dressed like a slob in shorts, sandals, and tank top—and the transvestite represent the inverse of ideal Honduran masculinity. These men are long-haired, effeminate, messily dressed, and rude. The old woman (*anciana*), who represents a traditionally feminine Honduran Catholic, doesn't seem bothered by them because she wants their business and is protected by the saint statues. The transvestite, the gringo, and the anciana are all distracted—the two men by their interest in the shared newspaper and the old lady by her belief that the saints will protect her business. The men's attention to the newspaper parallels the woman's faith in the saints.

The written word and the statues of the saints represent forms of authority—the first being associated with the modern intellectual power of the gringo and the latter with the traditional religious power of Catholicism. Both are opposed to the physicality of the young men. Hence, the gringo is associated with the transvestite. They sit together and flirt. The newspaper draws the attention of the gringo and transvestite away from their food. The saints' theft of food is a critique of the efficacy of words and icons and an affirmation of materiality, which is associated with males. The newspaper readers are effeminate buffoons, implicitly contrasted with the young male actors who portray them. Honduran men are present only as the critical authors and performers of the skit. The actors are saying that the transvestite, the gringo, and the old woman are too caught in their respective forms of false consciousness to notice that they are being robbed of the substance of life (food) by their belief in media. The symbolic (words and icons) is associated with a benighted, somewhat benign, femininity, while the material (the production of food) is associated with masculine physicality.

The message of this skit bears much in common with the extreme materialist view of religion as mystification, an interpretation that Marxian anthropologists have long struggled to overcome. This view separates social reality into a "base" of relations of material production that determines symbolic representations and social consciousness. These representations ultimately reinforce the dominant relations of production, "mystifying" dominated classes so that they accept the terms of domination as the way of the world.

One virtue of the Marxist critique of religion is that it links cultural or symbolic systems with social relations and emphasizes that religious beliefs can have ideological effects that disguise social inequalities. However, this theory understands society primarily as a system of material production rather than one that also produces values, beliefs, and collective representations that are *equally* important to the organization of social life and not secondary to material production. The interplay between religious doctrines in La Quebrada shows that the desire for a sense of power is not only about materiality, but about the ability to give meaning to social reality. In times of great doubt, the experience of individual power provides religious believers with a comforting certitude. Both the Pentecostal Church and CEG provide adherents with a sense of power and control over their lives. For the Pentecostals, this power comes from the ability to access a transcendent Holy Spirit. Members of CEG are empowered by the liberating doctrine of Dr. José Luis de Jesús Miranda.

Christian Citizenship and the Power to Act

Although I have stressed that the appeal of new religious movements in La Quebrada rests on their tendency to empower the individual, the theological debates above attest to the difficulty of defining what *individual empowerment* actually is. The debate centers on whether or not each religion offers a true, viable vision of the power of the individual, or whether that power is constrained or hidden by a set of mystifying doctrines or forces.

This is a fundamental issue in social theory: Does religion, as an institution, give meaning to social reality, or does it hide that reality behind alienated, overly simplistic models of the social world? The meaning-oriented view of religion is foregrounded in Clifford Geertz's famous definition of *religion* as a "system of symbols that . . . formulates a general order of existence" (1973, 90). Here, religion serves to articulate a people's sense of their place in the world by giving a systematic, symbolic vision of how the world works. Marxian theories of religion, on the other hand, focus on the hard surface of truth that is partially hidden by religious ideology. In this view, religious thought is a fetishized or alienated symbolic medium for an external theoretical construct called "society."[9] People project their own powers as agents onto divine beings and thus deny their own capacity, as agents, to transform the world (see, e.g., Feuerbach and Eliot 1989; Sangren 1991, 1993, 2000).

Certainly, religious narratives in La Quebrada distorted or occluded the complexity of the migration phenomenon by focusing on individual moral and personal issues rather than higher-level political economic forces or collective processes of social production. However, in La Quebrada, I would suggest that the narrative content of these religions was less important than the act of mediation itself. To hear one's name from a tiny speaker in a computer, spoken from a soundstage in Miami, or to foreswear the temptations that might emanate from that very screen, enables one to formulate a definition of the relationship between the town and the United States. No matter how simplistic, illusory, or downright bizarre these narratives may have seemed, they provided people with a sense of mastery and control in a changing world.

As Sidney Mintz (1974) argued, the idea of power that emanates from the individual, rather than a defined group, is especially appealing in times of abrupt social change. In a classic essay on the origins of religious authority, Max Weber wrote that in times of social, political, or economic distress, "natural leaders . . . have been holders of specific gifts of the body and the spirit; and these gifts have been believed to be supernatural, not accessible to everybody" (Weber 1958, 245). Weber's concept of *charisma* was based on the idea that the most fundamental form of religious power is directly opposed to any social hierarchy. It is rooted in the capacities of a specific individual who is able to transcend the dominant social order. In periods of perceived crisis, when the social order is in question, people whose power is not determined by position within power structures become appealing leaders. Individual unstructured power, Weber believed, is the basis of charismatic authority.

However, charisma is given meaning only when it is witnessed and communicated by a social group. Jacques Derrida (2001) has argued that modern Christianity rests on a uniquely mediated religious experience of charisma. *Mediation,* in this context, is any experience that is perceived by an audience through the prism of religious icons, priests, televised services, or photographs (or perhaps language itself). In contrast, unmediated belief is based on a direct experience of divinity. Unlike Judaism and Islam, Christianity rests on knowledge of divinity through a "third"—the mediating figure of Jesus Christ. Derrida argues that Christianity is *uniquely* dependent on mediation—the communication of religious experience through symbols—rather than direct experience.

Derrida's key point is that in periods of doubt, social bonds must be reconstructed on the basis of mutually recognized faith in something that *appears* to be absolutely certain. In the absence of collective ideologies that seem to "fit" reality, people look for direct sensory experiences that establish that certitude. For Christians, this often involves bearing witness to miracles as a spectator. The "truth" of religious power is established through a performance.[10] Spectators experience the miracles of the evangelist qua medium, which makes evangelical Christianity especially well-suited to television.

Derrida's argument emphasizes that charisma attains meaning in mediated form, but the process of mediation is elided or hidden behind the appearance of directness.[11] This theory of religious power is especially relevant to proselytizing religions that explicitly believe in the power of faith to resolve life's problems. That proselytization is so often based on access to miraculous power suggests that people are drawn to faiths that present them with the power to assert greater control over their lives. They experience this power in *relatively* unalienated or direct form because it is not mediated by priests, icons, or formal church rituals—and this is part of its appeal.

In La Quebrada, the new churches emphasize what Steven Sangren (1993) calls the "subject's own powers of self-production" in totally different ways. Taken to its logical conclusion, the idea that relatively "unalienated" religions emphasize individuals' power to determine the course of their own lives suggests a libertarian philosophy that runs the risk of becoming a doctrine of absolute autonomy. As the interplay between ascetic and libertarian faiths in La Quebrada suggests, the way that religions conceptualize this problem can contribute to an anthropological understanding of the relationship between theology and citizenship. The key challenge is to understand *why* collective representations take *specific* forms in different cultural situations. The fact that both the Pentecostals and members of CEG conceive of divinity as the power to improve the lives of individuals reflects a desire for solutions to social crisis that are based on individual acts.

Religious Modernity and Postmodernity

Placed in historical context, these representations of power fit well with contemporary visions of the role of the individual as citizen. This chapter began with a description of the popular religious movements that developed during the era of modernization and agrarian reform in the 1960s and 1970s. In the mid-twentieth century, the secularization of Honduran society—specifically the rise of modern, national political parties—changed the nature of religious practice (White 1977). Various religions embraced "popular empowerment," understood as the expanding involvement of a broad coalition of classes to reform society for the collective good. Reformist groups promoted cooperative agricultural production and land reform, while radical groups focused on overcoming economic dependency and class inequality, leading land-seizures and projects that "brought the peasantry to consciousness." Despite their philosophical differences, these populist movements envisioned power within the sphere of *national society.* In the reformist case, Catholic leaders stressed the need for a democratic class compromise to be achieved through agricultural modernization and land reform. In the radical case, they stressed the power of the *campesino* (rural peasantry) class that would be led by a revolutionary vanguard, taking violent action in order to be liberated. The key similarity is that both the reformist and radical versions of Catholic Social Movements had some overarching vision of "society." In contrast, the contemporary religious movements ignore "society" and focus exclusively on individual power, however conceived.

"Traditional" Honduran Catholicism emphasized the power of specific patron saints that protected a specific community. These saints, represented in carved wooden statues or icons, were collectively worshiped during ritual feasts that guaranteed divine protection while cementing social bonds between different sectors of a community. The integrative function of saints' feasts has been well documented in the ethnographic literature on Mesoamerica (see, e.g., Cancian 1965). The collective power of local communities was embodied in the saints and worshiped each year, and the religious fiestas redistributed wealth and brought various sectors of the community together. The specific representation of power was based on a localized, village-based vision of the social whole.

As the modern state developed, the Virgin of Suyapa became the symbol of the Honduran nation, replicating the relationship between saint and community at a national level. Fittingly, the shrine of Suyapa was located on the outskirts of Tegucigalpa, the city that became the country's political capital after independence.[12] The Catholic clerical elites remained in the country's colonial capital, Comayagua, while the new secular center of the country was constructed around mining concerns in Tegucigalpa. It was no coincidence that the "miracle of Suyapa" occurred on the outskirts of Tegucigalpa at the same time (late eighteenth century) that new national elites were wresting power from the colonial aristocracy in Comayagua. The story of Suyapa allowed the postindependence leaders to shift the country's symbolic center away from Comayagua and to the new capital of Tegucigalpa. The religious patron of the nascent Honduran nation found a home just outside the new capital. Throughout the modern history of Honduras, the symbolic expression of religious power has tended to follow patterns in the development of the nation-state.

As the role of secular government expanded, political parties replaced territorial communities as the basic unit of social affiliation, and secular, diachronic visions of progress began to guide sociopolitical life. Religion, of course, remained a vital part of everyday life, but the state surpassed the church as the fundamental social institution in all but the most isolated parts of the country. Through the 1960s, popular religious movements followed the basic fault-lines of secular politics—democratic modernization theory and Marxism. By the 1980s, "popular Christianity" slowly withered away, alongside popular politics in general. Evangelical Christianity developed in its wake, assisted by the U.S.–Honduran military alliance, which feared any form of populist politics in the countryside.

Contemporary religious movements frequently formulate individual choice as the source of social problems and their potential solution. As Martín Hopenhayn (2001, 15) cogently argues, these religions translate the ideology of postmodernity into the religious sphere:

> A suggestive hypothesis is that the withdrawal of physical and discursive forces of socialist liberation has provoked a deployment of diverse spaces for variously reinserting [political energy]. These spaces promote the accelerated expansion of popular religious currents in which *individual liberation is quite independent of collective change* [my emphasis].

In contemporary popular religion, there is no notion of "the popular" or "the social" beyond the immediate kin-group and the local church. Secular political debates have been replaced by a focus on depoliticized individual morality. At a time when the Honduran state has given up on agrarian reform, and the logic of market competition has replaced any overarching vision of collective progress, this individualized concept of power reflects secular changes in the relationship between nation and state. Just as "modern" political theories were reflected in popular religious movements in the 1960s and 1970s, "postmodern" theories found a religious counterpart in the evangelical movements. Religious representations of the power of the individual in society, even ones as different as those of the evangelicals and CEG, ideologically reproduce the dominant vision of society. In this case, the historically specific form of religious symbolism is related to the absence of a guiding collective political project for rural Hondurans and the transformation of the social contract between state and nation. Both the sober, morally upright Pentecostals and the libidinous libertarians of CEG view themselves as iconoclasts. Their respective faiths restore the power to act to individuals, abstracted from any wider totality.

In chapter 5, I describe how a similar process of individualization occurred within the global coffee economy. It may seem strange to draw a connection between religion and economic life. However, efforts to *regulate* the global coffee market are premised on an institutionalized social bond between coffee producers and consumers.[13] One of the central tenets of social anthropology is that religion and law perform a similar function: They both control the conduct of individuals in the name of *social solidarity*—the preservation of a human group that defines the identity and shapes the conduct of members within that group. The *specific* human group in question could be a tribe, a village, a nation, a community of believers, or even a universal human brotherhood, but, in all cases, there must be some conscious moral system that binds individuals together. Markets can be regulated in the name of a variety of collectivities. Under the fair trade system, which I discuss in chapter 5, individual consumers become responsible for regulating the global coffee market. Individuals perform a function that was once carried out by nation-states and international cartels. In its emphasis on individual moral choice as a strategy of social reform, I argue that fair trade bears much in common with evangelical religion.

5

Justice at a Price

Risk and Regulation in the Global Coffee Market

A coffee economy is inherently risky. Prices swing wildly. Bad weather or disease can kill an entire crop. Farmers have assets such as land, buildings, machinery, and vehicles that are not insured. In case of fire or theft, they have nowhere to turn. Many live in a perpetual state of debt, so the profits of the boom years go to paying off interest accrued during the bust years. For hired pickers, the risks are omnipresent as well. There is always a chance that a fall in the fields will put a picker out of work for the season. The slopes are mossy, steep, and covered with mud and slippery roots, and it is common for people to trudge up and down them with hundred-pound loads on their backs. Injuries are common, and there is no "safety net" for workers, save the generosity of kin, friends, neighbors, or church members. Coffee farmers accept that they will have some bad years and some good years, and that risk is a fact of life. The idea of "stability" or economic security is so contrary to their lived experience that I never heard a coffee farmer mention it as a goal. The business is necessarily volatile, and, in general, coffee growers do not consider risk to be a problem.

Javier Montoya was my closest friend in the field, and I had great re-spect for his honesty and business savvy. I spent virtually every day with him, and he became my de facto guide to life in La Quebrada. He taught me about the risks of coffee farming and continually assured me that there was nothing wrong or unfair about the business—I just didn't think like a coffee farmer. Javier is a tried and true realist. He never mentions any abstract principles in which he believes. He believes in Jesus, but does not go to church often. His home contains religious posters and he listens to religious music, but he never talks about the content of his religious beliefs. He does not complain about the coffee business and sees it as a speculative endeavor with a potential for great individual success or failure, depending on some combination of personal ability, fate, luck, and Providence.

To me, Javier seemed almost ridiculously comfortable with risk. I once told him that I couldn't handle so much uncertainty and chance in my own life with his sense of serenity and calm. He laughed and said, "If you only knew how many times I've made money and then lost it all. . . . That's the way life is when you grow coffee. That's how it works here." He thought that people who complain about low coffee prices simply do not under-stand that every bust is followed by a boom. He had lost his shirt several times, but that was the nature of the business.

Javier sees nothing "unfair" about the coffee industry in general. I asked him about whether low prices to growers are fair, and he said, "Look, when I worked in the United States, I looked for the cheapest coffee I could find. . . . We all [Honduran migrants] bought the huge refillable mug from the gas station mini-mart or Sam's Club. It was like ninety-nine cents, and you get to keep the cup. . . . If I'm buying coffee, I want it cheap. If I'm selling it, I want it to be expensive." For Javier, coffee was a business with clear rules.

A few years later, Javier was visiting me in Massachusetts when we stopped at a high-end specialty coffee shop. Javier had never been to such a place before because he tended to live as simply and frugally as possible when he was in the United States, saving money for his return home. As we entered the café, we saw the patrons huddled over laptops and books, or chatting at their tables as soft music played. Javier looked at the menu and became agitated by the scene. He asked to leave, and we quickly walked out onto the street. I asked him why he wanted to depart, and he said that he didn't like the place, refusing to elaborate. I got the feeling that there was something troubling about coming face to face with wealthy Americans spending five dollars per cup of coffee on the very product that could not provide him with an income sufficient to live contently in Honduras (Moodie 2007).[1] This may be why Javier blocked out ethical issues when it came time to buy coffee in the United States. He simply looked for the cheapest possible coffee to drink. However, when he came to visit me, he brought me a plastic shopping bag filled with ten pounds of coffee from his farm.

Javier inherited three acres of low-quality coffee land from a grandparent in 1996, when he was still in his teens. During the 1997–1998 harvest, coffee prices were extremely high, with growers being paid as much as $1.50 per pound. Javier, then only nineteen years old, made a significant amount of money. Thinking that coffee prices would remain high, he took out a loan from a local moneylender to purchase an additional plot of high-altitude coffee land at a time when land prices were high due to the optimism in the coffee sector. Javier and his wife, who was then pregnant with their first child, built a nursery and replanted thousands of high-yielding *catuai* plants themselves, "on their hands and knees," banking on a positive future for coffee.[2] He thought that he was making a wise investment.

In the 1998–1999 harvest, coffee prices plummeted to seventy-five cents per pound, and Hurricane Mitch hit in October, just before the start of the harvest. Although Mitch did not destroy Javier's crop, it made the roads impassable for almost a month, making it costly to transport his crop for sale. Even if his crop arrived at a mill or wholesaler, they could not transport it to the coast for export, so many exporters stopped buying coffee altogether. Javier could not pay his debt (at 5 percent monthly interest) and decided to immigrate temporarily to the United States to make some money to pay off the debt. Javier was able to secure a tourist visa because he owned a considerable amount of land and employed the common strategy of using the funds of friends and family members to pad his bank account so that it would appear to embassy officials that he was far wealthier than he actually was, therefore helping his chances of obtaining a visa.

Javier ended up in Denver, Colorado, where a friend from vocational school lived and worked. A trained electrician, Javier worked as an electrician's assistant in the suburbs and earned enough money in one year of work in Denver to repay his debt and return to Honduras. In 2003–2004, he did not need to borrow money to fertilize his field in the off-season, which is rare for all but the wealthiest farmers. He hired a year-round foreman for an annual salary of about $1,500 U.S., who managed the pruning, weeding, and fertilization of the fields, as well as the timing of the harvest. Javier paid his pickers two dollars per hundred pounds of coffee cherries. This was the "going rate" at the height of the harvest. Some of the pickers were relatives or neighbors, and some were migrants who came to La Quebrada during the harvest season. He paid his cousins and other relatives the same amount that he paid strangers, indicating his lack of sentimentality when it came to coffee production.

In 2003, he sold hundred-pound bags of unprocessed cherries for $7.50 to a local miller.[3] Each bag would yield about eighteen to twenty pounds of processed green coffee beans. He sold at a guaranteed price, known as a *depósito,* which is essentially an unwritten futures contract. Prior to the harvest, he agreed to sell his whole crop to the miller at that rate in order to mitigate risk. Both he and the miller were satisfied with that price, although either one could lose out depending on how the price moved in the following months. If it rose above $7.50, Javier would lose, and if it dropped below $7.50, the miller would lose. Both sides use the *depósito* contract as a hedge against price volatility. In this case, the market price dropped to $6.50, so Javier came out on top.

Assuming that Javier sells one hundred pounds for $7.50, he makes a modest profit. Subtract the costs of harvesting, fertilizer, transportation, and the labor of a foreman, and he makes a profit of three dollars per hundred pounds of cherries, which is only one dollar more than the pickers earn for harvesting that same quantity of coffee. He produced about 100,000 pounds of coffee in 2003, so his profit would have been roughly $3,000 for the year. This provides a relatively high standard of living in rural Honduras. It requires little physical labor for the landowner and provides several months of leisure time. Javier wasn't getting rich, but he had no reason to complain.

The miller is responsible for washing, depulping, drying, bagging, and transporting the beans to be exported in San Pedro Sula, a large industrial city near Puerto Cortés, the Caribbean port from which coffee is shipped to New York, Hamburg, or New Orleans. The exporter processes the beans a second time, ensuring that the dried hulls are removed and that the coffee is dried to correct moisture content. The exporter then sorts and bags the beans for export. Once the coffee arrives in port, it is sold at auction. The price set by the New York Board of Trade is the most important determinant in the going-rate for coffee. The buyers at auction could be small boutique roasters or multinational corporations. Javier's coffee is a mild, washed *arabica,* which is more valuable than the bitter *robusta* variety.[4] However, his crop is not specialty-grade.[5] It is not good enough to interest a high-end specialty coffee company, so it is most likely sold to big roasters that blend coffees from all over the world, companies such as Folgers, Maxwell House, Nescafé, and Chock full o' Nuts. All of these brands are part of large corporations: Maxwell House is owned by Kraft Foods, and was owned by Phillip Morris from 2000 to 2007; Folgers is owned by the J. M. Smucker Company, and was formerly owned by Procter and Gamble; Chock full o' Nuts is owned by Massimo Zanetti, and was formerly part of Sara Lee Foods; and Nescafé is part of Nestle Foods.

The local miller has a large capital investment in the mill machinery, and pays labor, overhead, and transport costs. During the 2003–2004 harvest, the miller was selling beans to the exporter at forty dollars per hundred pounds. At this price, he lost money on Javier's coffee. Like Javier, he was constantly speculating, buying coffee low and holding it until he could make a modest profit. He had to sell small amounts at the low prices to cover his operating costs, but he held a lot of his stock in anticipation of increases. Although he lost money on Javier's coffee, he purchased from other growers at lower rates, and ended up making a small profit for the season.

In this case, the miller sells his coffee to Molinos de Honduras, an exporter that is a subsidiary of Volcafe, the world's third-largest green coffee trader.[6] Volcafe sells to the major coffee roasters—publicly traded corporations such as Procter and Gamble, Sara Lee, Nestle, and Starbucks. Volcafe is a subsidiary of London-based ED&F Man Holdings, one of the world's largest corporations and operator of a commodities hedge fund worth tens of billions of dollars. It would be futile to trace the chain of profit across all of these intricate networks, from Javier's farm, to New York, to the bank accounts of ED&F Man's investors or shareholders in publicly traded companies like Kraft. However, this provides a sense of the intricacies of the global coffee chain and the difficulty in locating the source of exploitation or "fairness" at any one point in that system.

Javier has no interest in fair trade because he says he would never join a cooperative, which is a requirement for fair trade certification. In La

Quebrada, personal trust is absolutely essential to the coffee business, and it is hard for Javier to think of the business in nonpersonalistic terms. Personal trust is especially important within the weak Honduran legal system. If someone writes a bad check or fails to comply with a contract, the dispute is rarely settled in court, except in the cities, due to corruption, a lack of legal titles, and high levels of illiteracy, which make people prefer verbal agreements over written ones. Sometimes, disputes are resolved by the threat of violence, or actual violence, between disputing parties. Usually, one party just loses out and the offending party's reputation is damaged through word of mouth. In such a situation, business is always personal. Javier will sell his coffee only to buyers who have not burned him in the past, people with whom he has an established friendship, and who are known as honest brokers. There are about a dozen *beneficios* (coffee mills) in town, but Javier does business with only one of them. When I asked him why, he recounted the one time he went with another miller who offered him a better price, but the miller paid with a check that bounced at the bank and never paid Javier for the coffee. Javier values his ability to make independent judgments above all else. He could never trust the leaders of a cooperative with his crop.

Javier was against fair trade because he would rather have independence than stability. The risk of losing everything was a part of life, and he used temporary migration to the United States to manage financial risk in the coffee business. The only injustices in the coffee industry, for him, were products of the weak rule of law in Honduras. His rather positive view of the coffee trade should not be attributed to a narrow perspective because he had experience in almost every aspect of the business and had lived and worked in the United States, where he was a habitual—and frugal—coffee consumer. He understood the business quite well, but he accepted the risks and inequalities as the rules of the game. In this sense, his vision of "fairness" basically parallels the neoliberal vision, in which a strong rule of law and legal transparency ensure that "the rules of the game" are upheld, and individuals can freely compete in an inherently risky marketplace.

I am still puzzled by Javier's negative reaction to our visit to the specialty coffee shop. I think our visit forced him to confront some aspects of the relationship between coffee producers and consumers that he had previously blocked out or had not seriously thought about. He had come to the United States to work building homes, and he had left his family and his coffee farm behind to do so. The sight of real people spending between four and six dollars on a cup of coffee must have prompted him to reflect on the overall justice of the system in a new way. He would never put it in those terms, however, because I have never heard him consider *justice* as an abstraction. His vision of ethics is resolutely personal and contextual.

Over the course of nine years, I saw how Javier used cyclical migration to the United States to generate capital to put back into his coffee farm in Honduras. When the coffee price was low, he would leave for the United States, spending anywhere from six months to one year working as an electrician. He would also buy one or two used vehicles from auto auctions in the United States and would drive them to Miami and put them on a ship to Honduras, where a friend would pick them up at the port and sell them for a profit. In making his decision to migrate or stay in Honduras, Javier would consider several factors: As the U.S. housing market crashed in 2008, he speculated that there wouldn't be much construction work in the Colorado suburbs. He knew about the increasingly inhumane treatment of immigrants in the United States during the Bush and Obama administrations, and considered this information when he thought about leaving Honduras. When he visited my home in Massachusetts, he planned to fill a shipping container with recycled computers and monitors, purchased at an auction, to send back to Honduras and sell. All the while, he remained socially rooted in life in La Quebrada, never thinking that he would stay long term in the United States. He always viewed his work in the United States as a way to support and enhance the profitability of his small coffee farm in La Quebrada.

Over the years, little by little, Javier sent money home to construct a house that was a replica of a home he had helped to build in a suburban development outside of Denver. In Colorado, the house sold for about $800,000; Javier would be able to build it in La Quebrada for about $50,000. The home had four bedrooms, a large attached garage on the bottom floor, and a modern kitchen with a built-in range. It also had a traditional outdoor kitchen with a wood-burning *comal* (cooking surface) under a tin roof, and this is what Javier's wife preferred to cook on because the *comal* gets hotter than the indoor range, and the smoke from tortillas or roasting coffee doesn't infiltrate the house.

While working on a Colorado home in 2005, a group of construction workers scratched a Jacuzzi that they were installing. Javier bought the scratched tub at a deep discount and put it in the bed of a truck that he shipped to Honduras. He installed the Jacuzzi in his home, but did not use it. He and his family didn't even have hot water in their previous home and didn't particularly enjoy hot water baths. Javier also shipped home two full-sized streetlights that he purchased at a public works auction when they were being replaced on a Colorado street. The street in front of his home had—by far—the brightest lights in town, and people were instantly able to recognize that he had prospered in the United States.

The built-in range, the Jacuzzi, and other modern accoutrements were certainly status symbols, but they seemed like exotic specimens brought back from a foreign land, trophies of success, rather than modern conveniences. While one would expect Javier and his family to congregate in the luxury of their fancy new home, it was just as common to see them relaxing in the home of his in-laws across the street, a dirt-floored shack with no running water or electricity, located on a dangerous, muddy hillside, directly under a cell-phone tower, on land that Javier leased to the phone company for a hundred dollars a month.

Coffee under the Radar

Building 45 in the cargo area of John F. Kennedy International Airport (JFK) is, aesthetically, about as far as one can get from a Starbucks. It looks like a warehouse on the outside, and the inside has the feel of a decrepit public school—fluorescent lights, tiled walls, and squeaky floors obsessively buffed by bored-looking janitors. The building houses Port Authority Police and U.S. Customs officials, and holstered pistols far outnumber laptops. Behind a door simply marked "Coffee" in a glorified break-room on the building's first floor, Tony Chan sells some of the world's most interesting coffee.

Tony sells his product for $1.25 per cup, one size only. The coffee is grown on Tony's farm in La Quebrada. A Taiwanese immigrant who became a coffee farmer after being fired from McDonald's, Tony ships his coffee to the United States, roasts it himself in the JFK cargo area, and sells it to airport workers from three small outposts, one of which is run by his wife. His coffee is specialty-grade, grown at high altitude and under shade, and meticulously managed at all stages of the production process. He has one paid employee in the United States and a full-time field boss in Honduras, and he serves the coffee himself, seven days a week.

Tony's coffee is of excellent quality, a high-grown, hard-bean arabica suitable for both espresso and American breakfast styles. Its path from farm to cup is much more direct than the complex web of transactions that Javier's coffee passes through. In this case, the coffee chain is vertically integrated: It is grown, shipped, roasted, and sold by the cup by Tony. He has seen the coffee trade from almost every angle and, like Javier, is an unsentimental realist who values his independence above all else.

I first met Tony in La Quebrada late in my fieldwork in 2004. I had heard occasional rumors about *el chino,* a "Chinese" coffee farmer living up in the mountains who had supposedly made millions selling his product in the United States. Given that this rumor was told amidst the most severe coffee crisis in the past half-century, I doubted its veracity. It was unlikely that anyone was getting rich off coffee because the market price was so low. At first, I chalked the rumor up to small-town jealousy and the myth of easy money in the United States. There was an element of racism and xenophobia to the rumors, blaming one of the community's only ethnic outsiders for exploitative practices.

I also doubted the rumor that Tony exported his own coffee; it is rather difficult for a coffee farmer to obtain an export license from the Honduran government. They usually must work through several established companies, selling to a miller or an exporter, as in Javier's case. Although I had heard farmers speak wishfully about exporting their own coffee, I had never seen it done. Later, I learned that the story was partly true. Tony did grow, transport, roast, and retail his own coffee. He had spent several years working to get the export license and had finally done so, but he was not getting rich. Far from it. He barely broke even.

Tony is a hardened entrepreneur. He became a coffee farmer after being fired from McDonald's in 1993 after eighteen years of employment. He began working at the restaurant at sixteen, making minimum wage. He worked his way up the ladder at McDonald's, eventually becoming a regional supervisor in Queens. He hoped to one day own a McDonald's restaurant himself, but he was fired, replaced by a younger employee as a way of cutting costs. As he puts it, "I was making too much money for McDonald's. I had been to Hamburger University [a McDonald's training center] twice. I knew everything. How many napkins to order, how many ketchup packets we needed. . . . I had it down to a science. But I made too much money, man. They threw me out and hired some kid out of college making twenty thousand."

Tony's wife, a Honduran woman whom he had met at McDonald's, heard about a coffee farm for sale in her home country. Out of work but fueled by a mix of ambition and bitterness, Tony used all of his savings and much of his McDonald's pension to buy the property. At first, Tony knew nothing about coffee and viewed his farm merely as a way to turn a profit. But he soon became caught up in the romance of farming, and he now seems to make a constant effort to repress his sentimentality and view his livelihood with the cold objectivity of the shrewd businessman he desires to be. He tells me, "You don't know what being a farmer is like until you do it. You live and die with your plants. If they die, my family dies. I didn't know anything about coffee, but now I love my farm. It's my life." But then he catches himself and says, "Man, I just want to grow this stuff, bring it to the States, and sell it. That's it, man."

The romantic side takes over while we walk through his farm, early one morning during the harvest. Set in a beautiful cloud forest where the temperature rarely rises above seventy-five degrees, Tony's farm is twenty miles from a telephone and about ten miles from the electrical grid. His fields are filled with tropical fruit trees, birds, and snakes. Pure spring water bubbles out of the ground near his mill, and he has built a house with beautiful views in a clearing at the high point of his farm. In every sense, it is the opposite of his bustling, workaday life in Queens. Families walk up the dirt roads with their picking baskets, on the way to work. Schools are closed during the harvest, and people come from all over the country to participate in the harvest. In his Queens-by-way-of-Taiwan accent, he describes his property as, "paradise, man" and tells me how he wants to move here permanently with his family and lead a pastoral farmer's life.

Tony would do so, if only people did not want to kill him so badly. In the past few years, his home has been burned down three times, his crop has been stolen out of his barn, and he has been attacked by a family of machete-wielding thugs in the central plaza of a nearby town. While I was in Honduras, his field boss was attacked while driving through the farm by two men who shot at him with pistols, leaving bullet holes in the driver side door of his red Nissan pickup. Fortunately, Tony's right-hand man was unscathed, but the next time Tony goes to visit his farm, he will wear a bullet-proof vest.

The causes of the violence against Tony are complex, but they reveal quite a bit about the politics of the global coffee market. From 1994 to 1999, coffee prices were over one dollar per pound, but they dropped below sixty cents from 2000 to 2003. Tony pays his pickers slightly above the going rate of about $2.50 per hundred pounds of coffee cherries, but he is singled out as an exploitative outsider, while other coffee growers are not, because he is a foreign, absentee landlord and the locals believe that he makes millions selling coffee in New York. He balks at the idea that he is exploiting workers. If he were making a profit, they would be paid more. But how can he pay them any more when he is not making a profit? Tony, who arrived in the United States as an unskilled immigrant worker, sympathizes with his employees, but believes the violence against him is motivated by a misunderstanding of the system, for which he is unjustly singled out. He says to me, "Picking coffee all day in the sun, carrying sacks on your back up and down hills, that's no life, man. . . . And then they got nothing to do for the rest of the year, it's no wonder they hate us." I sense some tinges of guilt and ask him if he feels any. "Fuck it, man. I feel *nothing*. I'm just trying to run a business and support my family. I don't want to live like a dog. I've done it before. It's the system we live in."

Tony dreams of expanding his business to the JFK passenger terminal, but concessions for spots in the terminal are open only to national brands. In 2004, he roasted only about 10,000 of the 100,000 pounds he produced, and sold the rest to a Honduran exporter for the market price of about sixty-five cents a pound. Although Tony would love to receive a higher price for his coffee, he is against fair trade. As he sees it, "fairness" should be based solely on the quality/cost ratio of coffee, without regard for sentiment or altruism. He is proud that he can manage every part of the process himself and would hate to involve intermediaries like certification outfits or cooperatives in the process.

He believes that a "fair" market would be one where marketing and branding were not part of the value equation. He cringes when I mention Starbucks, saying that their coffee is overpriced and overhyped by advertising, and that, in a taste test, he is sure customers would prefer his brew. Tony believes that his coffee could compete with the Starbucks of the world if he was given a concession to open in the passenger terminal.

His coffee is the most unmediated product imaginable, but unless he tells his story through clever marketing, his coffee has little cachet. "Directness" must be mediated to have symbolic value. As it is, Tony is struggling. He expects to make a decent profit, since he now has three locations in the airport, but he has lost money in the two previous crop years.

The common theme in both Javier's and Tony's stories is the belief that the coffee business is inherently risky. One party always wins at the expense of another, and that's just the way it is. This is most apparent in Tony's resigned acceptance of the violence directed against him. He understands what it is like to be an exploited worker, and he understands the hopelessness the pickers on his farm face. Yet he feels powerless to change anything. ("I feel nothing. . . . It's the system we live in.") Tony has created an efficient and direct coffee production business, but he is barely scraping by. He treats his workers the same as other growers in La Quebrada do, but he is perceived as a carpetbagger who makes millions in the United States.

Just as Tony's neighbors unfairly target him as the source of their problems, he directs his anger toward the advertisers and marketers who, as he sees it, hype inferior coffee and keep him from relocating to the JFK passenger terminal. The symbolic side of the coffee value chain is the one element that he does not understand or control. He is frustrated that he grows, transports, roasts, and sells his own coffee yet still loses out to the Starbucks of the world, who claim to have close relationships with coffee farmers, yet rely on "hype" to sell their coffee. If people really cared about coffee farmers, he reasons, they would avoid the flashy brands altogether because farmers barely participate in their business.

Javier, on the other hand, locates the problems in the coffee trade at the most immediate level. He would like to see a better enforcement of contracts in Honduras, and a less corrupt legal system, so that he would not have to deal only with the small circle of people whom he trusts. He sees the structure of the coffee industry as being inherently unequal and risky, but there is nothing "unfair" about it.

Javier is a medium-sized grower by Honduran standards, owning about fifteen acres of land; Tony is a relatively large-scale grower. At 125 acres, Tony's farm is large by Honduran standards but small compared to the large *fincas* (plantations) found in other parts of Central America. Unlike Guatemala or El Salvador, Honduras has no class of coffee elites, and the majority of farms are in the hands of small-scale farmers. Both Javier and Tony have lived and worked in the United States, and both have seen the coffee trade from a variety of perspectives. Their worldly experiences have given them insight about the inequalities inherent in the world coffee market and provide a sense of its complexity.

People like Tony and Javier lead the kind of transnational lives that led anthropologists of globalization, such as Arjun Appadurai (1996), to focus on the movements of people and things across borders to understand the contemporary social world. It would be impossible to grasp something as seemingly simple as a ten-acre coffee farm in La Quebrada without tracing out connections to a McDonald's in Queens or a new suburban development in Colorado. The lives of these individuals are integrated into transnational circuits as complicated as those that bring the coffee beans they grow from Honduran mountaintops to supermarket shelves. These transnational livelihoods are strategies used to cope with extreme volatility in the liberalized coffee market. Although migration certainly provides a way for some people to live out new media-fueled lifestyle possibilities, for people like Tony and Javier, migration is simply a way to generate capital. The experiences of people like Javier and Tony lead one to wonder about how, and indeed *if*, the coffee market could be regulated to provide a stable source of income for farmers like them. Both men used transnational migration as way to manage risk and volatility in the market, and neither one expressed any faith in the potential of collective forms of market regulation.

Fair Trade and Private Regulation

Fair trade coffee drew me to La Quebrada. In 2001, the community was abuzz over the potential of *comercio justo* (fair trade). At that time, the town was in the midst of the most severe decline in world coffee prices in the past century, and participation in the fair trade system provided a potential way out of the crisis for struggling farmers.

Fair trade is one of the most well-known examples of the transnational secular concept of social justice. It is a form of international market exchange that combines normative concepts of fairness with liberal economics.[7] Fair trade is a process that certifies and labels commodities, notably coffee, that are produced under "fair" conditions, as determined and enforced by a nongovernmental auditing body, the Fairtrade Labelling Organizations International (FLO). In general, "fair" certification guarantees that farmers have been paid a minimum price of $1.29 per pound of coffee and that workers are treated fairly on farms. Fair trade producers must fit into country-specific definitions of "small farmers" developed by the FLO. Fair trade is an alternative to agro-industrial food production and is marketed toward urbanites who can afford to pay between ten and thirteen dollars for a pound of coffee. With the addition of a "fair trade certified" label, fairness becomes an attribute of the commodity, similar to its country of origin, flavor characteristics, or caffeine content. Under fair trade, consumers enforce labor standards outside the boundaries of any national political system, using market choice rather than legal means. In its rhetoric, fair trade rests on affective bonds between producers and consumers in international commodities markets. The question is: Is this possible? Can international consumers develop and enforce a standard of fairness outside of political institutions?[8]

The fair trade system guaranteed a minimum price of $1.29 per pound of coffee, which is almost exactly the amount that had been guaranteed by the International Coffee Agreement before it collapsed in 1989. In 2001, Honduran coffee farmers were getting less than thirty cents per pound on the open market, so fair trade held obvious economic benefits. As mentioned in the introduction, I came to La Quebrada in 2001 as a marginal part of a development project that was designed to help coffee growers establish an ecological cooperative and access the fair trade market in the United States and Europe. I was "marginal" because the organizers of the project knew that I was skeptical about fair trade, and they encouraged me to be critical in my writings about the project in the interest of institutional self-critique. At the time, I was planning to begin a coffee commodity chain study as doctoral research, and this project provided a convenient point of entry. Although the project paid my way to Honduras, I was not really "inside" the project in a bureaucratic or professional sense because I had no professional commitment to the project's organizers. Like many graduate students looking for a research topic, I was an unusually fortunate academic tourist, poking around a small town for selfish reasons, trying to do something useful, but not quite sure how to do it. To the people in Honduras affiliated with the fair trade project from the beginning, I was probably more of an annoying interloper than anything else.

On an early visit to an evangelical church, the pastor spotted me in the audience, and he associated me with the burgeoning fair trade co-op. He decided to base his sermon on a passage from Psalms 11, which read "El fruto del justo es árbol de vida, y él que gana almas es sabio." (The fruit of the just is a tree of life, and he who wins souls is wise.) In Spanish, coffee cherries can be called *fruto,* so the pastor's biblical passage, referencing *el fruto del justo* (the fruit of the just or righteous) was a subtle theological nod in my direction. Although the sermon didn't provide me much intellectual guidance on the matter, I continually pondered whether the "the fruit of the just" could indeed be considered a potential tree of life for La Quebrada.

As I described in the introduction, the fair trade cooperative in La Quebrada never really got off the ground. The cooperative was never fair trade certified. Fair trade requires a farm to be audited and certified by an independent, third-party agency—a process that can be very expensive and time-consuming.[9] The average landholdings of the cooperative members were too high for them to be considered "small farmers" by the standards developed by the Fairtrade Labelling Organizations International (FLO) for Honduras. In theory, the cooperative could have denied membership to large- and medium-sized growers, but Hernán, one of the co-op's leaders, could not qualify under the small-farmer guidelines. He could not keep other relatively large-scale landholders out without being labeled a hypocrite. Given his already polarizing presence in town politics (described in chapter 3), this would have only confirmed the suspicions that he was a fraud. The co-op could have tried to attract small landholders, thereby lowering its average acreage, but small coffee-farmers lived on the edge of survival and were the least likely group to join a risky, fledgling cooperative that had a strong chance of failure. After a year or two of successful harvests, they may have been willing to join, but the first group of co-op members was embarking on an unknown path. As it happened, the cooperative's members were stuck between two categories: They were too small to profitably produce export coffee, but they were too large to be eligible for "fair trade."

The second cause of the co-op's failure (and one that I cannot emphasize enough) was the worldwide crisis in coffee prices that occurred between 2000 and 2003. During these years, the average price paid to Honduran coffee farmers dropped by one half. Because the co-op could not be fair trade certified, they tried to be certified as organic. Organic certification would have enabled them to receive a higher price for their crop. The transition to organic production takes at least two full crop-seasons and needs to be monitored by a third-party certification program. During this transitional phase, crop yields for the co-op dropped significantly (by more than 30 percent) at the same time that prices were at historic lows. During its first crop season, the co-op had to sell its crop at a price that was far below the cost of production. After this failure, almost all of the members quit the co-operative and felt they could no longer trust its leadership.

Given the short lifespan of the fair trade experiment in La Quebrada, it may seem strange for me to spend time exploring this topic. However, as a model of transnational citizenship, fair trade provides an important lesson about both the positive potential and the limitations of individual action as a transnational strategy for social reform. Earlier, I referred to fair trade as a "secular analog" of evangelical religion, a strategy for citizenship that attempts to transform an expansive collectivity through individual moral choice. This is more than a rhetorical analogy. The regulation of coffee has followed a similar historical trajectory as did the religious movements described in chapter 4. During the twentieth century, states and international institutions played an increasingly important role in managing the coffee trade in the interest of society. As part of a broad trend toward liberalization, these institutions were dismantled in the late 1980s, and new individualized strategies emerged to regulate coffee in the vacuum left by neoliberal reforms. The inability of nation-states to manage a global market gave way to private strategies for social reform. To reiterate, fair trade provides an important example through which we can think through the strengths and limitations of "systems of global private regulation" (Neilson 2008).

Fair Trade I and II

To illustrate just how novel contemporary fair trade is, it's helpful to examine the modern history of coffee in more detail. In the early twentieth century, a consumer-driven movement called fair trade emerged among urbanites in the United States. It was intended to challenge the power of large corporations who paid coffee growers an "unfair" price.[10] Consumers in the United States became involved in the affairs of coffee growing countries in Latin America, and they clamored for political changes that would establish a fair coffee price. American politicians leveled charges of exploitation against Latin American coffee growers, whom they considered exploitative profit-mongers.

A hundred years later, the issue of fair trade coffee reemerged among U.S. consumers. Again, it was an urban-based consumer movement that challenged corporate power and the prices paid to coffee growers in Latin America. These two movements, however, had opposite concepts of fairness. "Fair Trade I" believed that coffee growers were paid unfairly *high* prices that hurt *consumers* by price gouging; "Fair Trade II" believes that coffee *producers* are paid unfairly *low* prices that threaten the livelihood of small-scale farmers. Under Fair Trade I, coffee-producing nations instituted subsidies or price floors that stabilized the industry and helped their own agricultural sectors. Under Fair Trade II, coffee consumers establish price floors and voluntary subsidies for coffee growers *outside* of the borders of their own countries. Under Fair Trade I, the standards of "fairness" were determined by political processes within individual nation-states. Under Fair Trade II, nongovernmental institutions, rather than states, establish and maintain the definition of fair trade through a nonpolitical process. Both movements were led by consumers fighting for moral concepts of fairness, but there could hardly be a more drastic reversal of philosophies of social justice. The difference between these two understandings of fair trade is a telling example of the differences between modern and postmodern concepts of justice.

Under Fair Trade I, states developed various policies that ran counter to abstract "pure" capitalism, such as protectionist tariffs and subsidies intended to benefit particular nation-states or classes within them. Although specific policies may have been international—as in the case of favorable tariff rates for strategic allies or investment in international development projects—such endeavors were promoted in the name of national security or strategic interest rather than moral obligation. Although moral rhetoric has often been used (e.g., "promoting the cause of freedom"), the political interests of the Cold War overshadowed the moral element of these efforts until the 1990s. The rhetoric of moral obligation was often used to justify economic aid, but such policies were clearly guided by national interest rather than a disinterested concept of right.

Agricultural subsidies are perhaps the clearest example of a policy that abandons pure market logic in the interest of national economic stability. Tariffs and duties are other means by which individual nation-states can protect their own citizens, or those of strategic allies, through policies that counteract pure market forces. Subsidies provide a stable supply of goods for consumers, while protecting producers from foreign competition and market volatility. Most state-directed social policy has been conducted in the name of *national* interests, or as a means for democratic governments to curry the favor of certain interest groups within the population.[11]

In contrast, contemporary fair trade (Fair Trade II) is transnational. The centers of demand for fair trade are Western Europe, the United States, and Japan, three places where coffee is not produced (with the exception of Hawaii and Puerto Rico). These countries are the world's largest coffee consumers by volume. Fair trade consumers are thinking about the well-being of people outside of their own nations and trying to develop transnational strategies to address their concerns. In addition, fair trade is a trans-class movement. The people fighting for fair trade are educated, wealthy consumers who can afford to pay twelve dollars for a pound of coffee beans, yet they are supporters of agrarian politics in the developing world. From a purely economic standpoint, fair trade raises the price of coffee for consumers. In Fair Trade I, producers fought for higher prices and consumers fought for lower prices, acting in accordance with economic self-interest. Fair Trade II is *relatively* nonpolitical and nondemocratic, compared to systems of governance within modern democracies. The FLO has voting members of boards and committees, but its standards are ultimately developed by a set of "expert" stakeholders that are ultimately accountable to only the members of their own voluntary organization (Renard 2005; Jaffee 2007). Fair Trade II is based on raising incomes for producers without the involvement of political structures in the producing countries. Fittingly, fair trade grew in popularity in the 1990s—after the International Coffee Agreement, an international political cartel that stabilized the industry through quotas and price supports—fell apart (Bates 1997).

That the fair trade movement originates among coffee consumers in nonproducing countries, coupled with its nondemocratic decision-making process, open it to the accusations of feel-good paternalism that tend to be leveled against any populist movement driven by elites. I have heard these criticisms of fair trade many times, especially in Honduras, and here

I have simplified them for dramatic effect. First are the accusations of naïve moralism; for example, "Why don't you look at the low-paid workers in your own country, like the janitors who clean up after you at Starbucks? Why turn coffee brokers into the bad guys?" Second are the accusations of paternalism; for example, "What do Americans (or Europeans) know about what's best for coffee farmers? How do you know if your version of fairness is the same as theirs?" These criticisms raise important questions about the viability of fair trade. Not incidentally, statements against fair trade parallel criticisms of "internationalist" meddling that are leveled against human rights workers, environmentalists, and other activists working in the developing world that perceive transnational movements as challenges to national sovereignty. The final line of criticism questions the consumerist elements of the movement; for example, "How can you save the world by shopping? Isn't this just a form of instant gratification that ignores the 'big questions'?"

The questions above identify criticisms that have been leveled against many kinds of "ethical consumerism" or consumer politics. At this point, I should clarify that my critical discussion of transnational consumer movements should not be taken to mean that they are "bad" or that I am personally against them as a political movement. I simply seek to trace the emergence of consumer politics back to the macro-level changes in the relationship among state, economy, and society that I have described throughout the book. For farmers like Tony and Javier, who face systematic risks that arise from participation in an essentially unregulated transnational market, the key question is: What kind of institution, if any, could best manage or regulate that market? For Tony and Javier, the answer is simple: It's up to the individual. When placed in historical context, however, this view—individuals participating in an expansive global system with no collective institution to mediate between the individual and the market—appears rather unique.

The Contradictions of Consumer Politics

That the fair trade movement is based on the changing symbolic meaning of coffee does not, by itself, limit its potential as a means to transform the politics of trade. "Consumer citizenship" has, historically, been

an effective strategy through which large numbers of people have organized to effect political change (D. Frank 1999; L. Cohen 2003; Micheletti
2003; Foster 2008). Indeed, two of modern history's most important revolutionary movements, the American Revolution and the struggle for Indian independence, both depended on the power of consumers to redefine
the meaning of commodities. These two movements provide instructive
points of comparison to fair trade.

Boycotts: Conspicuous Non-Consumption

Since the late eighteenth century, boycotts have been a common and effective form of public political action. Fair trade follows in the tradition of the
boycott, but shifts the politics of consumption from the public to the private spheres. Most examples of consumer activism are inherently public,
such as the anti-English boycotts leading up to the American Revolution
(D. Frank 1999; Breen 2004) and the Swadeshi movement in India (Cohn
1996; Goswami 1998). In both examples, individuals communicated their
political affiliation through "conspicuous non-consumption," making individual sacrifices to communicate participation in a broader public.[12]

T. H. Breen's *The Marketplace of Revolution* (2004) provides a detailed
history of how a boycott of English goods shaped the American Revolution. Breen makes a strong argument that the decision to forgo the purchase of imported British goods was a key idiom through which American
colonists expressed support for the revolutionary cause. The language of
personal sacrifice and the ability to overcome temptation were vital parts of
this movement. The ability to forgo drinking tea, an addictive drug-food,
displayed political commitment. Breen writes:

> [T]he colonists' shared experience as consumers provided them with the
> cultural resources needed to develop a bold new form of political protest.
> In this unprecedented context, private decisions were interpreted as politi-
> cal acts; consumer choices communicated personal loyalties. Goods became
> the foundation of trust, for one's willingness to sacrifice the pleasures of the
> market provided a remarkably visible and effective test of allegiance. (xvi)

To not drink tea, which required great discipline and restraint, showed
commitment to the revolutionary cause. Breen argues that consumer

choice served as a public display of political sentiment and that such acts were an important stimulant for collective anti-English action in the then-inchoate nation. Breen argues that the Boston Tea Party and other public acts served as symbolic redefinitions, and "private consumer experiences were transformed into public rituals" (329).

Whereas tea had been a valued sign of refinement, civilization, and status (like most other imported goods), the tea boycott turned it into a symbol of dependency and tyranny, inverting the symbolic order of colonialism. The emergence of a capitalist market had created a new language of consumer choice in the expanding colonies, and Breen argues that this new language was used to communicate revolutionary political sentiment.

The Indian *swadeshi* movement is another example of a boycott that redefined British goods in protest to colonial dependency. *Swadeshi* (Sanskrit for "of *our* land or country") was a call to purchase locally made goods *and* to boycott imported ones, so it could be seen as both a sacrifice and a virtuous indulgence. Its power sprang from the decision to forgo imports that could not be substituted with Indian-made ones. The locally made textiles were simple, homespun garments, as opposed to the prestigious Lancashire cottons that were worn by the British. Manu Goswami (1998) cites a popular *swadeshi* song written in 1870 that exemplified the movement's spirit of abstinence, saying "We will eat our own coarse grain and wear the rough, home-spun cloth. What do we care for lavender and imported trinkets?" (625). The public display of sacrifice became even more apparent after 1907, when, under Mahatma Gandhi's leadership, the *swadeshi* movement became even more radical. Bernard Cohn (1996) writes:

> The [goals of the *swadeshi* movement in Bengal, 1903–1908] were complex, but one aim was to encourage the development and use of indigenously produced goods through a boycott of European manufactures. As the movement developed, there was increasing discussion and propaganda to encourage Indian weavers and to revive the hand spinning of cotton thread. These ideas were taken up and formalized by Mahatma Gandhi in the next decade. . . . Gandhi continually articulated and elaborated on the theme that the Indian people would only be free from European domination, both politically and economically, when the masses took to spinning, weaving, and wearing homespun cotton cloth, khadi. (148–149)

Like the American "symbolic redefinition" of tea, the Indian boycott of imported English goods turned the symbols of virtue into markers of tyranny. The success of boycotts rests in their power of "symbolic redefinition." By turning imported goods from signs of wealth and refinement into signs of dependency and injustice, boycotts shift the terms of political debate. In these examples, nonconsumption signified solidarity with nascent nationalist movements.

The Ethical Consumption Model

The ethical consumption model is the opposite of the boycott. Rather than calling for a prohibition of certain goods, this type of action calls for consumers to purchase products that conform to a particular set of values. This type of action has been less successful than boycotts in effecting political change, mainly because it is a private act that does not establish a community through the suppression of individual gratification. In these cases, individual choices are interpreted as political acts, but these acts do not communicate a message outward.

The union-labeling movement, which began in the 1870s, presents an illustrative comparative case to fair trade. One of the most important unions in U.S. history, the Cigar Makers' International Union (CMIU) of America, initiated a campaign to advertise certain cigars as "union made" to differentiate them from cigars made by Chinese immigrant labor.[13] This union was led by a young Samuel Gompers, who would later become the most influential figure in U.S. labor history. In 1872, the CMIU placed a blue stamp on boxes of cigars that said, "This certifies that a cigar has been made by a first-class workman, a member of the Cigar Makers' International Union of America." This program was an attempt to improve union-members' working conditions by appealing to anti-Chinese sentiment and nationalism. At that time, large numbers of Chinese immigrants were producing cheap cigars in New York City, and the CMIU, consisting of mostly European immigrants, used both racism and nationalism to promote their cause.

By the early twentieth century, the union label discourse had changed, using public outcry against monopoly trusts—rather than cheap immigrant labor—to arouse support. In 1905, badges and posters in support of the CMIU read, "Don't Support the Trust. Buy Blue Label Cigars." At that time, there was considerable controversy surrounding the monopolistic control of the American Tobacco Company, a trust controlled by the Duke family. The "union label" purchase was a statement against big business, and it came at a point in history when the U.S. government was enacting antitrust legislation and other Progressive-era policies, such as the Pure Food and Drug Act, designed to curtail the power of large corporations in the interest of the public good. This is the political platform that I have earlier referred to as "Fair Trade I."

In the late twentieth century, the union label reappeared, and it symbolized an explicitly nationalistic agenda. Through the 1960s and 1970s, U.S. manufacturing had lost considerable clout as production moved overseas and the domestic economy shifted toward the service sector. In 1975, the "union label" advertising campaign appeared in television and radio spots. Its lyrics are:

> Look for the union label
> when you are buying that coat, dress or blouse.
> Remember somewhere our union's sewing,
> our wages going to feed the kids, and run the house.
> We work hard, but who's complaining?
> Thanks to the I.L.G. we're paying our way!
> So always look for the union label,
> it says we're able to make it in the U.S.A.!
>
> (Frank 1999, 137)

This song is meant to appeal to nationalism and "family values." The International Ladies Garment Union highlights that wages go "to feed the kids, and run the house" and that its products are made in the United States. This effort would lead to the "Made in the USA" and "Buy American" campaigns that became popular in the 1980s. These movements developed within a recessionary economic climate and a cultural milieu that stressed the sunset of U.S. economic power and the escalating power of Japan (Frank 1999). As economic integration made foreign manufacture and assembly an inescapable part of life, "patriotic spending" became the latest incarnation of the ethical consumption model.

By the 1990s, economic prosperity and the sunny future of "globalization" had turned such nationalistic projects into anachronisms, and the

"Made in the USA" movement faded considerably after the passage of the North American Free Trade Agreement (NAFTA) in 1992. Even the Democratic Party, a longtime advocate of protectionist measures, began to embrace free-marketism. By 2000, at the height of the millennial optimism toward globalization, the *New York Times Magazine* published a feature article by Nicholas Kristof and Sheryl WuDunn, arguing that American consumers could do their part to help the cause of global development by purchasing goods from foreign sweatshops.[14] Global economic integration became the dominant vision of progress, and protection of the economic interests of particular nation-states was seen as an obstacle to global prosperity and stability. As images of McDonald's in Moscow flickered across the screens of American households, "Made in the USA" disappeared from public discourse.[15]

These examples suggest that "negative" acts of prohibition, such as boycotts, have had considerable political impact, while "positive" acts of ethical consumerism have had less success. Nonconsumption is far more public than virtuous consumption. The decision to forgo tea or imported clothing is visible to other people and sends a powerful symbolic message. In contrast, only the consumer knows if he or she has "looked for the Union Label" or bought fair trade coffee because these are not apparent in the physical properties of the commodity, and the consumer still smokes cigars or drinks coffee. Only the buyer and seller witness the quasi-political act, making virtuous indulgence a basically private phenomenon.

For almost a century, nation-states developed various protectionist measures and international alliances to regulate coffee. This political process culminated with the institution of the International Coffee Agreement (ICA), which regulated coffee prices for almost thirty years, from 1962 to 1989. The ICA involved stakeholders from all aspects of the coffee trade in its organization, which allowed it to grasp the industry at a systemic level. The ICA's demise was largely due to pressure from powerful member states who placed their own national political interests over the interests of the industry as a whole, and it became dominated by internal conflicts and the hegemonic interests of the two largest coffee-producing nations, Brazil and Colombia (Bates 1997). Additionally, the centralized marketing boards that controlled the coffee trade in many countries were beset by corruption and inefficiency. The most notorious examples of coffee *rentierism* (system where the government collects a "rent" for all coffee grown within its borders) were in Zaire (Talbot 1997b, 77) and Uganda (Bates 1997, 167), where the government paid coffee farmers a fraction of the international coffee price and used the surplus to enrich themselves. The ICA was far from perfect, but, as Robert Bates has convincingly argued, it did provide a relatively effective system of international regulation for almost thirty years.

In contrast, the most recent International Coffee Agreements, signed in 1994 and 2001, have turned away from the entire regulatory project that guided the first ICA. The International Coffee Organization, which is mandated by International Coffee Agreement, now provides statistical information about the industry, promotes coffee consumption, and formulates strategies for farmer competitiveness. It is designed to stimulate and streamline the coffee trade according to free-market principles, but it has no regulatory power. In the wake of the end of the international regulatory system, fair trade consumers attempt to regulate the coffee market by choice.

Here, it is useful to return to John Talbot's (1997b) study of the production and retention of surplus value in the global coffee commodity chain. Talbot has shown that the major consequence of the cessation of the International Coffee Agreement was a transfer of income from coffee-producing countries to coffee-consuming countries. Five transnational corporations control more than 60 percent of the world coffee market (Talbot 1995, 120). These companies have seen their share of the total surplus created along the coffee commodity chain rise by about 20 percent since the end of the ICA in 1989, while the share of the surplus retained in the producing countries has fallen. Talbot concludes that the collapse of the ICA led to a "huge transfer of surplus out of the producing countries" toward transnational corporations (86). But Talbot's analysis does not attempt to explain how the profits of the transnational corporations are used. More than half of the outstanding shares of stock of Procter and Gamble, Sara Lee, and are owned by financial institutions (as much as 73 percent in the case of Altria), which include mutual funds and private capital funds. The dividends created by growing profits are concentrated in large banks and brokerage firms. A tiny percentage of this income may wind up in the hands of small individual investors, but this is insignificant compared to the profits of the financial companies.

The universalist version of the social contract that guides fair trade suggests great potential for a form of transnational (as opposed to international) regulation of the coffee trade that might be able to avoid the flaws of international cartels, but it provides no coherent vision of what such an institution would look like. In fact, proponents of fair trade almost never acknowledge the existence of the ICA and tend to downplay that they are performing a similar regulatory function. Not one promotional flyer or information packet on fair trade mentions the existence of the ICA or the fact that it collapsed just as fair trade began to grow in popularity.

The tendency to rely on private action to address systemic concerns derives from the incredibly complex and fragmentary nature of the contemporary global division of labor. In the absence of a viable theory of how postindustrial capitalism works, individual solutions become the best available option for change. The rising concern over transnational labor issues, expressed by advocates of fair trade, demonstrates the popular potential for the formation of new social bonds between international producers and consumers (Foster 2008). Frequently, this potential has been focused on private consumer behavior rather than governmental strategies, such as trade or labor policy. Consumers embrace a symbolic opposition to neoliberalism, but provide no alternatives other than individual acts.

The Myth of Fair Trade

To be clear, I am not taking the absolutist position that small steps are not worth taking; nor am I espousing a totalizing solution to the injustices of capitalism. However, I do believe that the contradiction that limits the potential of fair trade—recognition of an expansive global economy that can be managed only at the individual level—is characteristic of more general tendencies of contemporary social theory and political practice.

By comparing fair trade with consumer boycotts and national trade policies, I argue that fair trade places the responsibility for the maintenance of justice upon individual consumers and thus represents the epitome of market-driven forms of social justice (Micheletti 2003; Foster 2008). Under fair trade, justice is quantified in the terms of money. Fair trade assigns a cash value to morality and sociality, synthesizing the two incompatible value-spheres of market and religion, objectivity and affect, as originally conceived by Max Weber. Though ideologically concerned with social justice and the well-being of commodity producers in the developing world, fair trade plays into the hand of the very process it seeks to redress. By incorporating morality into the exchange value of a commodity, fair trade reinforces the terms of pure calculative rationality by expressing fairness in terms of exchange value. In this sense, it epitomizes what I have called postmodern theories of social justice.

For fair trade to have a lasting impact, it must be based on a clear theory of social justice and exploitation. This would require an accurate understanding of the coffee commodity chain. The coffee industry is an exceptionally complex case. Coffee is traded on the global commodities market, and its price is determined by a complex set of forces that reach far beyond basic supply and demand, including currency exchange rates, the investment strategy of hedge funds and other structured financial products, not to mention weather, transportation, and the politics of trade factors. To determine who is exploited, if anyone, one must look at all the links in the commodity chain in order to understand how surplus value is produced (Talbot 1997b). Fair trade's efforts to pay coffee farmers a bit more money is a pragmatic, local-level solution, but it makes no attempt to grasp the system at its highest levels. Its version of "social justice" is too simple to truly "re-embed" exchange in social relations. Like the narratives of exploitation developed by the workers on Tony's farm, or Tony, or Javier, this concept of "fairness" is based on a limited perspective that locates social problems and their possible resolutions at an immediate level.

Over the course of this study, I spoke with many fair trade consumers who expressed a sentiment that rang true to my own experiences as an occasional fair trade buyer: Consumers recognized the great inequalities inherent in global capitalist markets, but they didn't know how to ameliorate them. They realized that fair trade was only a small symbolic step in the right direction, but it felt good and had a simple philosophy that seemed to produce tangible benefits. It did not solve the problem of global inequality, but it surely didn't add to it. The main argument of this chapter is that fair trade is a basically private act that has no adequate political platform to address systemic inequalities. The desire to know the conditions under which one's food is produced is a result of the alienating aspects of life in the postindustrial world, and the direct producer-to-consumer narrative on which fair trade depends is a mythic construction that simply explains the incredibly complex nature of the global economy with a reassuring image of the coffee farmer, living a life of rustic tranquility. Like all myths, it provides a coherent yet simple explanation of social reality, and much of its meaning comes "in the telling" or, in this case, "in the buying, brewing, and drinking." Buying fair trade gives the consumer a reassuring—even empowering—feeling of control over the seemingly incomprehensible system.

6

GLOBAL SOCIALITY, POSTMODERNITY, AND NEOPOPULISM

A disturbing—even tragic—finding of my research in La Quebrada was that undocumented Honduran immigrants were frequently blamed for social and economic decline in their hometowns in Honduras. These people were motivated by a desire to *support* their families and communities, yet they were criticized by the very people who depended on them. They are the same immigrants who are often the targets of virulent, racist, and accusatory political rhetoric in the United States, where they are accused of "stealing jobs" or "not playing by the rules" of the U.S. labor market, while simultaneously being subjected to extreme forms of exploitation. Honduran migrants therefore suffer the double indignity of being blamed for socioeconomic decline in their hometowns *and* in the U.S. communities to which they migrate in search of a decent wage. In this sense, there is something about the figure of "the immigrant" that is charged with intense metaphoric value as a symbol of systematic economic changes that affect Honduras and the United States.

The tendency to blame "the immigrant" for problems on both sides of the border is a symptom of the anxieties and social dislocations caused by *uneven* processes of economic integration, which allow global capital to move around the globe in search of profits but limit the mobility of people to seek out opportunities, weakening the political position of workers around the globe. Globalization has been marked by an imbalance: While the world has become integrated economically, socially, and culturally, it remains *politically* fragmented by nation-states and relatively weak systems of international governance. In a situation where nation-states seem incapable of mediating between individuals and the global economy, systematic political and social frustrations are often displaced onto symbols "that condense the vast multitude of anonymous forces that determine us" (Žižek 2006, 557).

The ideology of globalization is based on the idea of a borderless world, where participation in a single market erases markers of identity such as nationality, language, and locality. However, *responses* to globalization invariably invoke the preservation of some meaningful social community— be it Americans clamoring to stop outsourcing to "keep American jobs at home," or rural Hondurans trying to preserve the long-term viability of their community by stemming the tide of emigration. Ultimately, the "protectionist" response to liberalization requires some check on the freedom of individuals in the name of social preservation. The question is: Who or what is to be protected? In many cases, "the nation" is the community that people seek to preserve through policies of economic nationalism;[1] for others, the meaningful social group may be the tribe, the village, or the family.

Writing in the 1940s, Karl Polanyi (1957, 132) identified this phenomenon as the "double movement" of capitalist liberalization, which he defined as "the action of two organizing principles in society . . . the principle of economic liberalism, aiming at the establishment of a self-regulating market . . . [and] the other, the principle of social protection aiming at the conservation of man and nature as well as productive organization." In other words, every attempt to organize society according to the principles of economic liberalism, in which all differences are erased in the name of a "level playing field" and individual freedom of choice will be met by a "conservative" countermovement that tries to preserve the organization of some meaningful social unit, ultimately limiting individual freedom in the name of social cohesion.

Polanyi traces the various forms that this antiliberal (or conservative) countermovement has taken throughout the history of European capitalism, from Poor Laws designed to protect English parishioners from poverty and homelessness in the 1700s, to the birth of the modern welfare state in the nineteenth century, to restrictive immigration laws in the twentieth century. Polanyi ultimately describes the origins of European fascism as a response against utopian free-marketism, arguing that:

> Freedom's utter frustration in fascism is, indeed, the inevitable result of the liberal philosophy, which claims that power and compulsion are evil, that freedom demands their absence from a human community. No such thing is possible; in a complex society this becomes apparent. This leaves no alternative but either to remain faithful to an illusionary idea of freedom and deny the reality of society, or to accept that reality and reject the idea of freedom. The first is the liberal's conclusion; the latter the fascist's. No other seems possible. (1957, 257)

Polanyi correctly points out that the antiliberal drive to "protect" or "preserve" some meaningful social unit can take both positive and negative forms. It can take a moderate form like social welfare law, which is based on some institutionalized bond between laborers and employers, or a more radical form like fascism, where all freedom is denied in the name of "order." But any "society" requires some limits on individual freedoms to preserve social solidarity. While some might see these bonds of sentiment and social solidarity as irrational barriers to efficient functioning of the free market, most anthropologists would see these bonds as defining elements of human life.

The key anthropological question is how and why people formulate *particular* understandings of the social community of which they are a part. Human beings are never completely conscious of the totality of relationships in which they act, so—by necessity—they rely on symbols that explain their place in the world (such as religions, philosophies, or stories). These symbols are often called "collective representations," "forms of social consciousness," or "cultural narratives" by social scientists. For example: Latin American immigrants are blamed for systemic problems in the U.S. economy; the coffee industry is singled out as an illustrative example of the injustices of global agro-food systems. These are partial explanations that come to symbolize larger structural problems that escape the limits of human consciousness. In the simplest possible terms: Symbols take the place of the whole.[2]

In this work, I have focused on three different responses to the economic liberalization that, since the 1990s, has almost universally come to be called *neo*liberalism. In each of the cases I have described—criticisms of migrants, religious narratives of crisis and redemption, and consumer activism—people attempt to assert collective principles of sociality or justice in response to economic change. Families in La Quebrada struggle with social disintegration caused by transnational migration and articulate principles of social solidarity through gossip and personal accusation. They blame individual migrants for their community's crisis, emphasizing the migrant's *social responsibility* to family. The evangelicals try to counter social disintegration by cultivating adherents' personal relationship with God, while members of Creciendo en Gracia (CEG) translate liberal individualism into the religious sphere, viewing individual moral conduct as the solution to social ills. Fair trade tries to regulate the global coffee industry through consumer choice, enforcing principles of economic and social justice through individual acts of consumption. All of these phenomena are, in one sense, examples of the kind of countermovement to liberalization described by Polanyi. They are based on moral understandings of community that move from the most local to the most global levels of social structure. Anti-migrant sentiment is a decidedly *local response* to a systemic issue, while fair trade inherently relies on some notion of *global* citizenship. However, they ultimately replicate the individualist ethic of the market by denying the transformative power of collectivities. In all of these cases, collective social projects are framed as the consequences of individual choices. When viewed in historical context, the narrow ideology on which these practices rest is clear. In each case, the declining importance of the nation-state as a category of social identification reverberates through various domains of social life.

The three responses to crisis I have described in this book exemplify the postmodern tendency to view individual choice as the basic engine of social reform and to ignore or downplay political philosophies that reach beyond the individual. I call these movements "postmodern" because they recognize the individual's participation in an expansive global society but locate the source of the potential transformation of that society at the most personal level. These phenomena are examples of the kind of "dispersed energies" that, according to Martín Hopenhayn (2001, xiii), mark the transition of Latin American politics from modernity to postmodernity. In his words, neoliberal globalization led to "the delegitimation of the State as the propeller of development and the builder of society" (2001, ix):

> The defeat of the revolutionary or egalitarian utopia entails a search for alternative forms of gratification and self-affirmation. Facing a future in which the fleshed out image of social revolution has lost the appearance of truth, liberating energies dissipate in a cloud of alternatives that don't add up to a single project or total discourse. Rather, they bring to society the fresh air of new searches: popular religious feeling, grass roots movements, diversified consumption in the growing cultural industry.

Hopenhayn's synthetic treatment of Latin American political philosophy argues that political energies that historically were directed toward the collective dream of socialist or capitalist modernization are now channeled toward more narrowly focused projects for the betterment of individuals or relatively small social groups. He sees the demise of the political goal of "integration" into modernity as marking the transition to postmodernity in Latin American politics.

Private Regulation and Postmodernity

To avoid analytical imprecision, at this point I need to elucidate why I have consistently referred to religion, fair trade, and other "systems of private regulation" (Neilson 2008) as "postmodern"—a term (like "modernity" itself) that has taken on so many meanings and connotations as to become almost meaningless. The transition to modernity is usually associated with the development of secular law, defined and enforced by a nation-state. Across the broad sweep of human history, the regulatory function of the state was performed by either religious institutions or kinship-based political systems before the emergence of the modern state (Fried 1967). While religious or kinship-based ideas of morality and virtue always exist alongside secular law, and continually shape the law's content, the state retains the ultimate power over law and order in modern societies. In capitalist economies, for example, we see regulatory codes that mandate proper treatment of workers, the enforcement of contracts, and environmental protection, among many other collectively helpful values. These laws institutionalize secular ideas of justice, which, historically speaking, were the province of religious precepts.

The possibility of creating equitable social institutions *within* (rather than against) the capitalist economy has been a central problem in modern social theory. Capitalism has often been described as being fundamentally incompatible with religious precepts—which Max Weber (1958) called the "ethic of brotherliness."[3] Theorists such as Karl Marx, Max Weber, and Emile Durkheim believed that the ethical requirements of capitalism (impersonal rules, competition, and abstract calculation) clashed with the requirements of collective social life, which were rooted in the value of interpersonal relationships, traditional social hierarchies, and other systems of belief that inhibited absolute individualism. Capitalism required people to view each other as fundamentally equal under the laws of the market, which clashed with the human need to see people as members of meaningful social groups. The central crisis of modernity lay in the social disintegration, class conflict, alienation, and anomie brought about by the rise of industrial capitalism and bureaucracy. How could social solidarity be maintained within a capitalist system, which sought to erase all social ties by viewing all individuals as equal participants in markets?

These thinkers sought to explain the radical cultural shifts that followed the Industrial Revolution in Europe, focusing on the rise of capitalist modernity in relation to previous world-historical epochs. Each one focused on some form of social decay brought about by the Industrial Revolution: Marx believed the rise of capitalism led to individual alienation and class polarization; for Weber, capitalism brought the rationalization of social life through bureaucratization; and for Durkheim, the rise of capitalism led to the breakdown of social cohesion, which was manifested in individual anomie caused by an increasingly fragmented and complex division of labor, which caused people to lose touch with their place within a collectivity. All three theorists shared a common concern for how best to resolve the tension between capitalist competition and the public good. They sought to understand how the incredible productive forces brought about by capitalism might lead to a more equitable, egalitarian society.

Of the three thinkers, Weber was the most pessimistic about the possibility of resolving the crisis of capitalist modernity. Although he clearly and brilliantly identified the crisis, he saw no way out of it. Industry, technology, and bureaucracy were here to stay, and he saw no reformist or revolutionary platform that might make capitalism more equitable in the future. In Weber's words, "The more the world of the modern capitalist economy follows its own immanent laws, the less accessible it is to any imaginable relation with a religious ethic of brotherliness" (Weber 1958, 331). For Weber, the value-spheres (*wertsphären*) of the market and religion were oriented toward opposing types of action, the former toward impersonality and rational individual maximization, and the latter toward human compassion and morality. Market logic was inherently dispassionate—based on abstract principles—and moral logic was inherently compassionate—based on human "brotherhood," the affective bonds formed between members of a community. For Weber, modern formal rationality was unique in that it relied on universal abstract laws, which, in pure ideal-typical form, were impersonal and therefore contrary to the "ethic of brotherliness." Modern social relationships were governed by impersonal legal contracts rather than affective principles of personal status.

Economic rationality denied the ethic of brotherliness, and there was no way out of this trap. In Robert Bellah's words, *modernity* was characterized by "the increasingly irreconcilable conflict between [value-spheres], a differentiation which leads to the 'polytheism' of modernity, a 'war of the gods,' which is the result of the entire process of rationalization, Weber's central preoccupation during his last and most fruitful period" (Bellah 1999, 277). The war of modernity pitted the god of the market versus the god of love (or, sentiment, to put it mildly), and the market was winning the war.

Bellah argues that the essay "Religious Rejections of the World and Their Directions" is "perhaps the key text in explaining Weber's entire corpus" (Bellah 1999, 277). Weber's bleak view of humanity's future as an "iron casing" emerged from his belief that the ethic of capitalist competition would progressively destroy the ethic of brotherliness, which, to some degree, had organized all precapitalist societies.[4] This ethic of brotherliness gradually lost its relative importance as humanity moved toward rational modernity, as the importance of kinship ties was eclipsed by more abstract notions of self and citizenship. The future would hold an impersonal, unfeeling world in which the cold objectivity of calculative rationality would dissolve the personal bonds between people, the social contract voided by the laws of the market.

Rationalization was, for Weber, based on politics that was depersonalized via bureaucracy and written law, an economy that was depersonalized through the use of money, and a religious morality that was depersonalized through belief in sacred texts that applied laws to all people. In all three domains of life, abstract logic replaced personalistic bonds. Following Henry Maine, Weber argued that "the sib," or kin group, is the historical basis of all social identification. He believed that society developed from simple forms to more complex ones. Weber, like Durkheim, argued that individuals in small-scale societies have reciprocal obligations to the kin group, which are legitimated through ritual. People become conscious of their place in a social collectivity through ritual practice and more mundane forms of reciprocal action. As cities began to develop (800 to 200 BC), salvation religions replaced kinship ties with ties of faith to an abstract "brotherhood" of believers. Such an allegiance required a person to renounce "organic" ties to the immediate kin group in the name of the bonds of faith and symbolic brotherhood, usually established through belief in a religious text.

The "world religions"—Christianity, Islam, and Buddhism—gave ultimate value to abstract "acosmistic" love, which is a concern for all people, regardless of language, nationality, or social position. Such a belief requires one to behave in ways that may conflict with the interests of the immediate kin-group in the name of religious creed. A person's allegiance expands beyond the boundaries of the "sib" because it is based on faith in a religious text that applies to *all* believers. This requires an inherently *abstract* concept of the social totality.

For Weber, the central problems of modernity were that nationalism had become the most important form of collective social identity and that nationalism served the interests of bellicose states that strove for power and rarely acted in the interest of the nation. Rhetoric aside, states were concerned only with the expansion of their own power. During Weber's lifetime, the modern welfare state began to rein in "pure" competitive capitalism in the name of the public good by enforcing labor laws and using taxes to benefit the citizenry as a whole (through, for example, education, health care, recreation, and the arts). Germany, for example, developed the world's first social security system in 1889. But Weber was cynical about the welfare state. Weber saw the measures of the welfare state as coercive policies designed to enhance state power, which were ideologically disguised as ethical policy. He wrote, "In the final analysis, in spite of all 'social welfare policies,' the whole course of the state's inner political functions, of justice and administration, is repeatedly and unavoidably regulated by the objective pragmatism of 'reasons of state' " (Weber 1958, 334). He drew an analogy between bureaucratic law and money—both created an abstract, impersonal system. "[T]he political man acts just like the economic man, in a matter of fact manner 'without regard to the person' . . . without hate and therefore without love" (1958, 334). Weber's pessimistic attitude toward the welfare state demonstrates his general pessimism toward the future of capitalist society.

Weber's work has clear parallels with Durkheimian sociology, although Durkheim had much greater faith in society's ability to manage capitalism for the greater good. Durkheim argued that all concepts of morality were based on an individual's awareness of his or her place within a social collectivity. Moral concepts formed the basis of all religious thought, which was a predecessor of scientific thought. Science and religion were abstract ways of explaining the world that recognized human collectivities as governed by forces that reached *beyond individuals.* The human faculty for abstract reasoning was a product of social relations, and universal logic required a *universal* concept of humanity to which such logic would apply. Unlike Weber, Durkheim saw the trend toward more abstract and expansive understandings of society as a positive development. In the conclusion to *The Elementary Forms of Religious Life,* originally published in 1912, he writes:

> There is no people, and no State, that is not engaged with a more or less undelimited society that includes all people and all States with which it is indirectly or directly in contact; there is no national life that is not under the sway of an international collective life. The more we advance in history, the larger and the more important these international groupings become. (1995, 428)

He continues,

> As that international life broadens, so too does the collective horizon; society no longer appears as the whole, par excellence, and becomes part of a

whole that is more vast, with frontiers that are indefinite and capable of rolling back indefinitely. As a result, things can no longer fit within the social
frames where they were originally classified; they must be organized with
principles of their own. (1995, 446)

The great challenge of modernity, according to Durkheim, was to develop legitimate social institutions to integrate an ever-expanding complex
society. Durkheim believed that social science could contribute to the development of a political institution that would rise above national interests
and class struggle, and his sentiments at the end of *The Elementary Forms,*
written on the brink of World War I, presage the idea of "world government" that would grow out of that war and lead to the establishment of the
United Nations. For him, modern states had the potential to act in the interests of society, but only if they were guided by positivist social science.

The impersonality of capitalist exchange is a central element of Marx's
definition of commodities as well. Marx defined commodities as represent-
ing a specific quantity of *abstract* (and therefore impersonal) social labor.
The universal exchangeability of goods requires a quantifiable abstract
measure of value, symbolically expressed in a specific quantity of money.
Similarly, Weber writes that "money is the most abstract and 'impersonal'
medium which exists in human life" (1958, 331). Money, as a symbolic
expression of a specific quantity of abstract labor, allows capitalism to
function as a rational system because, through the symbolic medium of
money, value can be objectively quantified according to universal standards. Despite the vast theoretical differences among Weber, Durkheim,
and Marx, all three agree that an abstract, impersonal standard of value
is a defining characteristic of the capitalist economy. When value is expressed in abstract terms, the human (i.e., personal) element of market
behavior fades to the background or, in Weber's more bleak predictions,
disappears completely.

Universal or global social movements—for human rights, fair labor
standards, environmental justice—have expanded the ethic of brotherliness beyond the boundaries of nation-states, adapting the religious ideal of
universal brotherhood to *secular* international politics. Secular concepts of
universal human rights and global standards of fairness have transcended
individual countries or regions in the name of social justice. These universal concepts of human morality existed in the past within the religious

sphere, but only recently have the so-called global New Social Movements developed a secular, transnational moral platform.[5]

I have argued that the ideology of modernity has been based on an ever-expanding concept of the social whole and a belief in some kind of social bond between different classes in society, conceived differently by various political philosophies. For much of modern history, the nation-state was the institution best able to institutionalize that social bond. However, the realities of globalization have weakened the ability of any nation-state to control and regulate its economy, leading to a process that Akhil Gupta (1998) and Terence Turner (2002) call the "de-hyphenization" of the nation-state. As a result of this "de-hyphenization," people have created new strategies of citizenship designed to institutionalize the social contract in a global context. As Douglas Holmes (2000, 11) writes, "As fast-capitalism nullifies the instrumental relationship binding the poor and disadvantaged to a wider social nexus, an all encompassing conception of society is increasingly difficult, if not impossible, to sustain." The key contradictory tendency of postmodernism is the recognition of the existence of a single global society without any collective "global" theory or political institution to regulate or transform society, beyond the logic of the market (Graeber 2001; Turner 2002).[6] Under these conditions, the logic of the market—individual choice—becomes the basic organizing principle of social life. Even movements that try to assert coherent principles of sociality, such as new religious movements and fair trade, ultimately reflect this essentially individualist ethos, albeit in vastly different ways.

The Particularist Case

One way to understand the origins of the social changes discussed in this book would be to focus on the *particular* history of Honduras. For example, why was migration such an attractive option to people in La Quebrada in the early 2000s? The violence of the 1970s and 1980s foreclosed most secular and religious platforms for change that focused on "society" and could therefore be linked to socialism or communism. Specific actors—supported by the Central Intelligence Agency (CIA)—fostered the growth of evangelical religion as an ideological counterweight to Marxism in the 1980s. Despite their questionable origins, new churches offered many tangible, realistic benefits for rural people at a time of insecurity and crisis, and, despite the history of evangelical growth in Honduras, people no longer associated the churches with the Cold War struggle against Communism. The breakdown of the International Coffee Agreement (ICA) in 1989, and the more sweeping structural adjustment platform of which it was a part, led to great economic instability in La Quebrada. In the years that followed, communications and travel became cheaper and easier, the U.S. economy prospered, and migration presented an attractive alternative to coffee farming. The post-ICA turmoil and the damage caused by Hurricane Mitch added to the appeal of migration, which offered socioeconomic rebirth, and contributed to the growth of the new religious movements, which offered spiritual rebirth. By 2000, migration was perceived as the most viable "way out" for many people, and the Honduran government basically agreed, viewing migrant remittances as a short-term resource that would benefit the poor and inject badly needed *dólares* into the struggling economy.

The imprint of all of these experiences lives on in the memories of people in La Quebrada and shapes their perceptions and actions. Given the turmoil of the past fifty years, there is good reason why this historical process has precipitated a culture of individualism and politically resigned pragmatism. Similar processes of depoliticization have been observed around the world since the end of the Cold War. When participation in collective political movements puts people at risk of imprisonment, torture, or death, these movements will tend to wither away. Given the history of corruption and false promises that has marked twentieth-century Honduran political history, people have turned to other philosophies that offer more pragmatic solutions at the individual or local level. The story of Hernán López, presented in chapter 3, is an instructive case in point.

This explanation of cultural change focuses on how historical experience informs the present-day activity of people in La Quebrada. It explains the demise of collective politics by focusing on the cultural meaning of political participation in a specific context. However, it fails to capture the systemic nature of the changes observed in La Quebrada. After all, this pattern has been found all over the world, not only in places that directly experienced Cold War violence. In addition, the failures of previous eras of statist democratic development or Marxism do not *necessarily* lead to the rise of their depoliticized opposites. Under different conditions, the new economic and social bonds formed through globalization could just as likely have produced a political response that focused on revamping international cooperation or increased global governance, rather than the narrowly oriented movements that have actually emerged, not only in Honduras, but across the globe.

The Case for Structure

At this point, I must return to the theoretical questions posed at the beginning of this work: Why did globalization so quickly emerge as an intellectual category, and what need did it fill? Throughout this work, I have shifted back and forth from the micro-level (individual biographies) to abstract theoretical topics. Most of the ethnographic profiles highlight processes of global sociocultural integration in La Quebrada: From Santos Orellana, the man who used an Internet phone to call a Long Island deli from Honduras looking for work, to Tony Chan, the Taiwanese-immigrant coffee farmer who roasts his coffee at JFK Airport, to the members of Creciendo en Gracia who huddle together in a small, dusty room at night to watch their apostle give sermons over the Internet from Miami, all of these stories demonstrate that we are truly living in a uniquely interconnected world in which space and place have taken on new meanings. Following "global flows" allows us to understand the complexities of the contemporary world. At the same time, the combination of socioeconomic integration and political/ideological involution is too widespread to be explained only by an analysis of particular cases. I have argued that all of these movements have been symptoms of a common cause: the breakdown of the bond between nation and state that has accompanied globalization.

The rhetoric of globalization is based on the idea that we live in a single global society organized by the market, in which states should basically enforce the laws that enable markets to function, such as currency stabilization, financial transparency, and protection of property rights. At the same time, the logic of consumer choice has underlain the ideology of globalization since its very beginnings. Theodore Levitt, a prominent management scholar, coined the term "globalization" in 1983 in an article that boldly proclaimed: "Companies must learn to operate as if the world were one large market—ignoring superficial regional and national differences" (1983, 92). Levitt's main point was that multinational companies could succeed by using mass marketing to homogenize consumer tastes around the globe. The drive for expanded corporate profits that drove the process of globalization from its origins in the recession of the late 1970s has, at times, been lost in the shuffle, and the global spread of Western consumer capitalism came to be seen as a natural (and neutral) historical consequence of technological integration. The metaphor of the "global village"—with its connotations of harmony, unity, and kinship—exemplifies the ideology of globalization as an integrative process.

By the 2000s, it became clear that globalization, which was once viewed by anti-structuralists such as Arjun Appadurai and George Marcus as a "complex," "chaotic" process of movement, flux, and hybridity, had a clear ordering structure.[7] Here, the analysis of structuralists such as Terence Turner (2002), Gérard Duménil and Dominique Lévy (2004), and David Harvey (2005)—who view globalization as a system with a well-defined political economic structure—is useful. Duménil and Lévy, whose ideas were expanded on by Harvey, analyze the rise of globalization as the project of a particular class, finance, which managed to achieve political hegemony in the late 1970s and early 1980s. Their interpretation traces the origins of neoliberalism back to a single day, October 6, 1979, which serves as a turning point, ushering in changes that would lead to the "resurgence" of global capital and lay the groundwork for global neoliberalism. On that day, the U.S. Federal Reserve Bank radically changed its policies in an effort to curb long-term inflation and low real interest rates that had led to a crisis in profitability for financial companies. Rising wages had led to high rates of inflation in many of the core countries, and finance was losing profits due to low (in some cases, negative) real interest rates. According to Duménil and Lévy, the so-called coup of 1979 allowed finance to overcome a structural crisis that had led to declining profit rates through the 1970s. In their decision to fight inflation by "shock therapy," the Federal Reserve reestablished the hegemony of finance that had existed during the nineteenth century but had weakened through much of the twentieth due to Keynesian policies designed to promote full employment and social stability. This event ushered in the resurgence of global financial capital, which effectively freed itself from national regulatory constraints. As Dana Frank puts it,

> In the era of NAFTA [North American Free Trade Agreement] and GATT [General Agreement on Tariffs and Trades], U.S.-based corporations have

pushed free trade in order to liberate themselves from the boundaries and regulations of nation-states altogether. In all these periods, the "freedom" of free trade has meant, in effect, corporate liberty to call the shots of international economic relations in whatever manner has best suited their profit rates at a given moment. (1999, 250)

The virtue of a systematic, structural approach to globalization is that it views the liberalization of financial markets and the subsequent drive to decrease the role of the state in order to fight inflation as the project of a particular class, enabled by purposeful political decisions that could be transformed under the right conditions. Rather than viewing "globalization" as a complex or indeterminate set of processes with no guiding logic, it, at the very least, provides a systematic understanding that could provide the basis for political change. The great political challenge of the contemporary world is to apply the principles of social equity that guided modernist policies at the national level to the transnational realities of globalization.

Neopopulism in Latin America

As I have argued, the individualized forms of politics that I describe in La Quebrada exemplify a political movement that occurred throughout Latin America in the 1990s and early 2000s, when the "old" politics of socialism or state-driven democratic modernization gave way to so-called "new social movements" (Escobar and Alvarez 1992; Castañeda 1993; Hopenhayn 2001) that dispersed political energies toward more narrowly focused agendas for social change. In the recent past, the trend toward New Social Movements has shifted drastically, as many parts of Latin America have experienced a resurgence of left-wing populism that seizes on the perceived failure of the kinds of narrowly focused strategies for social change described throughout this book. Populism presents a strong alternative to the political movements I have described because it tends to be based on the strengthening of the state, appeals toward economic protectionism, and a strong, vocal opposition to neoliberalism, especially the power of global finance. It also rests on a strong ideological connection between nation and state, which is in contrast to the tendencies I describe here.

Looking back, it is now clear that the social and political forces I describe in La Quebrada anticipated the populist turn of Honduran president Mel Zelaya, a onetime conservative who was ousted in a coup d'état in June 2009. At the height of the neoliberal era in Honduras, the rural poor felt no ideological connection to a government that viewed practices such as undocumented migration and sweatshop labor as beneficial economic resources rather than social problems. People turned to churches and NGOs to address their everyday concerns, and the government was perceived as the agent of an increasingly narrow faction of the population that was integrated into the global economy. The Honduran gross domestic product (GDP) grew throughout the 2000s, but this growth was accompanied by the political marginalization of the nonmigrant rural poor.

Mel Zelaya used this political marginalization to his advantage. When Zelaya took office in 2006, it would have been difficult to imagine him as an enemy of the Honduran establishment. Zelaya was a quintessential political insider within the Honduran Liberal Party, which had advocated market-friendly, neoliberal policies since the early 1990s and had enjoyed good relations with the United States during the administrations of Carlos Roberto Reina (1994–1998) and Carlos Flores Facussé (1998–2002). Under President Flores, Zelaya oversaw the country's post–Hurricane Mitch redevelopment plan, Fondo Hondureño para Inversión Social (FHIS). In the 2005 presidential elections, Zelaya began to establish his credentials as a populist (under the guidance of U.S.-based political consultants affiliated with the Democratic Party) to separate himself from his right-wing opponent, Porfirio "Pepe" Lobo, who was ahead in the polls.

Zelaya campaigned on a platform of "Poder Ciudadano" (citizen power) and utilized rural populist themes in his campaign, intending to establish a symbolic connection with the country's rural poor. At the time, this seemed more a matter of presentation than substance, a consultant-driven media ploy to cultivate a populist image for a political insider, à la George W. Bush on his ranch. Despite the rise of left-wing populism throughout Latin America at the time, most saw Zelaya's early populism as a calculated means to an end—a way to win the election against the right-wing National Party—that would have little impact on actual policy once he took power.

Throughout his term in office, Zelaya moved toward the left, distancing himself from the leaders of his own party and the Honduran

Congress in the process. In 2007, Zelaya entered Honduras into Petrocaribe, an alliance that provides preferential prices for Venezuelan oil for member countries. In 2008, Zelaya entered into the Bolivarian Alternative for the Americas (ALBA), a regional trade alliance led by Venezuela and Cuba that is explicitly positioned as a socially equitable alternative to the neoliberal Washington Consensus and planned to develop its own currency to cut itself off from dependency on the dollar and the Euro. Many within the Honduran establishment worried that Zelaya was strategically aligning Honduras with Hugo Chávez and Fidel Castro, a move that could possibly sour both commercial and political relations with the United States, Honduras's largest trading partner and closest military ally. There was also widespread concern that the United States might crack down on Honduran immigration even more strongly than it had up until that point, which would have strong negative effects on the Honduran economy if remittance levels were to decrease. At an institutional level, Zelaya was blatantly opposing the power of the Honduran Congress by entering into ALBA without their consent. It is worth noting that entrance into ALBA was presented to the Honduran people as a way to acquire cheap petroleum and food at a time when oil and gas prices reached record highs. Zelaya's approval ratings were plummeting due to the rising costs of staple items, and he needed to do *something* about rising costs for items upon which the entire populace depended.

In perhaps his most important political move, Zelaya raised the Honduran minimum wage by almost 60 percent in early 2009, again without the legally mandated support of Congress.[8] This move was wildly popular among Hondurans. It was the first truly systematic piece of social legislation that had been implemented in decades, but it was also the first piece of legislation that posed a real threat to neoliberal hegemony in Honduras. After all, the country relied on cheap, reliable, and productive labor as an economic resource that attracted manufacturing facilities (sweatshops) and other export industries. A dramatic rise in the minimum wage would threaten the loss of contracts for export products and could lead to the potential loss of jobs and profits. Leaders of the Honduran business community argued that foreign companies that chose to produce goods in Honduras due to its cheap labor and political stability would now take their business elsewhere.

Without dwelling on the minutiae of Honduran party politics and constitutional due process, the decision to raise the minimum wage set in motion a series of events that led to a coup d'état on June 28, 2009. Zelaya's opponents claimed he was trying to illegally extend his term in office by holding a popular referendum. The referendum would have asked the people to vote on whether or not to hold a constituent assembly that *potentially* could amend or rewrite the Constitution. On the day the vote was to be held, the armed forces stormed the presidential mansion and detained Zelaya, claiming that he was unlawfully attempting to revise the Constitution of the Republic.

After the coup, Honduras held democratic elections, and Pepe Lobo, the National Party candidate, took power. This likely would have been the outcome had the coup *not happened* because the primary elections had been held prior to the coup and Lobo was polling well ahead of Elvin Santos, the Liberal Party candidate. However, this should by no means indicate that "nothing changed" as a result of the coup. The coup led to a massive popular resistance calling for Zelaya's return, which mobilized, perhaps repoliticized, sectors of Honduran society that had been marginalized. Labor unions, intellectuals, *campesino* organizations, human rights groups, environmentalists, the lesbian, gay, bisexual, and transgender (LGBT) community, and some religious organizations coalesced into a broad-based resistance movement, often in the face of intimidation, death threats, and violence. In the process, these groups formed new connections with international social movements and harnessed new media to create a counternarrative to news stories about the coup that were coming from the mainstream Honduran press. As of 2011, it is too soon to know what kind of long-term impact this repoliticization of Honduran society will have. The key question will be whether the resistance movement that developed after the coup d'etat will open up political space for their agenda *within* mainstream political institutions.

Neopopulism as a Response to Globalization

Readers will rightly ask whether the turn to populism in Latin America should be seen as a turn *away* from the kind of postmodern politics I have described. Although populism tends to rest on a strong association between nation and state, a return to economic nationalism is not the most viable way to respond politically to the problems of economic integration.[9] In fact, a resurgent nationalism reverses the tendency toward more expansive forms of governance for which I have argued. Forms of governance and regulations must become more expansive, translating the political energies that now exist in the nongovernmental sphere into legitimate political entities. As Turner has suggested, "concerted action by states remains the most likely basis for the imposition of a new global order, capable of regulating financial and corporate capital for social and political ends. This would take a concerted political movement that could re-take control of state policy-making from the current neoliberal hegemony" (2002, 78). If we indeed participate in a single global *system,* there is no reason why forms of regulation, such as minimum wage laws, should not be subject to global standards enforced by international bodies like the International Labor Organization (ILO).[10] The kind of international cooperation that led to the establishment of the International Coffee Agreement created a global regulatory system for coffee that functioned—albeit imperfectly— for almost three decades. The treaty effectively established a price floor for coffee that is now enforced by a nongovernmental system.

Many of the social dislocations I have described in La Quebrada could be ameliorated by a more humane U.S. immigration policy that accepts the realities and demands of participation in a global labor market. People must be able to relocate legally, along with their families, with the same ease that capital can move across borders. One way to accomplish this would be through the World Trade Organization (WTO), which should require immigration reform as a precondition for countries to enter into bilateral free trade agreements such as NAFTA and Dominican Republic–Central America Free Trade Agreement (DR-CAFTA). International bodies also have the potential to develop an international system for managing labor migration, as the United Nations already does for the refugee population. At a more concrete level, the U.S. government needs to develop realistic immigration quotas to account for the estimated number of undocumented immigrants already living within its borders, rather than using quotas as a punitive measure to effectively punish populations that rely on migrant flows. There must be a path to legal citizenship for unauthorized immigrants and their families, and the distribution of seasonal visas must enable workers to go back and forth across borders without risking their lives.

As a more general goal, governments must not lose sight of the place of the economy within the total process of social reproduction. Although capital may be "deterritorialized," and therefore able to relocate with ease, this process comes at a tremendous social cost for people. La Quebrada exemplifies the type of social disintegration that occurs when people have to be separated from families and communities in order to earn a decent wage. The care and education of children and the elderly, the integration of families into broader communities, and the maintenance of some form of collective life cannot be sustained in a deterritorialized economic system. The constant search for increased profit and efficiency that drives the movement of capital comes at a tremendous cost for society.

Strengthened international governance remains the most viable way to manage globalization's social tensions. Returning to Polanyi's "double movement" concept, the key question is how some kind of "social order" can be protected without opening the door to racism, xenophobia, fascism, or other political movements that place unacceptable limits on individual freedom. In Europe, for example, an old, stable social order that was protected by a strong state has, in many cases, been disrupted by immigration and other forms of international integration. Holmes (2000) and Žižek (2006) have argued that this change has produced a right-wing backlash in which class-based anxieties are displaced onto racial and ethnic minorities, especially immigrants. A similar process has occurred in the U.S., where anti-immigrant sentiment is found on both right and left, with the right frequently lamenting the loss of cultural identity caused by Hispanic immigration and one faction of the left worrying that immigration lowers wages and weakens the power of trade unions. This is a far more extreme version of the anti-migrant sentiment in La Quebrada, in which systematic economic tensions are displaced onto individuals. Žižek (2006, 552) affirms this idea. On the infusion of new immigrants into Western Europe, he writes:

> Even those elements that appear as pure rightist racism are effectively a displaced version of workers' protests. Of course it is racist to demand the end of immigration of foreign workers who pose a threat to our employment; however, one should bear in mind the simple fact that the influx of immigrant workers from post-Communist countries is not the consequence of some multiculturalist tolerance. It effectively is part of the strategy of capital to hold in check the workers' demands. (552)

This quote reminds us of the importance of a structural approach to globalization. The turn to neoliberalism over the past twenty years has systematically allowed global capital to escape the regulatory control of nation-states. Even relatively poor countries like Honduras, which are supposed to benefit from this system by attracting foreign capital and sending workers abroad, recognize that this is a socially disastrous and unsustainable economic system. On the other side of the spectrum, workers in the advanced capitalist countries face a new economic threat that is often expressed through racism or nationalist rhetoric. These sociopolitical conflicts are symptoms of the same cause—the "de-hyphenization of the nation-state."

Looking Toward the Future

In La Quebrada, the social costs of migration are just beginning to appear, but the frustration is palpable. Young people who depend on remittances from absent parents are often angry. They feel no bond with Honduras, knowing that their absent parents left the country to earn a decent wage and that the government has no real platform for rural development beyond migrant dependency, epitomized in various programs designed to "make remittances work" for rural development without addressing the underlying causes of emigration.

On June 28, 2009, the day of the Honduran coup d'état, I was chatting online with Jorge Orellana (profiled in chapter 1). After more than ten attempts at crossing the U.S. border, he had made it to New Jersey and was working in a car wash by day and a country club by night. Jorge had relatively little interest in politics, and it was not something we spoke about much. I asked him why he thought Zelaya had been deposed. He responded simply, "The rich people didn't like him because he raised the minimum wage."

For people like Jorge, a 60 percent increase in the minimum wage would be life-transforming. As a *jornalero* (day laborer) he made only about three dollars a day in Honduras in 2003. We can never know for sure if a higher wage would have kept him from risking his life to come to the United States. Nor do we know what impact Zelaya's minimum wage increase would have had on the Honduran economy. The increase may have indeed led to a loss of jobs, as manufacturers chose to produce products in countries with cheaper labor, such as China or Cambodia. The wage increase may have indeed led to decreased demand for Honduran products, or, most likely, the law may not have been enforced at all in rural villages such as La Quebrada. Symbolically, however, Zelaya's commitment to improving the social conditions of the Honduran rural poor meant something to the people. At the very least, it indicated that someone in power recognized that the current reality for people like Jorge—undocumented migration, sweatshop jobs, or survival wages in agriculture—was a social problem and *not* an economic resource.

Young people in La Quebrada have an ambivalent sense of animosity toward the United States. They depend on the United States economically, but they know that U.S. immigration laws have kept them separated from their parents and have prevented them from accessing the economic opportunities for which they long. In most cases, people just plod along, hoping to save the money to go to the United States, with a sense of bitter detachment. When these young people mature, they will have to migrate in order to support their own children. If they cannot, the stage will be set for growing popular resentment and hostility unless a political platform is developed to provide some sense of optimism and hope for rural Hondurans. Honduras was largely able to avoid the revolutionary violence that plagued its neighbors in the 1980s due to policies, such as agrarian reform, that *attempted* to integrate rural society into the national community. Although the modernist reform projects did not achieve their lofty goals, they were based on a philosophy that believed in the potential for people to collectively change society and provided people with a limited sense of optimism. The failure of the modernist project must not lead to a rejection of its guiding spirit. Instead, we must learn from previous mistakes so that they are not repeated.

Notes

Introduction

1. La Quebrada is a pseudonym for a town of approximately 4,500 people in central Honduras.

2. David Harvey's *The Condition of Postmodernity* (1989) was arguably the first work to grasp the systematic economic transformations that would lead to the erosion of the power of nation-states under globalization.

3. See the concluding paragraphs of chapter 3 and chapter 6 for more detailed discussion of these debates.

4. Honduras lies at the southern extreme of what Julian Steward called the "Mesoamerican culture area," which is characterized by the cultural influence of the Maya. However, most of Honduras does not fit within the Mesoamerican culture type due to its relative lack of Maya influence on present-day cultural life. Its marginal status in the postwar area studies model, developed by Steward and others, has led to its marginal status in the ethnographic literature. The anthropological study of Mesoamerica has meant the study of Maya cultures for the past half century, and studies of "acculturated" mestizo groups are comparatively scarce (see note 6). With the exception of the region surrounding Copán and the border with Guatemala, there is relatively little Maya cultural influence in rural Honduras: Spanish is the predominant spoken and written language; Roman Catholicism or Evangelical Protestantism are practiced without indigenous cultural syncretism; and there are few ritual practices linked to the Maya or any other indigenous tradition. There are some Mayan language terms used in daily conversation, such as *comal* (cooking surface or hearth), *milpa* (subsistence maize plot), *tecomate* (water jug made from gourd), and *cipote* (slang

for child), but there is far less indigenous cultural influence in rural Honduras than in the Mexican and Guatemalan communities that have tended to dominate the anthropological literature on Mesoamerica.

5. *Maquilas* are factories that assemble products for export, mainly to the United States. Honduran maquilas are located in special free trade zones called ZIPs (Zonas Industriales de Procesamiento para Exportaciones). Most ZIPs are located in the Department of Cortés, close to the city of San Pedro Sula. Factories in these zones are given tax breaks and provided with an abnormally high level of infrastructure (electricity, roads, security, etc.). Since the 1980s, they have been a major driver of economic growth in Honduras. In other parts of Latin America, they are called *maquiladoras*, and are often referred to derogatorily as "sweatshops" in English.

6. La Quebrada's citizens are mainly mestizo (alternately called *ladino*), people of mixed Native American and Hispanic ethnicity. There is one Lenca family living in town and one Garífuna family in a small hamlet that lies just outside of it, but apart from these exceptions, the town is rather homogeneous in its ethnic makeup. In this regard, La Quebrada is typical of most of inland Honduras, which is 90 percent mestizo. (See Euraque 1996b and Anderson 2009 for more information on ethnic and racial categories in Honduras.) Tegucigalpa is the country's political and cultural capital, while San Pedro Sula is Honduras's industrial and commercial center. Tegucigalpa's importance grew out of mining concerns that began in the Colonial period (1550–1820), while San Pedro Sula's growth has been linked to the twentieth-century banana industry and, more recently, to a boom in export-oriented manufacturing (Euraque 1996a). La Quebrada is provincial—the great majority of adults have traveled to cities at some point in their lives, and the town's commercial and political leaders do so weekly. Many coffee farmers rely on credit from urban banks or coffee brokers that buy and transport coffee from farm to market. Recent road repairs cut the travel time to both cities from nine hours to four hours, and since then a daily bus has traveled from La Quebrada to both cities, a development that has strengthened its links to the city.

7. Honduran politics is dominated by two parties. The Liberal Party (Partido Liberal de Honduras or PLH) is symbolized by the color red, and the National Party (Partido Nacional de Honduras or PNH) is symbolized by the color blue. Historically, the Nationalists have been on the right, and the Liberals on the left. The Liberals were historically tied to the interests of workers and merchants on the North Coast in the twentieth century, and the Nationalists were more connected with conservatives and the military. However, the ideological differences between these two parties are not nearly as stark as they are in other parts of Latin America, as I explain in detail in chapter 3. Both parties are now solidly capitalist and democratic, essentially on the center-right of the political spectrum.

8. I do not want to romanticize Honduran developmentalism in the twentieth century. Rural "stability" was a guiding ideological goal rather than a reality in Honduras. In this paragraph, I merely seek to signal a shift in the theory and practice of development that occurred after 1989, in which neoliberal values of entrepreneurialism, movement, and free choice became more highly valued than political stability or social solidarity in Central America.

1. American Dream, American Work

1. George Foster made a similar point more than forty years ago in his classic ethnography of the village of Tzintzuntzan in Chiapas: "Because of scientific communication media, formerly isolated peoples become merely marginal. They are increasingly dissatisfied with their lot but, sadly enough, it is extremely difficult to convert this dissatisfaction into purposeful seeking after new opportunities" (Foster 1967, 3).

2. Portes and Rumbaut (1996) support their claims with evidence from Mexico, the Dominican Republic (Bray 1984; Grasmuck 1984), and Haiti (Stepick and Portes 1986).

3. A number of social scientists have studied the relationship between economic restructuring and Latin American migration patterns; see, e.g., Gledhill 1998; Pedersen 2002, 2003, 2004, 2008; Binford 2003; Massey, Durand, and Malone 2003.

4. "People like me" is a self-deprecating comment, drawing attention to Wilmer's lack of education and "country" way of life.

5. In this context, a "Korean" maquila means a manufacturing facility that is owned and operated by Koreans. It could still advertise as an "American" company if it was contracted to produce goods by an American brand. Jobs in American maquilas (owned and operated by Americans) are generally considered preferable to those in Korean or Chinese maquilas because workers are treated better and the pay is higher. See Pine (2008, 180–191). In Honduras, there are American companies that recruit workers for legal temporary visas (H1-B), but employers usually work through for-profit middlemen and would never resort to passing leaflets at a bus station.

6. Neolocal postmarital residence is preferred, but people in La Quebrada do not follow strict preferences about whether the couple should reside near the bride or groom's family. The new couple resides near whichever family has a more comfortable, convenient space or needs domestic labor power. There is no clear rule about postmarital residence.

7. Wilmer frequently used the word *mojado* (wet). This word has become an acceptable slang term for "undocumented" among people in La Quebrada. Although the English version of the term, wetback (from the practice of crossing the Rio Grande River from Mexico to enter the United States), is extremely derogatory, Hondurans use the Spanish word to describe themselves in a slyly parodic way, indicating "cultural intimacy" (Herzfeld 1997) with the dangerous circumstances migrants face. *Cultural intimacy* recognizes an individual's deep familiarity with the predicament of a particular social group and creates a boundary between self and other through linguistic categories that can be used only by "insiders." See the cartoon in figure 3 for an example from one of the country's mainstream newspapers.

8. This was the infamous "Victoria 19" tragedy, which occurred on May 14, 2003, and was well publicized by the U.S. media. Popular journalist Jorge Ramos has written a book on this event, *Dying to Cross: The Worst Immigrant Tragedy in American History* (2005).

9. One of the most disparaging things a person could say about a male returnee was "No trajo nada" (He didn't bring anything back). A migrant needed to return with material commodities that provided proof of his hard work or he was considered a failure.

10. The word *corralón* is frequently used to describe immigrant detention centers in the United States. It is literally a large corral for livestock.

11. According to an AP news story, employees of this jail alleged that prisoners were inhumanly treated and were denied basic prisoners' rights (Associated Press, "Federal Officials Investigating Inmate Complaints," April 15, 2004).

12. An hour online in an Internet café costs between ten and fifteen lempira (seventy–eighty cents) in 2003–2004.

13. Literacy rates and figures for access to electricity, divided by rural and urban locations, are found in the 2006 UN Human Development Report for Honduras (United Nations Human Development Program, Programa de las Naciones Unidas para el Desarrollo [PNUD], Tegucigalpa, Honduras).

2. The Needy, the Greedy, and the Lazy

1. Maria Cristina García (2006) discusses the political implications of this dichotomy. *Economic migrants* are often denied the right to either asylum or refugee status because they are not directly motivated by political persecution.

2. The category "deportable aliens" is defined by the U.S. Office of Immigration Statistics as "An alien in and admitted to the United States subject to any grounds of removal specified in the

Immigration and Nationality Act. This includes any alien illegally in the United States, regardless of whether the alien entered the country by fraud or misrepresentation or entered legally but subsequently lost legal status," http://www.dhs.gov/files/statistics/stdfdef.shtm#3 (accessed March 18, 2011).

3. After the decline of the Maya around AD 1300, modern-day Honduras was colonized by Spain in the sixteenth century. The country, along with the other United Provinces of Central America, gained independence in 1823, led by modernizing liberals who were influenced by the North/South American and Haitian revolutions. Post-independence, Honduras was greatly affected by British mercantile interests and became heavily indebted to French and English banks after a failed attempt to build a transoceanic railroad during the California Gold Rush of the 1850s. By the twentieth century, U.S. mining corporations came to prominence, and, later, multinational fruit companies held sway until the mid-twentieth century, leading to the popular (and to Hondurans, deeply offensive) perception of Honduras as a "banana republic."

4. Darío Euraque (1996a, 13) demonstrates how a small group of nineteenth-century coffee elites based in the towns of Santa Bárbara and Comayagua abandoned coffee growing and relocated to the North Coast to invest in banana cultivation. See Euraque (1996a) and Williams (1986) for a detailed discussion of the role of coffee cultivation in the formation of the Honduran nation-state.

5. The Contras were a counterrevolutionary force that fought against the Sandinistas in Nicaragua from the 1979 Revolution until peace accords were reached in 1989. The Contras were funded by the CIA and trained and based in Honduras. See Grandin (2007) and LeoGrande (1998).

6. Entry without inspection (EWI) refers to coming into the United States without the authorization of an immigration official. This term is used in U.S. Department of Homeland Security (formerly INS) statistics to describe people who enter the United States without passing through a border inspection.

7. Temporary Protected Status (TPS) was extended again in 2010. There are between 50,000 and 110,000 Hondurans with TPS status, which constitutes a relatively small proportion of the total population of Hondurans in the United States.

8. Catherine Tucker (2008) has written the most detailed and important ethnographic analysis of Honduran coffee farmers. Her study is a long-term investigation of economic strategies in the village of La Campa in the Department of Lempira. Her work focuses on the ways that coffee farmers responded to the crisis of 1999–2003, but, in La Campa, emigration was *not* a common adaptation strategy for farmers (164).

9. Robert Bates (1997, 173–174) writes that a major cause of the termination of the ICA was the U.S. government's desire to increase the quota of coffee from the Central American countries (often called the "Other Milds" in the coffee trade). This would threaten the market share of the hegemonic coffee producers within the ICA, mainly Brazil, Colombia, and the Ivory Coast. It was widely assumed that the end of the ICA would stimulate production in Honduras, Guatemala, Nicaragua, and El Salvador, which were countries of great strategic interest to the United States at that time.

10. The story of these computers is interesting. They are late-1990s Pentium II models that were purchased at a used-equipment auction in the United States, shipped to Honduras, and sold for about $200 each. The machines in Internet Los Catrachos have stickers on them identifying them as the former property of the Pillsbury Corporation in the United States, part of the General Mills Company.

11. I use the term Internet café, although this business does not serve refreshments. The terms "cyber café," "cyber," or "café Internet" are common in Honduras.

12. For those who criticize undocumented immigrants for not following the law, consider that merely scheduling an interview for an immigrant visa requires the following: (1) Potential

migrants must go to a branch of a private bank (Banco Atlántida) and pay a large sum of money (at least $150 in 2010, depending on the kind of visa one requests) to schedule a *cita* (appointment) at the U.S. Embassy; (2) At the embassy, they must provide legal documents that many Hondurans do not have and would need to hire a lawyer to obtain (e.g., property deeds, birth certificates, bank statements, passports, support from relatives already in the United States); (3) They must make an expensive trip to Tegucigalpa, most likely by bus, and pay for lodging for at least two days. All of this is necessary to merely apply for the possibility of a visa, which is limited by a preference-based worldwide quota system to only 226,000 immigrants per year. Gaining a legal immigrant visa from Honduras is extremely unlikely for most residents of La Quebrada, and the visa application process presents insurmountable obstacles to the rural poor.

13. The concept of the "moral economy" is based on the idea that peasant societies value group solidarity and collective survival over individual gain. The work of Karl Polanyi (1957), George Foster (1965), and James Scott (1976) develop this concept. Following Wolf, I am suggesting that "the moral economy" ethic is *weaker* in coffee-farming communities than it is in subsistence or petty-export economies; however, some moral bond is still present between landowners and landless workers, which has been threatened by migration.

14. Wolf's study was conducted before the initiation of the International Coffee Agreement in 1962, which stabilized prices until it fell apart in 1989.

15. Elana Zilberg (cited in Andrade-Eekhoff and Silva-Avalos 2003; Zilberg and Lungo 1999) finds that this term is also used to describe young people who receive migrant remittances in El Salvador.

16. The definition from the 1737 edition of the Real Academia Española's dictionary reads, in Spanish: "El holgazán, floxo, perezoso y tardo en lo que mandan hacer. El P. Guadix citado por Covarr. dice que es voz Arábiga, y que vale tanto como él que canta quando hace calor: lo que ordinariamente executan los gañanes y peones, en que no estando el dueño de la hacienda presente, se echan a la sombra, y se están cantando u durmiendo sin trabajar. Lat. Defes, dis, Iners, tis. SANTIAG. Quar. Serm. 2. Salutac. El delinquente, el fullero, el blasfemo, y aun el hijo de vecino haragán, aprendiz destas virtúdes. Herr. Hist. Ind. Decad. 4 lib. 9. cap. 7. Ni quieren hacer heredades ni sembrar, porque son grandes haraganes," http://buscon.rae.es/ntlle/ SrvltGUILoginNtlle.

17. Marshall Sahlins's *Culture and Practical Reason* (1976) provides the intellectual foundation for this idea.

18. In addition to being wealthier, larger, and more populous than Honduras, Mexico also has more extensive infrastructure (roads, phones, information sources, banks, higher levels of literacy, etc.); is geographically closer to the United States (so undocumented migrants have to cross only one border, rather than three); and, overall, Mexico has a much higher baseline level of well-being than Honduras. It's hard to lead a transnational social life when one's hometown has no electricity, no phone, 50–60 percent nonliterate adults, and families that must take an expensive three-hour bus ride to arrange a remittance payment.

3. The Ashes of Progress

1. Jorge Castañeda's *Utopia Unarmed* (1993, 358 and *passim*) succinctly expresses the transformation that occurred in the ideology of the Latin American left. He argues that the "new, postsocialist agenda" of the Latin American left was predicated on "democratizing democracy," empowering grassroots movements, fighting corruption, and strengthening the institutions of local democracy.

2. Hugo Noé Pino, former director of the Central Bank of Honduras and ambassador to the United States, writes: "A principios de los años setenta la transformación agraria llegó a considerarse como el 'quehacer fundamental' del gobierno. Hoy, a lo sumo, se habla de una 'modernización'

que, para muchos analistas, no es más que la muerte de la reforma agraria" (Noé Pino 1992, 9). [At the beginning of the seventies, the agrarian transformation came to be considered the fundamental project of the government. Today, in sum, people talk of a "modernization" that, for many analysts, is nothing more than the death of the agrarian reform.]

3. See Paul Friedrich (1965) for a description of Mexican *caciques* (rural political bosses) during this time period.

4. There were some public schools, funded by municipalities, as early as the nineteenth century, but it wasn't until the postwar modernization of Gálvez and Villeda Morales that the national education system reached most rural areas.

5. Arturo Escobar (1995) argues that the Alliance for Progress, and modernization theory in general, turned "poverty" into a social disease that could be eradicated by applied technology.

6. General López Arellano is perhaps best known for his role in the "banana-gate" scandal. As president, he accepted bribes from the United Fruit Company.

7. On October 2, 1968, the Mexican Army opened fire on a student demonstration in Tlatelolco in Mexico City, killing hundreds of demonstrators. See Eric Zolov (1999) for an analysis of the origins of the massacre and its impact on Mexican politics and culture.

8. Honduras has made great strides in fighting corruption and enforcing human rights since the return of democracy, but they remain two of the most pressing issues for the country, and reports of human rights abuses have increased dramatically since the 2009 coup. Not one military or political leader has been convicted of human rights abuses despite the efforts of a national human rights commission.

9. Schelhas and Pfeffer (2008) document the role of Aldea Global in managing a Honduran national park, the Parque Nacional Cerro Azul Meambar. The park was managed by the COHDEFOR, the Honduran national forest agency, from 1987 until 1992, when management responsibility was turned over to Aldea Global.

10. The lack of a political project that reconciles global economic integration with state-level nationalism is especially apparent in the split between "new" free-trade Democrats in the United States, who favor market liberalization, and "old" factions of the party who seek to "keep jobs at home" and protect industrial workers from foreign competition with tariffs and subsidies. This division has come to the fore during debates over free-trade agreements such as the North American Free Trade Agreement (NAFTA) and the Dominican Republic–Central America Free Trade Agreement (DR-CAFTA).

4. The Devil Has Been Destroyed

1. Creciendo en Gracia (CEG) has not yet been subject to extensive scholarly analysis, but it has received much coverage in the popular media. Its leader, Dr. Miranda, was profiled in Bill Maher's spoof documentary on popular religion, *Religulous* (2008). CEG has also been covered in *Maxim* magazine, ABC News, MSNBC, and many other popular media outlets.

2. The relationship between evangelical religion and politics in Latin America has been the subject of some recent studies; see, e.g., Smilde 1998, 2007; Sánchez 2001; Chesnut 2003.

3. Several studies have focused on evangelical concepts of personal empowerment, including Harding 2000; Robbins 2004; Elisha 2008; McDougall 2009; Selka 2010.

4. This song was a huge hit throughout Latin America in the 1980s. I noticed that it appealed equally to active and passive Christians in La Quebrada. I twice saw people break into tears while singing along with this song on the radio.

5. The relationship between religion and mediation has become an increasingly popular topic of study, leading Matthew Engelke (2010, 371) to describe "the media turn" in the study of religion. Significant examples include Coleman 2006; Hirschkind 2006; Engelke 2007; Keane 2007.

6. The lack of attention paid to Papal authority is unlike the opposition to Catholicism found in Peter Cahn's ethnography of religious diversity in Chiapas, Mexico, where Catholics are called "romanistas" (2003, ix).

7. The poster incorporates a favorite joke that Miranda makes: The word *Honduras* means "depths," and Miranda calls it *Alturas* (heights) due to the rapid growth of CEG in the country.

8. The theater group is made up of local men with no formal training. Most have the equivalent of a high school diploma, but none have attended college. They perform unscripted short plays at local events, schools, and festivals.

9. Of course, these are not isomorphic definitions—a symbolic medium always has a communicative function, and communication always contains some degree of alienation or concealment.

10. On American televangelists, Derrida writes:

> To return to those American sessions of miracles on the set, one sees there a very elegant person who speaks well, a star of the stage. He comes and all of a sudden he makes ten persons rise, fall, get up again, falling and rising at the very instant he touches them, or even looks at them. There is no need to believe; one believes; no effort is necessary because no doubt is possible. Like the ten thousand persons in the auditorium, one is confronted with the thing itself.
>
> This is the argumentative strategy that is actually used in all the milieus of proselytism, of conversion. . . . It bets . . . on the fiduciary structure that enjoins that in any case faith is irreducible, that there is no society without appeal to faith, without "believe me, I am telling you the truth, believe me!" . . . [C]ertitude is there, in the immediacy of the senses. (Derrida 2001, 64)

11. The shortcoming of this argument is that it fails to account for the fact that charismatic power is often directly experienced by afflicted people during healing rituals and trances. As Thomas Csordas (2002) has emphasized, religious belief is often grounded in bodily experience rather than acts of witnessing. In these cases, the worshiper feels that he or she can directly access transcendent power. Derrida would likely argue that the experience of directness obscures the medium of the healer, but Pentecostals consistently believe that the Holy Ghost directly touches them and heals bodily afflictions. The healer may be present, but the act is experienced as the direct intervention of divinity.

12. There is often a close association between Catholic icons and national imaginaries, with Our Lady of Guadalupe in Mexico being the most obvious example. See Brading 2001 and Lomnitz 2001 for a discussion of Mexico. See Sánchez 2001 for a sophisticated study of the relationship between the veneration of saints, mediation, and populism in Venezuela.

13. The connection between coffee and religion is even closer than I detail here. Many churches in the United States hold fair trade coffee hours, in which they express solidarity with Latin American coffee growers. Daniel Jaffee (2007, 84–85) notes that coffee producer cooperatives were established in Mexico by Catholic priests associated with liberation theology and Catholic Social Action, before the fair trade system existed.

5. Justice at a Price

1. Ellen Moodie (2007) and David Pedersen (2008) both provide eloquent ethnographic descriptions of situations where El Salvadoran migrants confront their position in the global division of labor through anxiety-provoking encounters with commodities. My brief description of Javier's visit to Massachusetts builds on their efforts to unravel processes of exploitation in the global economy by defetishizing the commodity.

2. *Catuai* is a variety of Arabica coffee that is quite popular in the vicinity of La Quebrada. It can produce either red or yellow fruit.

3. I use the word *cherries* to refer to the ripe red or yellow fruit of the coffee plant, which, in its unprocessed state, looks like a fresh cranberry or small cherry. The raw cherries are washed, depulped, and dehulled in a machine at the *beneficio* or mill. The "bean," actually a seed, is then dried on patios to a moisture content of approximately 11.5 percent. This is the unroasted or "green" coffee that is eventually exported, after a final stage of minimal processing, cleaning, sorting, and storage, which is done by the exporter in the city of San Pedro Sula.

4. *Coffea arabica* coffee tends to be grown at higher elevations and produces a smoother, sweeter coffee than the bitter *Coffea robusta,* which thrives at low altitudes and is used as a cheap blending coffee for many of the largest roasters. At times when coffee prices are high, the proportion of *robusta* to *arabica* increases, and one can often taste the increased use of *robusta* beans in mass-produced coffee.

5. Javier owns two plots of land. One, which is at a higher elevation with ample natural shade, produces far better quality coffee than the lower, sunnier plot. However, the yields of the shade *finca* are lower than those of the sunny plot.

6. To avoid confusion: *Green* coffee means unroasted, dried coffee beans, which is the form in which all coffee is imported. It does not mean "environmentally friendly" coffee.

7. Fair trade is part of a broader movement that has come to be known as "alternative trade." Many examples of alternative trade, such as "local" currencies and Islamic finance, are based on antiuniversal or even antiliberal philosophies that grant "special" rights and entail specific obligations to particular social groups. Bill Maurer (2005) provides an extensive analysis of alternative trade.

8. Much scholarship on fair trade has emerged in a relatively short period of time. Scholars such as Marie-Christine Renard (1993, 2005), Laura Raynolds (2000, 2002; Raynolds, Murray, and Taylor 2004; Raynolds, Murray, and Heller 2007), and Elizabeth Barham (2002) tend to see fair trade as a corrective to contemporary free-market economics that re-embeds commodity exchange in concrete social relations. A group of scholars led by Laura Raynolds and Douglas Murray has conducted a number of studies on individual fair trade cooperatives around the world, generally finding that fair trade increases farmer incomes, though not as dramatically as would be suggested by its proponents. Daniel Jaffee (2007) has conducted an extensive village-based study on fair trade as a response to the 1999–2003 coffee crisis in Mexico. See also Lyon 2006, 2007a, 2007b; Fridell 2007; Luetchford 2008; Neilson 2008; Reichman 2008.

9. In Mexico, Jaffee (2007, 337) reports a cost of $2,431 for initial certification, $607 for annual recertification, and 2 cents for each kilogram of certified coffee that the cooperative sells. See Luetchford 2008 for an example of the challenges faced by Costa Rican cooperatives attempting to enter the fair trade market.

10. The twentieth-century fair trade movement was not limited to coffee, but the coffee industry was one of its targets. See Mark Pendergrast's discussion of the trade war between Brazil and the United States over Brazil's "unfair" attempts to regulate the coffee market (1999, 77–94).

11. In her study of the "Buy American" movement, Dana Frank shows that economic nationalism always suppresses class distinctions within the nation: "When we clear off the fog, the tariff debate turns out to have masked the real issues at stake in the economic nation; and economic nationalism masked divergent class interests just as it had during the American Revolution" (2003, 34).

12. "Sacrifice" is vital to the creation of publics and deserves more extensive discussion. I use the word *sacrifice* in the mainstream sense, meaning personal abstinence for the sake of an impersonal moral principle. People commonly say, "I make sacrifices for my family," "my country," etc. This sense of the word differs from the anthropological definition of *sacrifice,* which refers to communal feasts and other "positive rites" that are based not on prohibition but on communal consumption. The mainstream definition of *sacrifice* is more like Durkheimian "negative rites"

because they are based on *prohibition* rather than consumption (Durkheim 1995, 303–329). In the case of boycotts, the prohibition is not a ritual practice but a matter of choice that establishes a like-minded community. Durkheim saw positive and negative rites as directly related. Negative rites (boycotts/prohibitions) presuppose communal sacrifice because abstinence permits a person entrance into a specific cult by "fleeing the profane world" and "forgoing sensuous interests" (1995, 321). By abstaining from profane things, a person shows respect for the sacred collectivity by suppressing egoistic desire (1995, 326). "Negative rites" are necessary for the establishment of a cult, which, for Durkheim, was the most basic form of collective social unit beyond the immediate kin-group. A person must demonstrate that he or she acts according to the principles of the group through prohibition.

13. See Lizabeth Cohen (2003), Dana Frank (1999, 33–55 and passim), and Landon Storrs (2000) for more detail on union labeling, anti-immigrant sentiment, and economic nationalism.

14. "Two Cheers for Sweatshops," *New York Times Magazine*, September 24, 2000.

15. In the 2000s, the local and "slow foods" movements grew. At times, these movements are motivated by a political spirit that seeks to strengthen local and regional economies, which could be seen as a step away from the kind of globalism that marked the 1990s. Some of the appeal of local/slow foods, however, is based on food safety and the purported health benefits of nonindustrial food products rather than on a desire to express solidarity with members of a particular social group.

6. Global Sociality, Postmodernity, and Neopopulism

1. I follow Akhil Gupta's (1998) discussion of economic nationalism, which emphasizes national self-sufficiency and sovereignty as a modernist discourse that tends to emerge in response to imperialism or neocolonialism, a term that describes the relationship between nations that are not formal colonies, but have a de facto colonial relationship, such as Honduras and the United States during the height of the banana economy.

2. This paragraph gestures toward one of the most fundamental issues in social theory: the relationship between cultural or symbolic systems and social structure. Although this entire work has been framed by a concern with this issue, it deserves more specific treatment here. Broadly speaking, modern anthropology focuses on the processes through which systems of meaning (culture) are shaped by systems of power, be it through class relationships, gender differences, the power of the state, the mass media, or other social forces that shape the consciousness of individuals. Post-Marxist social thought has tended to follow one of three main pathways: One, following Pierre Bourdieu, argues that class relations are not only about control over material production but also about the ability to attribute meaning to reality. Social power lies in the ability to differentiate valued categories from their opposites—what Bourdieu refers to as a "separative" power to create dominant systems of classification. The second body of theory, which derives from the Frankfurt School (especially Theodor Adorno and Walter Benjamin) critiques the role of the mass media in the creation of social consciousness and focuses on "fetishism" as a way to critically analyze cultural forms. "The fetish" provides a way to analyze cultural symbols not as collective representations of social relations, but as seductive misrepresentations that obscure the conditions of their production (cf. Taussig 1980). A third variant of post-Marxist thought derives from Antonio Gramsci (1971) and Raymond Williams (1973). It is concerned with the historical creation of cultural systems as products of class hegemony at particular moments in time (cf. Roseberry 1989, 1991; Joseph and Nugent 1994). Whereas Bourdieu's approach is *synchronic*—focusing on how a structural model of class relations shapes cultural forms at a "frozen" moment in time—the latter approach is *diachronic*—focusing on how cultural systems change over time.

3. Dated language aside, we may safely assume that "brotherliness" applies to women as well since the word was intended to refer to generalized human compassion. My discussion of Weber draws greatly from Robert Bellah (1999).

4. Here, I follow Eric Wolf's suggestion that the standard translation, "iron cage," is incorrect (Wolf 1999, 41).

5. Jürgen Habermas (1989) is the most important theorist of secular transnational justice. He has generally espoused a form of politics that creates the conditions for rational communication between social groups, divorced from systems of coercion or power. One consequence of Habermas's theory of the "transformation of the public sphere" (1989) has been renewed attention to public participation in politics. However, the ideal Habermasian public sphere develops outside of the institutional confines of the nation-state.

6. Terence Turner writes:

> The globally-oriented elites who direct or strongly influence the policies of many contemporary states, and who act as mediators between the global economic system and the internal economy of the state . . . have little basis for identification or sense of national community with economically unproductive or uncompetitive elements of the national population. . . . They no longer depend on the legitimation of their power within the state or an ideological claim to represent all citizens of the nation. . . .
>
> The efforts of alienated citizens to create new vehicles for their civil and social values outside of the formal political structure, meanwhile, have led to the great multiplication of New Social Movements [which] stem directly from the quest by alienated citizens for forms of civic and political action commensurate with their social values, which they feel can no longer be realized through the institutional political structures of nation-states (2002, 65).

7. In a landmark set of essays on the anthropology of globalization, George Marcus (1998, 80) argued that the best way for contemporary anthropologists to grasp "the global" was to "acknowledge macrotheoretical concepts and narratives of the world system but not rely on them for the conceptual architecture framing a set of subjects" (80). Instead, Marcus argued that anthropologists should provisionally do away with "structure" and study the contemporary world by following material objects, people, ideas, or conflicts though multisited approaches that trace social processes across space and time to capture their complexity.

8. This is a simplification of a more complex set of changes. Honduran minimum wage law is based on a scale that establishes different minimum salaries for the rural and urban sectors, as well as enterprises of different sizes. Minimum wage laws, however, are generally not enforced in the rural agricultural sector, especially for enterprises that hire fewer than fifteen workers. Minimum wage laws have a far greater impact on urban salaried workers, such as government employees, and employees working in the *maquila* sector, than they have on rural laborers.

9. There are signs that point toward a new form of populism in Latin America that does not rely on economic nationalism. For example, the Bolivarian Alternative for the Americas (ALBA), an alternative regional trading bloc, has sought to create a system of international trade that provides open markets for member countries while offering greater social protection for workers than are offered by other regional trade agreements such as the Free Trade Area of the Americas (FTAA). On the other hand, the push for "food sovereignty" laws in countries such as Ecuador may indicate a turn away from export-led growth and open markets.

10. Dana Frank (2005) has demonstrated the political power wielded by transnational labor activism in Honduras. International worker solidarity movements may provide a significant source of political agency in the future. However, one could also look to the creation of the European Union, and the subsequent changes to national-level labor policy, as an example of both the promise and peril of international integration.

BIBLIOGRAPHY

Adams, Richard N. 1956. "Cultural Components of Central America." *American Anthropologist* 58:881–907.

———. 1957. *Cultural Surveys of Panama, Nicaragua, Guatemala, El Salvador, Honduras*. Washington, D.C.: Pan American Sanitary Bureau.

———. 1981. "Dynamics of Societal Diversity: Notes from Nicaragua for a Sociology of Survival." *American Ethnologist* 8(1): 1–20.

Anderson, Mark. 2009. *Black and Indigenous: Garifuna Activism and Consumer Culture in Honduras*. Minneapolis: University of Minnesota Press.

Andrade-Eekhoff, Katharine, and Silvia-Avalos, Claudia. 2003. "Globalization of the Periphery: The Challenges of Transnational Migration for Local Development in Central America." FLACSO working paper, April 2003, San Salvador, El Salvador.

Annis, Sheldon. 1987. *God and Production in a Guatemalan Town*. Austin: University of Texas Press.

Appadurai, Arjun. 1986. *The Social Life of Things: Commodities in Cultural Perspective*. New York: Cambridge University Press.

———. 1996. *Modernity at Large: Cultural Dimensions of Globalization*. Minneapolis: University of Minnesota Press.

Armony, Ariel. 2008. "Transnationalizing the Dirty War: Argentina in Central America." In *In from the Cold: Writing a New History of the Latin America Cold War*, ed.

Gilbert M. Joseph and Daniela Spenser, 134–169. Durham, N.C.: Duke University Press.

Babb, Florence. 2001. *After Revolution: Mapping Gender and Cultural Politics in Neoliberal Nicaragua*. Austin: University of Texas Press.

———. 2004. "Recycled Sandalistas: From Revolution to Resorts in the New Nicaragua." *American Anthropologist* 106(3): 541–555.

Bacon, Christopher M., V. Ernesto Méndez, Stephen R. Gliessman, David Goodman, and Jonathan A. Fox, eds. 2008. *Confronting the Coffee Crisis: Fair Trade, Sustainable Livelihoods, and Ecosystems in Mexico and Central America*. Cambridge, Mass.: MIT Press.

Barahona, Marvin. 1991. *Evolucíon Histórica De La Identidad Nacional*. Tegucigalpa, Honduras: Editorial Guaymuras.

Barham, Elizabeth. 2002. "Towards a Theory of Values-based Labeling." *Agriculture and Human Values* 19:349–360.

Bates, Robert. 1997. *Open-Economy Politics: The Political Economy of the World Coffee Trade*. Princeton, N.J.: Princeton University Press.

Baumeister, Eduardo. 1990. "El Café en Honduras." *Revista Centroamericana de Economia* 11:33–78.

Bellah, Robert. 1999. "Max Weber and World-Denying Love: A Look at the Historical Sociology of Religion." *Journal of the American Academy of Religion* 67(2): 277–304.

Bestor, Theodore C. 2001. "Supply-Side Sushi: Commodity, Market, and the Global City." *American Anthropologist* 40(2): 76–95.

———. 2004. *Tsukiji: The Fish Market at the Center of the World*. Berkeley: University of California Press.

Binford, Leigh. 2003. "Migrant Remittances and (Under)Development in Mexico." *Critique of Anthropology* 23(3): 305–336.

Boehm, Deborah A. 2008. "'Now I am a Man and a Woman!': Gendered Moves and Migrations in a Transnational Mexican Community." *Latin American Perspectives* 35(1): 16–30.

Bourdieu, Pierre. 1977. *Outline of a Theory of Practice*. New York: Cambridge University Press.

———. 1984. *Distinction: A Social Critique of the Judgment of Taste*. Cambridge, Mass.: Harvard University Press.

Brading, D. A. 2001. *Mexican Phoenix: Our Lady of Guadalupe: Image and Tradition Across Five Centuries*. Cambridge: Cambridge University Press.

Bray, David. 1984. "Economic Development: The Middle Class and International Migration in the Dominican Republic." *International Migration Review* 18:217–236.

Breen, T. H. 2004. *The Marketplace of Revolution: How Consumer Politics Shaped American Independence*. New York: Oxford University Press.

Brooks, David. 2000. *Bobos in Paradise: The New Upper Class and How They Got There*. New York: Simon and Schuster.

Brusco, Elizabeth. 1995. *The Reformation of Machismo: Evangelical Conversion and Gender in Colombia*. Austin: University of Texas Press.

Cahn, Peter S. 2003. *All Religions Are Good in Tzintzuntzan: Evangelicals in Catholic Mexico*. Austin: University of Texas Press.

Cancian, Frank. 1965. *Economics and Prestige in a Maya Community: The Religious Cargo System in Zinacantán.* Palo Alto, Calif.: Stanford University Press.

———. 1992. *The Decline of Community in Zinacantán: Economy, Public Life, and Social Stratification, 1960–1987.* Palo Alto, Calif.: Stanford University Press.

Cáritas, Pastoral Social. 2003. *Sueños Truncados: La migración de hondureños hacia Estados Unidos.* Tegucigalpa, Honduras: Editorial Guaymuras.

Carrier, James G., and Daniel Miller. 1998. *Virtualism: A New Political Economy.* New York: Berg.

Castañeda, Jorge G. 1993. *Utopia Unarmed: The Latin American Left after the Cold War.* New York: Alfred A. Knopf.

Castañeda, Jorge G., and Marco A. Morales. 2008. *Leftovers: Tales of the Latin American Left.* New York: Routledge.

Castillo, Rosalva Aída Hernández, and Ronald Nigh. 1998. "Global Processes and Local Identity among Mayan Coffee Growers in Chiapas, Mexico." *American Anthropologist* 100(1): 136–147.

Chesnut, R. Andrew. 1997. *Born Again in Brazil.* New Brunswick, N.J.: Rutgers University Press.

———. 2003. *Competitive Spirits: Latin America's New Religious Economy.* New York: Oxford University Press.

Cohen, Jeffrey. 2003. "Transnational Migration in Rural Oaxaca, Mexico: Dependency, Development, and the Household." *American Anthropologist* 103(40): 954.

Cohen, Lizabeth. 2003. *A Consumers' Republic: The Politics of Mass Consumption in Postwar America.* New York: Vintage Books.

Cohn, Bernard S. 1996. *Colonialism and Its Forms of Knowledge: The British in India.* Princeton, N.J.: Princeton University Press.

Coleman, Simon. 2006. "Materializing the Self: Words and Gifts in the Construction of Charismatic Protestant Identity." In *The Anthropology of Christianity,* ed. Fenella Cannell, 163–184. Durham, N.C.: Duke University Press.

Comaroff, Jean, and John L. Comaroff, eds. 2001. *Millennial Capitalism and the Culture of Neoliberalism.* Durham, N.C.: Duke University Press.

Coronil, Fernando. 1997. *The Magical State: Nature, Money, and Modernity in Venezuela.* Chicago: University of Chicago Press.

———. 2000. "Towards a Critique of Globalcentrism: Speculations on Capitalism's Nature." *Public Culture* 12(2): 351–374.

Csordas, Thomas J. 1992. "Religion and the World System: The Pentecostal Ethic and the Spirit of Monopoly Capital." *Dialectical Anthropology* 17(1): 3–24.

———. 2002. *Body/Meaning/Healing.* New York: Palgrave.

———. 2004. "Asymptote of the Ineffable: Embodiment, Alterity, and the Theory of Religion." *Current Anthropology* 45(2): 163–185.

Dávila, Arlene M. 2001. *Latinos, Inc.: The Marketing and Making of a People.* Berkeley: University of California Press.

Daviron, Benoit, and Stefano Ponte. 2005. *The Coffee Paradox: Global Markets, Commodity Trade and the Elusive Promise of Development.* New York: Zed Books.

Derrida, Jacques. 2001. "Above All, No Journalists." In *Religion and Media,* ed. Hent DeVries and Samuel Weber, 56–93. Palo Alto, Calif.: Stanford University Press.

Dow, James, and Alan R. Sandstrom. 2001. *Holy Saints and Fiery Preachers: The Anthropology of Protestantism in Mexico and Central America.* Westport, Conn.: Praeger.

Duménil, Gérard, and Dominique Lévy. 2004. *Capital Resurgent: Roots of the Neoliberal Revolution.* Cambridge, Mass.: Harvard University Press.

Durkheim, Emile. 1995. *The Elementary Forms of Religious Life.* Trans. Karen Fields. New York: Free Press. (Orig. pub. 1912.)

——. 1997. *The Division of Labor in Society.* Trans. W. D. Halls. New York: Free Press.

Eber, Christine. 2000. *Women and Alcohol in a Highland Maya Town.* Austin: University of Texas Press.

Elisha, Omri. 2008. "Moral Ambitions of Grace: The Paradox of Compassion and Accountability in Evangelical Faith-Based Activism." *Cultural Anthropology* 23(1): 154–189.

Engelke, Matthew. 2007. *The Problem of Presence: Beyond Scripture in an African Church.* Berkeley: University of California Press.

——. 2010. "Religion and the Media Turn: A Review Essay." *American Ethnologist* 37(2): 371–379.

Engelke, Matthew, and Matt Tomlinson, eds. 2006. *The Limits of Meaning: Case Studies in the Anthropology of Christianity.* Oxford: Berghahn Books.

Ensor, Marisa, ed. 2009. *The Legacy of Hurricane Mitch: Lessons from Post-Disaster Reconstruction in Honduras.* Tucson: University of Arizona Press.

Enos, Don, et al. 1984. *Displaced Persons in El Salvador: An Assessment.* Washington, D.C.: Bureau for Latin America and the Caribbean, Agency for International Development.

Escobar, Arturo. 1995. *Encountering Development: The Making and Unmaking of the Third World.* Princeton, N.J.: Princeton University Press.

Escobar, Arturo, and Sonia E. Alvarez. 1992. *The Making of Social Movements in Latin America: Identity, Strategy, and Democracy.* Boulder, Colo.: Westview Press.

Euraque, Darío. 1996a. *Reinterpreting the Banana Republic: Region and State in Honduras, 1870–1972.* Chapel Hill: University of North Carolina Press.

——. 1996b. *Estado, Poder, Nacionalidad Y Raza En La Historia De Honduras.* Tegucigalpa, Honduras: Subirana.

Fajans, Jane. 1998. *They Make Themselves: Work and Play among the Baining of Papua New Guinea.* Chicago: University of Chicago Press.

Ferguson, James. 1999. *Expectations of Modernity: Myths and Meanings of Urban Life on the Zambian Copperbelt.* Berkeley: University of California Press.

——. 2009. "The Uses of Neoliberalism." *Antipode* 41(1): 166–184.

Ferry, Elizabeth Emma. 2005. *Not Ours Alone: Patrimony, Value, and Collectivity in Contemporary Mexico.* New York: Columbia University Press.

Feuerbach, Ludwig, and George Eliot. 1989. *The Essence of Christianity.* Amherst, N.Y.: Prometheus Books.

Finn, Janet L. 1998. *Tracing the Veins: Of Copper, Culture, and Community from Butte to Chuquicamata.* Berkeley: University of California Press.

Fischer, Edward F. 1999. "Cultural Logic and Maya Identity: Rethinking Constructivism and Essentialism." *Current Anthropology* 40(4): 473–499.

Fisher, Bart S. 1972. *The International Coffee Agreement: A Study in Coffee Diplomacy.* New York: Praeger.

Foster, George. 1965. "Peasant Society and the Image of Limited Good." *American Anthropologist* 67:293–315.

——. 1967. *Tzintzuntzan: Mexican Peasants in a Changing World.* Boston: Little, Brown.

Foster, Robert J. 1995. *Social Reproduction and History in Melanesia: Mortuary Ritual, Gift Exchange, and Custom in the Tanga Islands.* New York: Cambridge University Press.

——. 2008. *Coca-Globalization: Following Soft Drinks from New York to New Guinea.* New York: Palgrave Macmillan.

Frank, Andre Gunder. 1969. *Capitalism and Underdevelopment in Latin America.* New York: Monthly Review Press.

——. 1999. "The Underdevelopment of Development." In *The Underdevelopment of Development: Essays in Honor of Andre Gunder Frank,* ed. Sing Chew and Robert Denemark. London: Sage Publications.

Frank, Dana. 1999. *Buy American: The Untold Story of Economic Nationalism.* Boston: Beacon Press.

——. 2005. *Bananeras: Women Transforming the Banana Unions of Latin America.* Boston: South End Press.

Frank, Thomas. 1997. *The Conquest of Cool: Business Culture, Counterculture, and the Rise of Hip Consumerism.* Chicago: University of Chicago Press.

Fraser, Steve. 2005. *Every Man a Speculator: A History of Wall Street in American Life.* New York: Harper Collins.

Freeman, Carla. 2000. *High Tech and High Heels in the Global Economy: Women, Work, and Pink-Collar Identities in the Caribbean.* Durham, N.C.: Duke University Press.

Frelick, Bill. 1991. *Running the Gauntlet: The Central American Journey Through Mexico.* Washington, D.C.: U.S. Committee for Refugees.

Fridell, Gavin. 2007. *Fair Trade Coffee: The Prospects and Pitfalls of Market-Driven Social Justice.* Buffalo, N.Y.: University of Toronto Press.

Fried, Morton. 1967. *The Evolution of Political Society: An Essay in Political Anthropology.* New York: Random House.

Friedrich, Paul. 1965. "An Agrarian 'Fighter'." In *Context and Meaning in Cultural Anthropology,* ed. Melford Spiro. New York: Free Press.

García, María Cristina. 2006. *Seeking Refuge: Central American Migration to Mexico, the United States, and Canada.* Berkeley: University of California Press.

García Canclini, Néstor. 1995a. "The Hybrid: A Conversation with Margarita Zires, Raymundo Mier, and Mabel Piccini." In *The Postmodernism Debate in Latin America,* ed. John Beverley, José Oviedo, and Michael Aronna. Durham, N.C.: Duke University Press.

——. 1995b. *Hybrid Cultures: Strategies for Entering and Leaving Modernity.* Minneapolis: University of Minnesota Press.

Garrard-Burnett, Virginia. 1998. *Protestantism in Guatemala: Living in the New Jerusalem.* Austin: University of Texas Press.

Garrard-Burnett, Virginia, and David Stoll. 1993. *Rethinking Protestantism in Latin America*. Philadelphia: Temple University Press.

Geertz, Clifford. 1957. "Ritual and Social Change: A Javanese Example." *American Anthropologist* 59:32–54.

———. 1973. *The Interpretation of Cultures*. New York: Basic Books.

Gledhill, John. 1998. "The Mexican Contribution to the Restructuring of U.S. Capitalism: NAFTA as an Instrument of Flexible Accumulation." *Critique of Anthropology* 18(3): 279.

Gonzalez, Nancie L. 1988. *Sojourners of the Caribbean: Ethnogenesis and Ethnohistory of the Garífuna*. Urbana: University of Illinois Press.

Goodman, David. 2008. "The International Coffee Crisis: A Review of the Issues." In *Confronting the Coffee Crisis: Fair Trade, Sustainable Livelihoods, and Ecosystems in Mexico and Central America*, ed. Christopher M. Bacon, V. Ernesto Méndez, Stephen R. Gliessman, David Goodman, and Jonathan A. Fox. Cambridge, Mass.: MIT Press.

Goswami, Manu. 1998. "From Swadeshi to Swaraj: Nation, Economy, and Territory in Colonial South Asia." *Comparative Studies in Society and History* 40(4): 609–636.

Graeber, David. 2001. *Toward an Anthropological Theory of Value: The False Coin of Our Own Dreams*. New York: Palgrave McMillan.

———. 2002. "The Anthropology of Globalization (With Notes on Neomedievalism, and the End of the Chinese Model of the Nation-State)." *American Anthropologist* 104(4): 1222–1227.

———. 2004. *Fragments of an Anarchist Anthropology*. Vol. 14. Chicago: Prickly Paradigm Press.

———. 2006. "Turning Modes of Production Inside Out: Or, Why Capitalism Is a Transformation of Slavery." *Critique of Anthropology* 26(1): 61–85.

Gramsci, Antonio. 1971. *Selections from the Prison Notebooks*. Ed. and trans. Quintin Hoarde and Geoffery Nowell-Smith. New York: International Publishers.

Grandin, Greg. 2007. *Empire's Workshop: Latin America, the United States, and the Rise of the New Imperialism*. New York: Henry Holt.

Grasmuck, Sherri. 1984. "Immigration, Ethnic-Stratification, and Native Working-Class Discipline: Comparison of Documented and Undocumented Dominicans." *International Migration Review* 18:692–713.

Gupta, Akhil. 1998. *Postcolonial Developments: Agriculture in the Making of Modern India*. Durham, N.C.: Duke University Press.

Gupta, Akhil, and James Ferguson. 1997a. *Anthropological Locations: Boundaries and Grounds of a Field Science*. Berkeley: University of California Press.

———. 1997b. *Culture, Power, Place: Explorations in Critical Anthropology*. Durham, N.C.: Duke University Press.

Habermas, Jürgen. 1987. "Modernity—An Incomplete Project." In *Interpretive Social Science: A Second Look,* ed. Paul Rabinow and William M. Sullivan. Berkeley: University of California Press.

———. 1989. *The Structural Transformation of the Public Sphere*. Cambridge, Mass.: MIT Press.

Hagan, Jacqueline. 1994. *Deciding to Be Legal: A Maya Community in Houston.* Philadelphia: Temple University Press.

Halperín Donghi, Tulio. 1993. *The Contemporary History of Latin America.* Durham, N.C.: Duke University Press.

Hamilton, Nora, and Norma Stoltz Chinchilla. 1991. "Central American Migration: A Framework for Analysis." *Latin American Research Review* 26(1): 75–110.

———. 2001. *Seeking Community in a Global City: Guatemalans and Salvadorans in Los Angeles.* Philadelphia: Temple University Press.

Hamilton, Sarah, and Edward F. Fischer. 2003. "Non-Traditional Agricultural Exports in Highland Guatemala: Understandings of Risk and Perceptions of Change." *Latin American Research Review* 38(3): 82–110.

Hannerz, Ulf. 1996. *Transnational Connections: Culture, People, Places.* New York: Routledge.

Harding, Susan. 2000. *The Book of Jerry Falwell: Fundamentalist Language and Politics.* Princeton, N.J.: Princeton University Press.

Hardt, Michael, and Antonio Negri. 2000. *Empire.* Cambridge, Mass.: Harvard University Press.

———. 2004. *Multitude: War and Democracy in the Age of Empire.* New York: Penguin Press.

Harvey, David. 1989. *The Condition of Postmodernity: An Enquiry into the Origins of Cultural Change.* New York: Blackwell.

———. 2005. *A Brief History of Neoliberalism.* Oxford: Oxford University Press.

Harvey, Neil. 1998. *The Chiapas Rebellion: The Struggle for Land and Democracy.* Durham, N.C.: Duke University Press.

Helmke, Gretchen, and Steven Levitsky, eds. 2006. *Informal Institutions and Democracy: Lessons from Latin America.* Baltimore: Johns Hopkins University Press.

Herzfeld, Michael. 1997. *Cultural Intimacy: Social Poetics in the Nation-State.* New York: Routledge.

Hirsch, Jennifer S. 2003. *A Courtship After Marriage: Sexuality and Love in Mexican Transnational Families.* Berkeley: University of California Press.

Hirschkind, Charles. 2006. *The Ethical Soundscape: Cassette Sermons and Islamic Counterpublics.* New York: Columbia University Press.

Holmes, Douglas R. 2000. *Integral Europe: Fast Capitalism, Multiculturalism, Neofacism.* Princeton, N.J.: Princeton University Press.

Holmes, Douglas R., and George E. Marcus. 2005. "Cultures of Expertise and the Management of Globalization: Toward the Re-functioning of Ethnography." In *Global Assemblages: Technology, Politics, and Ethics as Anthropological Problems,* ed. Aihwa Ong and Stephen J. Collier, 235–252. Malden, Mass.: Blackwell.

Hondagneu-Sotelo, Pierrette. 2001. *Doméstica: Immigrant Workers Cleaning and Caring in the Shadows of Affluence.* Berkeley: University of California Press.

———. 2003. *Gender and U.S. Immigration: Contemporary Trends.* Berkeley: University of California Press.

Hopenhayn, Martín. 2001. *No Apocalypse, No Integration: Modernism and Postmodernism in Latin America.* Durham, N.C.: Duke University Press.

Jaffee, Daniel. 2007. *Brewing Justice.* Berkeley: University of California Press.

Jones-Correa, Michael. 1998. *Between Two Nations.* Ithaca, N.Y.: Cornell University Press.

Joseph, G. M., and Daniel Nugent, eds. 1994. *Everyday Forms of State Formation: Revolution and the Negotiation of Rule in Modern Mexico.* Durham, N.C.: Duke University Press.

Keane, Webb. 2007. *Christian Moderns: Freedom and Fetish in the Mission Encounter.* Berkeley: University of California Press.

Kearney, Michael. 1986. "From Invisible Hand to Visible Feet: Anthropological Studies of Migration and Development." *Annual Review of Anthropology* 15:331–361.

———. 1995. "Local and the Global: The Anthropology of Globalization and Transnationalism." *Annual Review of Anthropology* 24:547–565.

———. 1996. *Reconceptualizing the Peasantry: Anthropology in Global Perspective.* Boulder, Colo.: Westview Press.

———. 2004. *Changing Fields of Anthropology: From Local to Global.* New York: Rowman & Littlefield.

Klein, Naomi. 1999. *No Logo.* New York: Picador Press.

Kottak, Conrad. 2005. *Assault on Paradise: Social Change in a Brazilian Fishing Village.* Boston: McGraw Hill.

Kray, Christine. 2001. "The Pentecostal Re-Formation of Self: Opting for Orthodoxy in Yucatán." *American Ethnologist* 29(4): 395–429.

Laclau, Ernesto, and Chantal Mouffe. 1985. *Hegemony and Socialist Strategy: Towards a Radical Democratic Politics.* London: Verso.

LaFeber, Walter. 1983. *Inevitable Revolutions: The United States in Central America.* New York: W.W. Norton.

Lancaster, Roger N. 1988. *Thanks to God and the Revolution: Popular Religion and Class Consciousness in the New Nicaragua.* New York: Columbia University Press.

———. 1992. *Life Is Hard: Machismo, Danger, and the Intimacy of Power in Nicaragua.* Berkeley: University of California Press.

Lauria-Santiago, Aldo, and Leigh Binford, eds. 2004. *Landscapes of Struggle: Politics, Society, and Community in El Salvador.* Pittsburgh: University of Pittsburgh Press.

Lears, T. Jackson. 1994. *Fables of Abundance: A Cultural History of Advertising in America.* New York: Basic Books.

Levitt, Peggy. 2001. *The Transnational Villagers.* Berkeley: University of California Press.

Levitt, Peggy, and Mary C. Waters. 2002. *The Changing Face of Home: The Transnational Lives of the Second Generation.* New York: Russell Sage Foundation.

Levitt, Theodore. 1983. "The Globalization of Markets." *Harvard Business Review* 61(3): 92.

Lewin, Bryan, D. Giovannucci, and P. Varangis. 2004. "Coffee Markets: New Paradigms in Global Supply and Demand." World Bank Agriculture and Rural Development Discussion Paper No. 3.

Lewis, David, and David Mosse, eds. 2006. *Development Brokers and Translators: The Ethnography of Aid and Aid Agencies.* Bloomfield, Conn.: Kumarian Press.

Lewis, Herbert S. 1998. "The Misrepresentation of Anthropology and Its Consequences." *American Anthropologist* 100:716–731.

Loker, William M. 2000. "Sowing Discord, Planting Doubts: Rhetoric and Reality in an Environment and Development Project in Honduras." *Human Organization* 59(3): 300–310.

——. 2004. *Changing Places: Environment, Development, and Social Change in Rural Honduras*. Durham, N.C.: Carolina Academic Press.

Lomnitz, Claudio. 2001. *Deep Mexico, Silent Mexico: An Anthropology of Nationalism*. Minneapolis: University of Minnesota Press.

Luetchford, Peter. 2008. *Fair Trade and a Global Commodity: Coffee in Costa Rica*. Ann Arbor, Mich.: Pluto Press.

Lyon, Sarah. 2006. "Just Java: Roasting Fair Trade Coffee." In *Fast Food/Slow Food: The Cultural Economy of the Global Food System*, ed. Richard Wilk, 241–258. New York: Altamira Press.

——. 2007a. "Fair Trade Coffee and Human Rights in Guatemala." *Journal of Consumer Policy* 30(3): 241–261.

——. 2007b. "Maya Coffee Farmers and the Fair Trade Commodity Chain." *Culture and Agriculture* 29(2): 58–62.

Macías, Miguel Alonzo. 2001. *La Capital De La Contrarreforma Agraria: El Bajo Aguán De Honduras*. Tegucigalpa, Honduras: Editorial Guaymuras.

Mahler, Sarah J. 1995. *American Dreaming: Immigrant Life on the Margins*. Princeton, N.J.: Princeton University Press.

——. 2003. "Engendering Transnational Migration: A Case Study of Salvadorans." In *Gender and U.S. Immigration: Contemporary Trends*, ed. Pierrette Hondagneu-Sotelo, 287–316. Berkeley: University of California Press.

Maine, Henry Sumner. 1959. *Ancient Law: Its Connection with the Early History of Society and Its Relation to Modern Ideas*. London: Oxford University Press.

Mandel, Ernest. 1995. *Long Waves of Capitalist Development: A Marxist Interpretation*. New York: Verso.

Marcus, George E. 1998. *Ethnography Through Thick and Thin*. Princeton, N.J.: Princeton University Press.

Martin, David. 1990. *Tongues of Fire: The Explosion of Protestantism in Latin America*. Oxford: Cambridge, Mass.: Basil Blackwell.

Marx, Karl, and Friedrich Engels. 1978. *The Marx-Engels Reader*. 2nd ed. Ed. Robert C. Tucker. New York: Norton.

Marx, Karl, and Martin Nicolaus. 1993. *Grundrisse: Foundations of the Critique of Political Economy*. New York: Penguin Books.

Massey, Douglas. 1990. "Social Structure, Household Strategies, and the Cumulative Causation of Migration." *Population Index* 56(1): 3–26.

Massey, Douglas, Jorge Durand, and N. Malone. 2003. *Beyond Smoke and Mirrors: Mexican Immigration in an Era of Economic Integration*. New York: Russell Sage Foundation.

Maurer, Bill. 2005. *Mutual Life, Limited: Islamic Banking, Alternative Currencies, Lateral Reason*. Princeton, N.J.: Princeton University Press.

McDougall, Debra. 2009. "Becoming Sinless: Converting to Islam in the Christian Solomon Islands." *American Anthropologist* 111(4): 480–491.

Mead, Margaret. 1973. *Coming of Age in Samoa.* New York: American Museum of Natural History.

Micheletti, Michele. 2003. *Political Virtue and Shopping: Individuals, Consumerism, and Collective Action.* New York: Palgrave Macmillan.

Migration News. 1998. "Central America: Hurricane Mitch." *Migration News* 5 (December): 12.

Miller, Daniel. 1998. *A Theory of Shopping.* Ithaca, N.Y.: Cornell University Press.

———. 2001. *The Dialectics of Shopping.* Chicago: University of Chicago Press.

Mintz, Sidney. 1974. *Worker in the Cane: A Puerto Rican Life History.* New York: Norton.

———. 1985. *Sweetness and Power: The Place of Sugar in Modern History.* New York: Viking.

———. 1996. *Tasting Food, Tasting Freedom: Excursions into Eating, Culture, and the Past.* Boston: Beacon Press.

Miyazaki, Hirokazu. 2003. "The Temporalities of the Market." *American Anthropologist* 105(2): 255–265.

Moodie, Ellen. 2006. "Microbus Crashes and Coca-Cola Cash: The Value of Death in 'Free-Market' El Salvador." *American Ethnologist* 32(1): 63–80.

———. 2007. "Dollars and Dolores in Postwar El Salvador." In *Money: Ethnographic Encounters,* ed. Allison Truitt and Stefan Senders, 43–55. Oxford: Berg Publishers.

Moore, Sally Falk. 1986. *Social Facts and Fabrications: "Customary" Law on Kilimanjaro 1880–1980.* Cambridge: Cambridge University Press.

Mosse, David. 2005. *Cultivating Development: An Ethnography of Aid Policy and Practice.* Ann Arbor, Mich.: Pluto Press.

Muñiz, Angel. 1995. *Nueba Yol.* Santo Domingo, Dominican Republic: Cigua Films.

Nash, June C. 1979. *We Eat the Mines and the Mines Eat Us: Dependency and Exploitation in Bolivian Tin Mines.* New York: Columbia University Press.

———. 2007. *Practicing Ethnography in a Globalizing World: An Anthropological Odyssey.* New York: Altamira/Rowman & Littlefield.

Neilson, Jeff. 2008. "Global Private Regulation and Value-Chain Restructuring in Indonesian Smallholder Coffee Systems." *World Development* 36(9): 1607–1622.

Nelson, Diane M. 2009. *Reckoning: The Ends of War in Guatemala.* Durham, N.C.: Duke University Press.

Neruda, Pablo. 1991. *Canto General.* Trans. Jack Schmitt. Berkeley: University of California Press.

Ngai, Mae. 2005. *Impossible Subjects: Illegal Aliens and the Making of Modern America.* Princeton, N.J.: Princeton University Press.

Nigh, Ronald. 1997. "Organic Agriculture and Globalization: A Maya Associative Cooperation in Chiapas, Mexico." *Human Organization* 56:427–441.

Noé Pino, Hugo. 1992. *Honduras, El Ajuste Estructural Y La Reforma Agraria.* Tegucigalpa, Honduras: Postgrado Centroamericano En Economía Y Planificación Del Desarrollo.

O'Neill, Kevin Lewis. 2010. *City of God: Christian Citizenship in Postwar Guatemala.* Berkeley: University of California Press.

Ong, Aihwa. 1987. *Spirits of Resistance and Capitalist Discipline: Factory Women in Malaysia.* Albany: State University of New York Press.

———. 1999. *Flexible Citizenship: The Cultural Logics of Transnationality.* Durham, N.C.: Duke University Press.

———. 2006. *Neoliberalism as Exception: Mutations in Citizenship and Sovereignty.* Durham, N.C.: Duke University Press.

Ong, Aihwa, and Stephen J. Collier, eds. 2005. *Global Assemblages: Technology, Politics, and Ethics as Anthropological Problems.* Malden, Mass.: Blackwell.

Ortner, Sherry B. 1984. "Theory in Anthropology Since the Sixties." *Comparative Studies in Society and History* 26:126–166.

Paley, Julia. 2001. "Making Democracy Count: Opinion Polls and Market Surveys in the Chilean Political Transition." *Cultural Anthropology* 16(2): 135–164.

Pedersen, David. 2002. "The Storm We Call Dollars: Determining Value and Belief in El Salvador and the United States." *Cultural Anthropology* 17(3): 431–459.

———. 2003. "As Irrational as Bert and Bin Laden: The Production of Categories, Commodities, and Commensurability in the Era of Globalization." *Public Culture* 15(2): 238–259.

———. 2004. "In the Stream of Money: Contradictions of Migration, Remittances, and Development in El Salvador." In *Landscapes of Struggle: Politics, Society, and Community in El Salvador*, ed. Aldo Lauria Santiago and Leigh Binford. Pittsburgh: University of Pittsburgh Press.

———. 2008. "Brief Event: The Value of Getting to Value in the Era of 'Globalization,'" *Anthropological Theory* 8(1): 57–77.

Pendergrast, Mark. 1999. *Uncommon Grounds: The History of Coffee and How It Transformed Our World.* New York: Basic Books.

Peterson, Linda S. 1986. *Central American Migration: Past and Present.* Vol. 25. Washington, D.C.: Center for International Research, U.S. Bureau of the Census.

Pew Hispanic Center. 2008. *Statistical Portrait of Hispanics in the United States.* Washington, D.C., http://pewhispanic.org/files/factsheets/hispanics2006/hispanics.pdf.

Pine, Adrienne. 2008. *Working Hard, Drinking Hard: On Violence and Survival in Honduras.* Berkeley: University of California Press.

Polanyi, Karl. 1957. *The Great Transformation: The Political and Economic Origins of Our Time.* Boston: Beacon Press.

Portes, Alejandro, and Rubén G. Rumbaut. 1996. *Immigrant America: A Portrait.* 2nd ed. Berkeley: University of California Press.

Puerta, Ricardo. 2002. "Remesas Para el Desarrollo." http://portal.rds.org.hn (posted February 2002).

———. 2003. "¿Cúantos hondureños viven en Estados Unidos?" http://portal.rds.org.hn (posted September 30, 2003).

Ramos, Jorge. 2005. *Dying to Cross: The Worst Immigrant Tragedy in American History.* New York: Rayo.

Raynolds, Laura T. 2000. "Re-Embedding Global Agriculture: The International Organic and Fair Trade Movements." *Agriculture and Human Values* 17:297–309.

———. 2002. "Consumer/Producer Links in Fair Trade Coffee Networks." *Sociologia Ruralis* 42(4): 404–424.

Raynolds, Laura T., Douglas Murray, and Andrew Heller. 2007. "Regulating Sustainability in the Coffee Sector: A Comparative Analysis of Third-Party Environmental and Social Certification Initiatives." *Agriculture and Human Values* 24(2): 147–163.

Raynolds, Laura T., Douglas Murray, and Peter Leigh Taylor. 2004. "Fair Trade Coffee: Building Producer Capacity Via Global Networks." *Journal of International Development* 16(8): 1109.

Redfield, Robert. 1965. *A Village That Chose Progress: Chan Kom Revisited.* Chicago: University of Chicago Press.

———. 1973. *Tepoztlán, A Mexican Village.* Chicago: University of Chicago Press.

Redfield, Robert, and Alfonso Villa Rojas. 1965. *Chan Kom: A Maya Village.* Chicago: University of Chicago Press.

Reichman, Daniel. 2008. "Justice at a Price: Regulation and Alienation in the Global Economy." *PoLAR: Political and Legal Anthropology Review* 31(1): 134–149.

Renard, Marie-Christine. 1993. "The Interstices of Globalization: The Example of Fair Coffee." *Sociologia Ruralis* 39(4): 484–500.

———. 2005. "Quality Certification, Regulation, and Power in Fair Trade." *Journal of Rural Studies* 21(1): 419–431.

Riles, Annelise. 2000. *The Network Inside Out.* Ann Arbor: University of Michigan Press.

Robbins, Joel. 2004. *Becoming Sinners: Christianity and Moral Torment in a Papua New Guinea Society.* Berkeley: University of California Press.

Roseberry, William. 1983. *Coffee and Capitalism in the Venezuelan Andes.* Austin: University of Texas Press.

———. 1989. *Anthropologies and Histories.* New Brunswick, N.J.: Rutgers University Press.

———. 1991. "Marxism and Culture". In *Politics of Culture,* ed. Brett Williams, 19–43. Washington, D.C.: Smithsonian Institution Press.

———. 1994. "Hegemony and the Language of Contention." In *Everyday Forms of State Formation: Revolution and the Negotiation of Rule in Modern Mexico,* ed. Gil Joseph and Daniel Nugent, 355–366. Durham, N.C.: Duke University Press.

———. 1996. "The Rise of Yuppie Coffees and the Reimagination of Class in the United States." *American Anthropologist* 98(4): 762–775.

Roseberry, William, Lowell Gudmundson, and Mario Samper Kutschbach, eds. 1995. *Coffee, Society, and Power in Latin America.* Baltimore: Johns Hopkins University Press.

Rouse, Roger. 1995. "Thinking Through Transnationalism: Notes on the Cultural Politics of Class Relations in the Contemporary United States." *Public Culture* 7(2): 353–402.

Sahlins, Marshall. 1976. *Culture and Practical Reason.* Chicago: University of Chicago Press.

———. 1993. "Goodbye to Tristes Tropes: Ethnography in the Context of Modern World History." *Journal of Modern History* 65(1): 1–25.

Sánchez, Rafael. 2001. "Channel-Surfing: Media, Mediumship, and State Authority in the María Lionza Possession Cult (Venezuela)." In *Religion and Media,* ed. Hent DeVries and Samuel Weber. Palo Alto, Calif.: Stanford University Press.

Sangren, P. Steven. 1991. "Dialectics of Alienation: Individuals and Collectivities in Chinese Religion." *Man* 26(1): 67–86.

———. 1993. "Power and Transcendence in the Ma Tsu Pilgrimages of Taiwan." *American Ethnologist* 20(3): 564–582.

———. 2000. *Chinese Sociologics: An Anthropological Account of the Role of Alienation in Social Reproduction.* Cambridge: Athlone Press.

Schelas, John, and Max J. Pfeffer. 2008. *Saving Forests, Protecting People? Environmental Conservation in Central America.* Lanham, Md.: Altamira Press.

Scott, James C. 1976. *The Moral Economy of the Peasant: Rebellion and Subsistence in Southeast Asia.* New Haven, Conn.: Yale University Press.

———. 1985. *Weapons of the Weak: Everyday Forms of Peasant Resistance.* New Haven, Conn.: Yale University Press.

———. 1990. *Domination and the Arts of Resistance: Hidden Transcripts.* New Haven, Conn.: Yale University Press.

———. 1994. "Forward." In *Everyday Forms of State Formation: Revolution and the Negotiation of Rule in Modern Mexico,* ed. Gil Joseph and Daniel Nugent. Durham, N.C.: Duke University Press.

———. 1998. *Seeing Like a State: How Certain Schemes to Improve the Human Condition Have Failed.* New Haven, Conn.: Yale University Press.

Selka, Stephen. 2010. "Morality in the Religious Marketplace: Evangelical Christianity, Candomblé, and the Struggle for Moral Distinction in Brazil." *American Ethnologist* 37(2): 291–307.

Sick, Deborah. 1999. *Farmers of the Golden Bean.* DeKalb: Northern Illinois Press.

Smilde, David. 1998. "Letting God Govern: Supernatural Agency in the Venezuelan Pentecostal Approach to Social Change." *Sociology of Religion* 59(3): 287–303.

———. 2007. *Reason to Believe: Cultural Agency in Latin American Evangelicalism.* Berkeley: University of California Press.

Soluri, John. 2005. *Banana Cultures: Agriculture, Consumption and Environmental Change in Honduras and the United States.* Austin: University of Texas Press.

Stepick, Alex, and Alejandro Portes. 1986. "Flight into Despair: A Profile of Recent Haitian Refugees in South Florida." *International Migration Review* 20:329–350.

Steward, Julian, ed. *The People of Puerto Rico.* Urbana: University of Illinois Press.

Stoll, David. 1990. *Is Latin America Turning Protestant? The Politics of Evangelical Growth.* Berkeley: University of California Press.

Stonich, Susan C. 1991. "Rural Families and Income from Migration: Honduran Households in the World Economy." *Journal of Latin American Studies* 23(1): 131–161.

———. 1993. *"I Am Destroying the Land!": The Political Ecology of Poverty and Environmental Destruction in Honduras.* Boulder, Colo.: Westview Press.

Storrs, Landon R. Y. 2000. *Civilizing Capitalism: The National Consumers' League, Women's Activism, and Labor Standards in the New Deal Era.* Chapel Hill: University of North Carolina Press.

Strathern, Marilyn. 1992. *After Nature: English Kinship in the Late Twentieth Century.* New York: Cambridge University Press.

Striffler, Steve. 2002a. "Inside a Poultry Processing Plant: An Ethnographic Portrait." *Labor History* 43(3): 305–313.

——. 2002b. *In the Shadows of State and Capital: The United Fruit Company, Popular Struggle, and Agrarian Restructuring in Ecuador, 1900–1995.* Durham, N.C.: Duke University Press.

——. 2005. *Chicken: The Dangerous Transformation of America's Favorite Food.* New Haven, Conn.: Yale University Press.

——. 2007. "Neither Here nor There: Mexican Immigrant Workers and the Search for Home." *American Ethnologist* 34(4): 674–688.

Striffler, Steve, and Mark Moberg. 2003. *Banana Wars: Power, Production, and History in the Americas.* Durham, N.C.: Duke University Press.

Talbot, John M. 1995. "Regulating the Coffee Commodity Chain: Internationalization and the Coffee Cartel." *Berkeley Journal of Sociology* 40:113.

——. 1997a. "The Struggle for Control of a Commodity Chain: Instant Coffee from Latin America." *Latin American Research Review* 32(2): 117.

——. 1997b. "Where Does Your Coffee Dollar Go? The Division of Income and Surplus Along the Coffee Commodity Chain." *Studies in Comparative International Development* 32(1): 56.

Taussig, Michael T. 1980. *The Devil and Commodity Fetishism in South America.* Chapel Hill: University of North Carolina Press.

Tax, Sol. 1953. *Penny Capitalism: A Guatemalan Indian Economy.* Washington, D.C.: Smithsonian Institution.

Taylor, Peter Leigh, Douglas L. Murray, and Laura T. Raynolds. 2005. "Keeping Trade Fair: Governance Challenges in the Fair Trade Coffee Initiative." *Sustainable Development* 13(3): 199.

Taylor-Robinson, Michelle M. 2006. "The Difficult Road from Caudillismo to Democracy: The Impact of Clientelism in Honduras." In *Informal Institutions and Democracy: Lessons from Latin America,* ed. Gretchen Helmke and Steven Levitsky, 106–124. Baltimore: Johns Hopkins University Press.

Tocqueville, Alexis de. 1856. *The Old Regime and the Revolution.* New York: Harper Brothers.

Topik, Steven, Carlos Marichal, and Zephyr Frank, eds. 2006. *From Silver to Cocaine: Latin American Commodity Chains and the Building of the World Economy, 1500–2000.* Durham, N.C.: Duke University Press.

Trouillot, Michel-Rolph. 1991. "Anthropology and the Savage Slot: The Poetics and Politics of Otherness." In *Recapturing Anthropology,* ed. Richard Fox. Santa Fe, N.M.: School of American Research Press.

——. 2001. "The Anthropology of the State in the Age of Globalization: Close Encounters of the Deceptive Kind." *Current Anthropology* 42(1): 125–138.

Tsing, Anna. 2000. "The Global Situation." *Cultural Anthropology* 15(3): 327–360.

——. 2005. *Friction: An Ethnography of Global Connection.* Princeton, N.J.: Princeton University Press.

Tucker, Catherine M. 2008. *Changing Forests: Collective Action, Common Property, and Coffee in Honduras.* New York: Springer Academic Press.

Turner, Terence. 1986. "Production, Exploitation and Social Consciousness in the 'Peripheral Situation.'" *Social Analysis* 19:91–115.

———. 1998. "Neoliberal Ecopolitics and Indigenous Peoples: The Kayapo, The 'Rainforest Harvest,' and The Body Shop." *Yale F&ES Bulletin* 98:113–127.

———. 2002. "Shifting the Frame from Nation-State to Global Market: Class and Social Consciousness in the Advanced Capitalist Countries." *Social Analysis* 46(2): 56–80.

United Nations Human Development Program. 2006. Human Development Report. Tegucigalpa, Honduras.

U.S. Department of Homeland Security. 2004–2009. *Yearbook of Immigration Statistics.* Washington, D.C.: U.S. Government Printing Office. http://www.dhs.gov/files/statistics/publications/yearbook.shtm.

U.S. Immigration and Naturalization Service. 1978–2001. *Statistical Yearbook of the Immigration and Naturalization Service.* Washington, D.C.: U.S. Government Printing Office.

———. 2001. Estimates of the Unauthorized Population Residing in the United States. Washington, D.C.: U.S. Government Printing Office.

U.S. Library of Congress. 1999. Library of Congress Subject Headings Weekly List 43 (October 27, 1999). http://www.loc.gov/catdir/cpso/wls99/awls9943.html.

Warren, Kay. 1998. *Indigenous Movements and Their Critics: Pan-Mayan Activism in Guatemala.* Princeton, N.J.: Princeton University Press.

Weaver, Erick. 1990. "La Diplomacia del Banano: El desarrollo de las relaciones entre los Estados Unidos y Honduras." In *Honduras: Pieza clave de la política de Estados Unidos en Centroamérica.* Tegucigalpa, Honduras: Centro de Documentación de Honduras.

Weber, Max. 1958. *From Max Weber: Essays in Sociology.* Trans. Hans Gerth and C. Wright Mills. New York: Oxford University Press.

Westbrook, David A. 2004. *City of Gold: An Apology for Global Capitalism in a Time of Discontent.* New York: Routledge.

White, Robert Anthony. 1977. "Structural Factors in Rural Development: The Church and the Peasant in Honduras." PhD diss., Department of Development Sociology, Cornell University.

Wilk, Richard, ed. 2006. *Fast Food/Slow Food: The Cultural Economy of the Global Food System.* New York: Altamira Press.

Williams, Raymond. 1973. *The Country and the City.* New York: Oxford University Press.

Williams, Robert. 1994. *States and Social Evolution: Coffee and the Rise of National Governments in Central America.* Chapel Hill: University of North Carolina Press.

Wolf, Eric R. 1956. "San José: Subcultures of a "Traditional" Coffee Municipality." In *The People of Puerto Rico,* ed. Julian Steward. Urbana: University of Illinois Press.

———. 1966. *Peasants.* Englewood Cliffs, N.J.: Prentice-Hall.

———. 1967. "Types of Latin American Peasantry: A Preliminary Discussion." In *Tribal and Peasant Economics,* ed. George Dalton. Garden City, N.Y.: Natural History Press.

———. 1969. *Peasant Wars of the Twentieth Century.* New York: Harper & Row.

———. 1982. *Europe and the People Without History.* Berkeley: University of California Press.

———. 1999. *Envisioning Power: Ideologies of Dominance and Crisis.* Berkeley: University of California Press.

Woodward, Ralph Lee, Jr. 1985. *Central America: A Nation Divided.* New York: Oxford University Press.

World Bank. 2003. Honduras: Country Assistance Strategy. Central America Country Management Unit, Latin America and the Caribbean Region.

Zilberg, Elana, and Mario Lungo. 1999. "Se han vuelto haraganes? Juventud, migración e identidades laborales." In *Transformando El Salvador: Migración, Sociedad, y Cultura,* ed. Mario Lungo and Susan Kandel, 39–94. San Salvador, El Salvador: FUNDE.

Žižek, Slavoj. 2006. "Against the Populist Temptation." *Critical Inquiry* 32(2): 551–574.

Zolberg, Aristide R. 2006. *A Nation by Design: Immigration Policy in the Fashioning of America.* New York: Russell Sage Foundation.

Zolov, Eric. 1999. *Refried Elvis: The Rise of the Mexican Counterculture.* Berkeley: University of California Press.

INDEX